INTEGRATING THE HUMAN SCIENCES

D1604362

What if we recognized that the human sciences collectively investigate a few dozen key phenomena that interact with each other? Can we imagine a human science that would seek to stitch its understandings of this system of phenomena into a coherent whole? If so, what would that look like?

This book argues that we are unlikely to develop one unified "theory of everything." Our collective understanding must then be a "map" of the myriad relationships within this large – but finite and manageable – system, coupled with detailed understandings of each causal link and of important subsystems. The book outlines such a map and shows that the pursuit of coherence – and a more successful human science enterprise – requires integration, recognizing the strengths and weaknesses of different methods and theory types, and the pursuit of terminological and presentational clarity. It explores how these interconnected goals can be achieved in research, teaching, library classification, public policy, and university administration. These suggestions are congruent with, and yet enhance, other projects for reform of the human sciences.

This volume is aimed at any scholar or student who seeks to comprehend how what they study fits within a broader understanding.

Rick Szostak is Professor of Economics at the University of Alberta. He is the author of 20 books, 60 journal articles, and dozens of book chapters and encyclopedia articles across a dozen fields, especially economic history, world history, interdisciplinary studies, knowledge organization, and future studies.

INTEGRATING THE HUMAN SCIENCES

Enhancing Progress and Coherence across the Social Sciences and Humanities

Rick Szostak

Routledge
Taylor & Francis Group

LONDON AND NEW YORK

Cover image: lvcandy via Getty Images

First published 2023
by Routledge
4 Park Square, Milton Park, Abingdon, Oxon OX14 4RN

and by Routledge
605 Third Avenue, New York, NY 10158

Routledge is an imprint of the Taylor & Francis Group, an informa business

© 2023 Rick Szostak

British Library Cataloguing-in-Publication Data
A catalogue record for this book is available from the British Library

Library of Congress Cataloging-in-Publication Data
Names: Szostak, Rick, 1959- author.
Title: Integrating the human sciences: enhancing progress and coherence
across the social sciences and humanities/Rick Szostak.
Description: Milton Park, Abingdon, Oxon; New York, NY:
Routledge, 2023. | Includes bibliographical references and index.
Identifiers: LCCN 2022016322 (print) | LCCN 2022016323 (ebook) |
ISBN 9781032230184 (hardback) | ISBN 9781032230177 (paperback) |
ISBN 9781003275237 (ebook) | ISBN 9781000689334 (adobe pdf) |
ISBN 9781000689341 (epub)
Subjects: LCSH: Social sciences–Research.
Classification: LCC H62 .S996 2023 (print) | LCC H62 (ebook) |
DDC 300.72–dc23/eng/20220602
LC record available at https://lccn.loc.gov/2022016322
LC ebook record available at https://lccn.loc.gov/2022016323

ISBN: 978-1-032-23018-4 (hbk)
ISBN: 978-1-032-23017-7 (pbk)
ISBN: 978-1-003-27523-7 (ebk)

DOI: 10.4324/9781003275237

Typeset in Bembo
by KnowledgeWorks Global Ltd.

Access the Support Material: www.routledge.com/9781032230177

CONTENTS

ILLUSTRATIONS

Figures

Tables

PREFACE

This book builds on a lifetime of reflection regarding the nature of human science. As a very interdisciplinary economic historian with an interest in big questions (my first two books were about the causes of the Industrial Revolution and the Great Depression, respectively), I became frustrated early in my career about how hard it was to find relevant information in other disciplines. I attended the annual conference of the Association for Interdisciplinary (then Integrative) Studies in 1997, and was hooked. I wrote books and articles about how we could collectively "map" human science over the next few years (Szostak 2001, 2003).

I had been suspicious of economists' reliance on just two methods, even in graduate school. Immersed in the community of scholars of interdisciplinarity, I came to reflect more deeply on the nature of the methods and theories employed across human science. As I began my second sabbatical, I had (what I at least think of as) a Eureka moment in which I appreciated that asking the Who, What, When, Where, and Why questions of science itself gave us keen insights into the nature of science, and of phenomena, data, theory, method, and practice (Szostak 2004).

Along the way, I published some works in economic methodology (especially Szostak 1999, inspired by my first sabbatical at the University of New South Wales, which at the time housed several methodologists, as well as several economic historians). These urged interdisciplinarity as well as theoretical and methodological flexibility. Several Nobel Laureates in Economics have voiced similar ideas since the financial crisis, but these were much less common when I wrote. Yet, as I became more interdisciplinary in my research, I came to question certain practices common in other fields. Economists tend to be very careful about defining terminology (economists fudge the definition of capital, to be sure, but are generally precise and logical). As I wrote Szostak (2003), I was horrified to find that scholars of culture accepted the fact that there were thousands of definitions of that term. And as someone who read widely for a host of integrative research projects, I came to appreciate that economists tend to give you a clear idea of their point in a paragraph or two, but scholars in other fields often bury any point they might have in impenetrable prose.

I still remember a day when people asked, "What is postmodernism?" at conferences. Now I suppose, people sometimes ask, "What was postmodernism?" I drafted Szostak (2007) because I had come to accept a whole array of postmodern critiques – they fit well with my methodological and theoretical pluralism, and my interdisciplinarity – but could not grasp why some postmodernists took the extreme view that progressive science – that is, a science that builds toward enhanced understandings – was simply impossible. I thought it important and obvious that we should recognize but seek to transcend the barriers to scientific progress.

Many of the key arguments in Chapter 2 have thus been gestating in my head for decades. I innovate in that chapter by both extending them and by tying them into one tidy bundle. Then in Chapter 3, I clarify them in the context of the latest thinking in the methodology of human science. I had in Szostak (2003) reflected a bit on the illogic of human science disciplines. This informs the novel exercise in Chapter 4 of describing logically how different fields of specialized research in human science should operate. Likewise, Chapter 5 is very new but builds on decades of writing about interdisciplinary teaching. Chapter 6 summarizes decades of my research in the field of Knowledge Organization – which in turn has reflected my continued concern that it is far harder to find relevant information in diverse disciplines than it needs to be. I have written a few pieces about public policy and have long been involved in conversations about policy issues. The key ideas in Chapter 7 reflect these conversations. In Chapter 8, I draw on both my published work on the administration of interdisciplinary programs and my (far too) many years as an academic administrator.

Most scholars specialize. They spend their careers applying a limited set of methods to a limited set of phenomena. This work is invaluable. Yet on its own, it can be biased and incoherent. It seems patently obvious that specialized research needs to be tied into a more coherent framework. Yet specialized researchers dominate academia, and so this obvious message is under-appreciated. I hope that specialized researchers can come to appreciate integrative research, just as integrative researchers necessarily appreciate the specialized research they draw upon. I will describe in this book a symbiotic relationship between the two.

One of the skills that an integrative researcher masters is to spot the good elements in opposing points of view. Though the recommendations in this book may strike some as revolutionary, I hope that I have struck a middle ground (a Golden Mean, in Aristotle's phrasing) in many ways: Valuing both specialized and integrative research; valuing diverse theories and methods; accepting postmodern concerns but seeking to transcend these; seeing value but also problems in all fields of human science endeavor; and encouraging a very rigorous form of interdisciplinarity. I value the many accomplishments of human science – I have drawn on insights from every field in my previous research – but argue that we can do much better. Most academics can continue doing research and teaching much as before, but their efforts can be rendered more productive through integration: Synthesizing the insights of different authors into a more comprehensive understanding. Integration may also suggest ways to improve specialized research and teaching.

In sum, this work builds on decades of research and reflection. This book is respectful but innovative. It outlines a path to a far more productive human science enterprise that will better teach our students and better inform our policies.

There are dozens of people associated with the Association for Interdisciplinary Studies who have influenced my thinking over the years. I will limit myself here to thanking those who I have co-authored with along the way: Allen Repko, Michelle Buchberger, Bill Newell, Julie Thompson Klein, Machiel Keestra, Tami Carmichael, and Jennifer Dellner. Co-authoring with Allen Repko multiple editions of two textbooks on how to perform interdisciplinary research has been one of the greatest experiences of my academic life. Among other things, it has resulted in invitations to speak at conferences in several countries, including Lebanon, Uganda, and Mexico, to serve on an international advisory committee for the new Université Gustav Eiffel in Paris, and teach a short course for the College of Europe in Warsaw. I learned much from these endeavors, and am immensely grateful to those who invited me. I received some great comments when I made a presentation on some of the ideas in this book at the 2021 AIS conference, hosted virtually by Southern Utah University (and a handful of other institutions in that state). I would also extend my thanks to many people at TD-Net in Switzerland; I have learned much at their conferences over the years. Gabriele Bammer of Integration and Implementation Sciences in Canberra has published some blog posts by me over the years, and I have benefited from both her editorial comments and the feedback from readers. Chapter 6 would not have been possible without my lengthy association with the International Society for Knowledge Organization: There are again dozens of scholars who I might thank, but I will limit myself to key co-authors: Claudio Gnoli, Maria Lopez-Huertas, Richard Smiraglia, and Andrea Scharnhorst. In recent months, a few people have given important advice on particular aspects of this project: Mark Ciatola, Merel Van Goch, Catherine Lyall, Michael O'Rourke, and Allen Repko. The book is far better because of their advice. Any remaining flaws reflect my own myriad limitations.

In recent years, I have published two books with Routledge, *Making Sense of World History* and *Making Sense of the Future*. These books also inform the present enterprise in important ways. They were both also a great pleasure to write. And it has been wonderful to work again on this book with Eve Setch and Zoe Thompson at Routledge (and to welcome Jennifer Morrow). I am immensely grateful to them. I close as usual by thanking my children: They each achieved important milestones while I have been writing this book, and I am immensely proud.

1

INTRODUCTION

This book asks a simple question: What if we recognized that human science (the humanities and social sciences) collectively investigates a few dozen key phenomena (that is, "things that we study") that interact with each other (and with some phenomena studied in natural science)? Can we imagine a human science that would seek to stitch its understandings of this system of phenomena into a coherent whole? If so, what would that look like? We will argue in this book that we are unlikely to develop one unified "theory of everything." Our collective understanding must then be a "map" of the myriad relationships within this large — but finite and manageable — system, coupled with detailed understandings of each causal link and of important subsystems (defined as a set of phenomena that interact with each other more than with other phenomena). If we wish to know, say, the impact of a particular cultural attitude on a particular political outcome, we follow the links from that attitude to a particular political phenomenon. We will, in such an endeavor, wish to have a good sense of which links are most powerful and under what circumstances (that is, realizations of yet other phenomena) they operate.

God, what a mess! However, if we reasonably doubt the possibility of a unified theory of everything, then it is obviously the best that we can do. If we give up because it seems hard, then we accept that forever the efforts of human scientists will be fragmented, and that we will never have any very good idea of how human societies function in all of their complexity. Indeed, if we do not attempt to integrate the human sciences, we can be confident that different scholars and different disciplines will reach quite different conclusions about particular phenomena and relationships without even being aware that they are disagreeing. This book will show that our vision of an integrated human science is feasible, and not quite as messy as it might at first glance appear. We will, of course, also highlight the myriad advantages of such an approach throughout.

DOI: 10.4324/9781003275237-1

The book is thus an exercise in metascience or the study of (human) science. It will ask what an integrated human science will look like and how we can achieve it. It will naturally suggest that we need to pay more attention to integration, to efforts to tie the research of individual scholars into a more coherent whole. It will outline how symbiosis between specialized and integrative work can best proceed. We will find that one key barrier to integration is the incredible looseness with which key terminology is defined across (much of) human science, and suggest how this can be remedied. We will find that different scholars favor different theories and methods, and urge a greater appreciation of the strengths and weaknesses of the different methods and theory types used across human science. It is not logical, but an accident of history, that human scientists investigate different causal links and subsystems with different methods and types of theories. Yet we will insist that all theories and methods – and strategies for integration – be applied properly. Methodological and theoretical diversity need not and should not be an excuse for superficial analysis. Yet in recognizing that no method is perfect (some human scientists may have just fainted), we need also to recognize the important place for human judgment in evaluating research results, and then discuss how we can find a place for judgment that does not totally destroy the scientific project through endless bickering. This will, I fear, involve occasional rather squishy invocations to clarity and honesty and humility – but as is well known a successful scholarly (or indeed any) enterprise requires a mix of the right institutions and the right attitudes.

The feasibility of this vision of the human science enterprise would be of little importance if we did not also establish that it is desirable. Our goal in this book is to improve the human sciences so that research is more successful, students are better prepared, and public policy advice is better given. Yet we want to do this while enhancing rather than restricting the ability of scholars to follow their curiosity and employ the theories and methods they find most appropriate. Along the way, we might also tamp down the culture wars.

Outline of This Book

Chapter 2 will make the general case for the arguments above. Chapter 4 will then drill down and examine each part of the map of human science. We will see time and again that communities of specialized researchers are not directly addressing the questions that would best inform the human science project. We will also generally find that they are not making use of the full range of theories and methods.[1]

What about Chapter 3? Here we relate our efforts to other recent works that suggest reforms to the humanities or social sciences. Our first point here is that our map guides us to engage with both the humanities and social sciences whereas most authors limit themselves to one or the other. We will find that the reforms we urge are broadly consistent with reforms urged by others, but provide solutions to challenges that they faced.

Chapter 5 turns our attention from research to teaching. If we can draw a map of human science that can guide our research, then we should share this map with our students. If we can appreciate the strengths and weaknesses of different theory types and methods in our research, we should communicate about these strengths and weaknesses to our students. Then we should teach them some epistemology so that they can appreciate the value of carefully amassing arguments and evidence from different theories and methods. I will also urge the teaching of World History and Future Studies to all, for these courses can – when properly taught – reinforce the key lessons above while giving students a strong sense of their place in the world. We will also discuss in Chapter 5 how to structure interdisciplinary and thematic Majors and how to teach in a comparative and integrative fashion.

Chapter 6 is relatively brief but raises an important issue: Our libraries are organized in a way that makes it hard for both scholars and students to identify relevant works in multiple disciplines. Libraries classify each discipline in a different way, and employ different terminology for the same thing in different disciplines. It would be quite feasible and desirable to organize libraries (physical and digital) around the phenomena we study, as identified in our map of human science (and a similar map of natural science).

Chapter 7 turns our attention to public policy. We first review two key advantages of the unified approach to human science research urged above. First, we can proffer less biased policy advice, for we can integrate the insights of specialized scholars into a more comprehensive understanding. Second, and related, we will be far less likely to fail to appreciate negative side effects of any policy we recommend because we will have explored its implications along multiple causal pathways. We will also recommend a different kind of integration: between academics and policy-makers. The more intensely that these collaborate around integrative scholarly understandings, the more likely we are to see beneficial changes in public policy. We close the chapter by discussing how our reforms to teaching will better prepare policy-makers.[2]

Then we will face the greatest barrier of all: academic inertia. As dissatisfied as many in the existing professoriate may be with the fragmentation of knowledge, and as much as many may want to see greater advances in human science understanding, they have made their careers within a system of specialized silos. We will reflect in the last substantive chapter on how to turn the human science "ship" onto a new course. How can administrators, granting agencies, professors, and students drive change? And what sort of administrative structure would best support an integrated human science?

Key Characteristics of This Book

One key point to stress at the outset is that this book sets out to stress the positive rather than the negative. It is not our purpose to be dismissive of existing practices but rather to suggest that these can and should be improved. We very much need to appreciate that the research of human scientists has already added much to the human understanding of humanity.[3] In my previous books and articles, I have been able to draw profitably upon research from every human science discipline.[4] Yet it is perhaps inevitable that large numbers of independent academic communities pursuing their own conversations do not add to our collective understandings as well as they could. This book provides a view from above and asks how each discipline and field might best add to our shared understanding of humanity. It is guided in particular by an appreciation that the phenomena studied by each discipline interact with the phenomena studied in other disciplines. It will turn out that this simple and obvious point has far-reaching implications for human science. The view from above also exposes the simple fact that none of the theories or methods employed in human science is perfect. This simple observation also has important implications.

I have occasionally engaged in methodological critiques of my original fields of economic history, economics, and history in the past. I quickly learned that suggesting "We should all do X" attracts a great deal of pushback that a more innocuous "More of us should do X" does not. With rare exceptions, this book will not call for us to stop doing anything that we do. Rather, it will urge us to do more of some things that we do too little of like integrating research into a more coherent whole. After all, research agendas that seem questionable from above may nevertheless produce great insights. Still, I think it is useful to at least query various research practices, and encourage researchers to reflect a bit more on why they do what they do.[5]

There is a well-known joke about an inebriated man who drops his house keys and fumbles around on the ground looking for them. A neighbor offers to help him and says, "So you dropped them around here?" The inebriated man responds that he dropped them over there but that the light is better where he is looking. I worry that we often "look where the light is" rather than where we should be looking.[6] We look where we find congenial data or where a certain theory points us. We do not reflect as much as we might about where we have collectively dropped our keys: What research questions would most advance our collective understanding? Where are the biggest gaps in that understanding? Therefore, I will from time to time query why we do certain things. Still, our main purpose is to prod us to do other things. Our view from above of the entire human science enterprise will readily identify research questions that merit greater attention in all fields within human science.

It is hopefully obvious from the above that I am a big believer in the pursuit of intellectual curiosity. I have followed my own curiosity across dozens of fields in my career (and in this book). Yet there have been points (especially early) in my career when I wondered what to do next. At such points in a scholar's career, some advice on questions that need to be answered, and on under-utilized strategies for answering questions, can be very useful. This book thus hopes to inspire curiosity in particular directions. We will not be particularly prescriptive in doing so: identifying good questions, and preaching the strengths and weaknesses of particular theories and methods, but leaving it to researchers to identify useful combinations of questions and approaches.

We mentioned the culture wars above. It is not our primary purpose to address these. Yet I will note that several of our proposals should serve to increase our collective reliance on arguments and evidence and decrease the scope for ideological posturing to pose as research. The very task of integration is important here, for in integrating across different points of view we must necessarily grapple with and try to transcend ideological and other sorts of biases.

This work grew out of a couple of paragraphs toward the end of my *Making Sense of the Future* (Szostak 2022) in which I spoke of how human science research could better inform our pursuit of a better future. The purposes of the two books are quite distinct and a reader might easily like one without much caring for the other. Yet it is useful for the reader of this book to understand the project of that book: to identify a set of strategies for building a better future *that could potentially achieve broad public support.* So there you have my own ideological predilection: to value all perspectives but pursue a "radical middle" of bold policies that are slaves to neither conservative nor radical ideologies. One need not share that predilection to appreciate the present book. Yet a human science with less space for ideological posturing, and more attention to complexity and integration, would naturally support the development of public policies that could be widely appreciated.

This book surveys a broad range of topics, addressing research, teaching, and public policy advice across all of human science. We will in Chapter 2 discuss the sort of standards that an integrative work such as this should pursue. We will note at that time that works pursuing breadth need to engage seriously with each field they draw upon but cannot be held to the unachievable standard of practitioner-level familiarity with each. I will sketch my sense of key debates in each field I draw upon. I do not strive for an unachievable perfection but for arguments that are "good enough": that cannot defend against every possible caveat but are firmly grounded in a variety of scholarly conversations.

The approach we take in this book of surveying the entire human science system is rare if not unique. This approach guides us to make a series of clear arguments in each chapter. We then summarize these key points at the end of each chapter. The reader should have no trouble identifying the key points made in this work.

I noted above that we will critique the use of vague terminology in many fields of human science. We will also worry from time to time that scholars sometimes bury silly or trivial arguments in impenetrable prose. This book is written in plain English. The combination of broad coverage and clear language may expose us to a range of criticisms. This is as it should be. I will not hide behind purposeful ambiguity or verbosity.

There is an irony at the heart of this work. We will argue that a theory of everything is not possible: that the best we can do is to integrate a set of understandings of diverse subsystems and causal links. Yet we will pursue an organizing structure for all of these diverse understandings. We thus simultaneously engage with all fields while urging others not to do so. The difference, of course, is that we are saying how human science should proceed rather than performing (for the most part) human science research – beyond the obvious fact that we employ human science understandings to explore human science itself.

Human Science and Natural Science

A comparison with natural science is useful. There is a more logical division among disciplines in the natural sciences. These are often distinguished by levels of analysis: physicists study atoms, chemists draw on understandings of atoms in exploring chemical reactions, and biologists draw on understandings of certain chemicals in exploring organisms. It is also often possible to completely isolate certain relationships in natural science. Natural substances behave the same in the lab as in the wild. This means that much of natural science can rely heavily on the experimental method and focus on a small set of relationships among phenomena at a time. Yet even there recourse to larger models and multiple methods is often advisable. If we think of the great insights in natural science, they generally involve a small set of phenomena: how certain chemicals react, how sub-atomic particles interact, how certain pharmaceuticals affect certain bodily organs or functions, and so on. Yet these little pieces of knowledge are stitched together: We know that chemical reactions reflect the bonding of atoms, and that biological practices involve complex chemical compounds. Attempts to develop one unified theory of natural processes have not proceeded very far but we nevertheless have a coherent body of understanding. There are gaps in that body of understanding of course – made clear precisely because of this coherence – and natural scientists noodle away at expanding our understanding, but there is a clear sense that our natural science understanding is both broadly coherent and steadily expanding. We strive in this book to enhance both the coherence and rate of advance in understanding in human science so that it more closely resembles natural science in these respects.

It will be useful at many points in this book to compare natural science and human science. At times, we can draw direct lessons from natural science for human science. Yet at other times, we must be cognizant of the key differences between the two and discuss how human science practice must necessarily differ from natural science practice. Human science, as Maxwell (2020, 48) has argued, is inherently more complex than natural science, precisely because it must grapple with a large number of phenomena that interact. We will find instances where human scientists could usefully mimic natural scientists (developing a more logical set of disciplines being one of these) and other instances where human scientists mistakenly think that they should.[7] In both cases, it is useful to reflect on how the two enterprises are similar and how they are not (keeping in mind that there is diversity within these two broad groupings also).

Why Do This?

The Preface explains how I came to write this book. Yet it is perhaps useful to summarize here the key experiences and attitudes that I bring to the present exercise. Most importantly, I have published in a dozen fields across (and beyond) human science, and thus have some understanding of many different academic communities. I have been a scholar of the theory and practice of interdisciplinarity, but one that has urged a type of interdisciplinarity that maintains rigorous academic standards (see my manifesto of interdisciplinarity, Szostak (2019), and my two co-authored textbooks Repko and Szostak (2020) and Repko, Szostak, and Buchberger (2020)). I have published two books (Szostak 2004; Szostak, Gnoli, and López-Huertas 2016) and several articles in the field of Knowledge Organization. These inform my efforts in this book to enhance the coherence of human science. I have appreciated the many biases and limitations to human science identified by scholars once known as postmodernists, but argued that we can and must seek to transcend these and carefully amass argument and evidence with an aim of eventual scholarly consensus (Szostak 2007). I have some familiarity with the literature on creativity (Szostak 2017a). I have explored public policy in many places, but especially Szostak (2022). I have spent my career integrating and seeking a middle ground between competing arguments, but that has never prevented me from suggesting creative solutions.

As an interdisciplinary scholar, I have usefully drawn upon research from every corner of the human sciences. Yet I have often been struck by the twin facts that research often does not focus on the questions of greatest interest to policy-makers or the public, and that research often reflects some critical misunderstandings about how productive academic inquiries are best pursued. As a teacher and sometimes administrator, I have likewise had cause to reflect that we do not always teach our students the most important information and skills for them to succeed in life.

This book highlights how we can do better. It is deeply respectful of what we have collectively accomplished. It focuses on constructive criticism: how we could ask better questions, communicate better, and better employ our theories and methods to aid human understanding. Yet we must at times explore the disadvantages associated with present practices: the failure to place specialized research in context, the sloppy efforts toward defining key terminology in many fields, and slavish adherence to particular methods.

In sum, *Integrating Human Science* aims to improve the human sciences so that research is more insightful and coherent, students are better prepared, and public policy advice is better formulated. Yet we do this while enhancing rather than restricting the ability of scholars to follow their curiosity, and to employ the theories and methods they find most appropriate.[8]

Such a book serves many potential audiences. It should most obviously be of interest to the sorts of scholars cited in Chapter 3 who themselves engage with questions of how to improve research in the social sciences or humanities.

Likewise, it addresses a set of issues of key interest to those who explore General Education or Collegium Generale curricula or who worry about what we should be teaching in (high schools and) universities. The book might be used as a text in courses in General Education, Collegium Generale, Liberal Studies, or Interdisciplinary Studies that explore the nature of the academy or of human science, in courses with a focus on understanding the social sciences or humanities, or in courses on the history and philosophy of human science. Those who worry about how to translate academic understandings into useful public policies should find Chapter 7 of particular interest; that chapter builds upon the analysis of the preceding chapters. University administrators also should find this book useful in informing curricula, research strategies, and efforts to influence public policy.

Most of all, though, this book is aimed at every scholar or student in the human sciences who wonders how the things they study fit within the bigger picture of human understanding (they may also gain insights into how universities and libraries are organized). It is hoped that in outlining the big picture, students will gain a broader understanding and scholars will be guided toward research that fills gaps in our collective understanding and (often) informs superior public policy.

Summary

- Human science involves the study of relationships among dozens of key phenomena. We need to integrate our understanding of particular (sets of) causal links into a coherent whole.
- We thus need a mix of specialized and integrative research.
- We also need clarity in terminology.
- We need to seek evidence from multiple theories and methods.
- These simple and inter-related arguments have profound implications for research (both generally and for each field of study), teaching, libraries, public policy advice, and university administration. These will in turn be the subjects of the next chapters.
- We will focus on constructive suggestions to improve human science practice, but occasionally criticize existing practices. We will focus on what we should do more of, and only rarely indicate that we should stop doing some things.
- We will pursue breadth of coverage but try to delve deeply enough into each topic to adequately reflect relevant literatures.
- We will often compare human science to natural science, indicating when we can follow similar practices and when we cannot.
- Our hope is to encourage research that is more productive, better educational outcomes, and superior policy advice.
- There are many audiences for this book, but it is aimed at any scholar or student who seeks to comprehend how what they study fits within a broader understanding.

Notes

1 Mattick (2020, 1) is far more pessimistic than us. He speaks of "a striking degree of agreement on the unsatisfactory state of social theory itself, not only among philosophical outsiders but among stock-taking anthropologists, sociologists, economists, and political scientists themselves." He says that outside of any school, there is no consensus on the questions to ask or theories and methods to employ. We hope to provide solid advice on both counts.

2 Boyer (1990) famously identified four types of scholarship: discovery, integration, application to the real world, and the scholarship of teaching. We will engage with each of these in this book, and show how they are related.

3 Elman, Gerring, and Mahoney (2020) in their introduction list a host of recent advances in social science methodology: machine learning, digitization, advances in experimentation, advances in causal modeling, GIS, and software for data analysis. They are still not sure that our understanding has advanced much.

4 My approach echoes Chambers' (2017, Preface) attitude toward his discipline of Psychology: "Despite its many flaws the castle has served me well. It sheltered me during my formative years as a junior researcher and advanced me to a position where I can now talk openly about the need for renovation. And I stress *renovation* because I am not suggesting we demolish our stronghold and start over."

5 Williams (2020, 202) voices a similar sentiment regarding his advocacy of different guidelines for social research: "Difference does not mean destruction of what is already good [in social scientific practice], but a questioning of how we think about the social world and consequently, how we investigate it."

6 Mahoney and Thelen (2015, 9) share this concern, and worry that advocates of particular methods urge us to investigate only the questions that their methods can shed light on.

7 Chambers (2017, Preface) warns of a scholarly "culture where the *appearance* of science was seen as an appropriate replacement for the *practice* of science."

8 "Let us insist in saying that such ability [for constructive scholarship] requires the definition of some general methodological rules that do not imprison human creativity in rigid procedures but nevertheless make possible both dialogue and co-operation among scholars as well as the recognition of real contributions to the advancement of knowledge" (Fusari 2014, 4).

2

RESEARCH IN HUMAN SCIENCE

The Map of Human Science

Imagine that you are teaching a course in North American geography. You describe the various regions in turn: Great Lakes, Rocky Mountains, Great Plains, and so on. On the final exam, you ask the students to describe the route from the Great Lakes to the Pacific and are disappointed when many wind up in Canada. If only they had had a map to guide them. Maps are so useful, for they allow us to draw connections and put places on the map in a broader perspective. Without a map of human science, it is hard – far harder than it need be – for both scholars and students to appreciate how one topic relates to another, or to appreciate how one phenomenon studied by one group of scholars fits within a broader view of science as a whole. Yet it turns out that it is straightforward to map human science.

Human science involves a set of relationships connecting some dozens of phenomena.[1] We will often use the phrase "causal link" in what follows to describe the effect that one phenomenon exerts on another. We have learned the hard way over the years that some people interpret "causal link" to mean that only one phenomenon exerts an influence on the other phenomenon. That is not at all our intent. Indeed, we will suggest that each phenomenon both influences and is influenced by several others. Every phenomenon is causally related to every other phenomenon, at least indirectly. So when we describe a causal link between phenomenon X and phenomenon Y we are stating only that X exerts some influence on Y, fully cognizant that other phenomena also influence Y.

We have not yet defined phenomena. This is quite straightforward: A phenomenon is a "thing that we study." A more precise definition will come in Table 2.1 when we list the key phenomena studied in human science. For the rest of this book, the word "phenomenon" refers exclusively to "one of those things

DOI: 10.4324/9781003275237-2

TABLE 2.1 The Phenomena

Main categories	Second-level phenomena	Third-level phenomena
Genetic predisposition	Abilities	Consciousness, subconsciousness, vocalization, perception (five, senses), decision-making, tool making, learning, other physical attributes (locomotion, eating, etc.)
	Motivations	Food, clothing, shelter, safety, sex, betterment, aggression, altruism, fairness, identification with group
	Emotions	Love, anger, fear, jealousy, guilt empathy, anxiety, fatigue, humor, joy, grief, disgust, aesthetic sense, emotional display
	Time preference	
Individual differences (Abilities:)	Physical abilities	Speed, strength, endurance
	Physical appearance	Height, weight, symmetry
	Energy level	Physical, mental
	Intelligences	Musical, spatial, mathematical, verbal, kinesthetic, interpersonal
(Personality:)	Sociability (extro/introversion)	Talkative, assertive, adventurous, enthusiastic vs. reserved, withdrawn
	Emotionality (stable/moody)	Contentment, composure, vs. anxiety, self-pity
	Conscientiousness	Thoroughness, precision, foresight, organization, perseverance vs. carelessness, disorderly, frivolous
	Affection (selfish/agreeable)	Sympathetic, appreciative, kind, generous, vs. cruel, quarrelsome, faultfinding
	Intellectual orientation (holistic/analytical)	Openness, imagination, curiosity, sensitivity vs. close-mindedness
	Other dimensions?	Dominant/submissive, in/dependent, strong/weak, future/present-oriented humor, aggression, happiness
	Disorders?	Schizophrenia, psychoticism, …?
	Sexual orientation	View of self, others, causal
	Schemas	relationships
	Interpersonal relationships	Parent/child, sibling, employee/r, romance, friendship, casual
Economy	Total output	Price level, unemployment, trade, individual goods and services
	Income distribution	
	Economic ideology	
	Economic institutions	Ownership (inheritance), production, exchange, trade, finance, labor relations, organizations
Art	Nonreproducible	Painting, sculpture, architecture, prose, poetry
	Reproducible	Theater, film, photography, music, Danced

(Continued)

TABLE 2.1 The Phenomena (*Continued*)

Themes	Second-level phenomena	Third-level phenomena
Social structure	Gender	
	Family types, kinship	Nuclear, extended, single parent
	Classes (various typologies)	Occupations (various)
	Ethnic/Racial divisions	
	Social ideology	
Politics	Political institutions	Decision-making systems, rules (including laws), organizations
	Political ideology	
	Nationalism	
	Public opinion	Issues (various)
	Crime	Versus Persons/Property
Technology and science	Fields (various)	Innovations (various)
	Recognizing the problem	
	Setting the stage	
	Act of insight	
	Critical revision	
	Diffusion/Transmission	Communication, adoption
Health	Nutrition	Diverse nutritional needs
	Disease	Viral, bacterial, environmental
Population	Fertility	Fecundity, deviation from maximum
	Mortality	Causes of death (various)
	Migration	Distance, international?, temporary?
	Age distribution	
Culture	Languages	By descent?
	Religions	Providence, revelation, salvation, miracles, doctrine
	Stories	Myths, fairy tales, legends, family sagas, fables, jokes
	Expressions of culture	Rituals, dance, song, cuisine, attire, ornamentation of buildings, games
	Values (Goals:)	Ambition, optimism, attitudes toward wealth, power, prestige, honor, recognition, love, friendship, sex, incest, marriage, time preference, physical and psychological well-being
	(Means:)	Honesty, ethics, righteousness, fate, work valued intrinsically, violence, vengeance, curiosity, innovation, nature, healing
	(Community:)	Identity, family versus community, openness to outsiders, egalitarianism, attitude to young and old, responsibility, authoritarianism, respect for individuals
	(Everyday norms:)	Courtesy, manners, tidiness, proxemics, cleanliness, punctuality, conversational rules, locomotion rules, tipping

(*Continued*)

TABLE 2.1 The Phenomena (*Continued*)

Themes	Second-level phenomena	Third-level phenomena
Non-human Environment	Soil	Soil Types (various)
	Topography	Land forms (various)
	Climate	Climate Patterns (various)
	Flora	Species (various)
	Fauna	Species (various)
	Resource availability	Various Resources
	Water availability	
	Natural disasters	Flood, tornado, hurricane, earthquake, volcano
	Day and night	Mode (various)
	Transport infrastructure	Offices, houses, fences, etc.
	Built environments	
	Population density	

Source: Szostak (2003, 2004).

in Table 2.1) or a component of one of those things)" – except on the rare occasions when we refer explicitly to natural science phenomena. We should stress here that a phenomenon is a "single thing that we study." We will also discuss the relationships among phenomena. However, a combination of phenomena and relationships is a causal link(s), not a phenomenon. Within our definition of these terms, it would be a mistake to describe, say, globalization, as a "phenomenon," for this term describes a set of causal links.

A subsystem is a set of causal links within our map of human science. It only makes sense to study such a subsystem if the causal links within the system are much stronger than the myriad causal links connecting the phenomena within the subsystem to phenomena beyond the subsystem. Only then is it likely that we will be able to detect regularities within our subsystem. Disciplines in human science often focus on subsystems. We will want in Chapter 4 to ask to what degree it does make sense to study these systems in isolation.

We keep using the word "map." We invite readers to envision a large map involving dozens of phenomena with thousands of arrows connecting these. Though we have not yet mentioned it, some of these arrows may themselves be complex, with two or more phenomena combining to exert a particular influence on another phenomenon. In practice, the map of human science is too messy to be drawn in a book (though a wall chart might make a nice gift to aspiring human scientists). In Figure 2.1, we do provide an abridged map focused on the main categories of phenomena in Table 2.1. One of the attractions of studying subsystems is precisely that they lend themselves to a far more manageable map (we will draw a couple of these in Chapter 4).

Even integrative research in human science generally engages only one smallish subset of the map of human science. Figure 2.2 reprises a picture of the causes of economic growth from Repko and Szostak (2020). We can see that a full appreciation of the sources of economic prosperity requires us to grapple with phenomena studied in multiple disciplines. Economists have

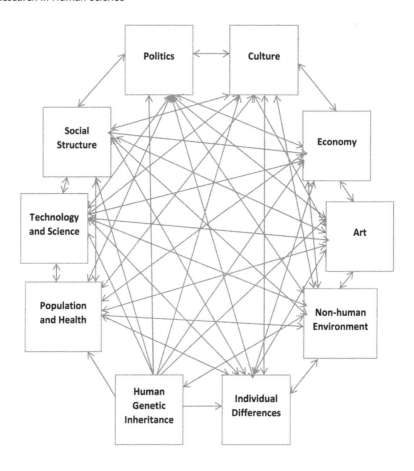

Note: There are potentially two-way arrows between any sets of phenomena, except for genetic inheritance.

FIGURE 2.1 An Abridged Map of Human Science.

often limited themselves to interactions among a handful of economic variables such as investment or trade. But why do some societies invest or trade (or
innovate) more than others? To answer questions such as these we need to look
far beyond economic phenomena. One notable feature of Figure 2.2 is the
large set of relationships *among* the various phenomena that influence economic
output. We cannot simply add up the influences that each phenomenon exerts
independently upon economic output but need to grapple with a large set
of inter-relationships: not just how investment and technological innovation
affect output but how they influence each other, and in turn how they operate
within a web of influences.

Note also that we have carefully avoided using the word "subsystem" in
describing Figure 2.2. Nobody has conjectured that this web of relationships

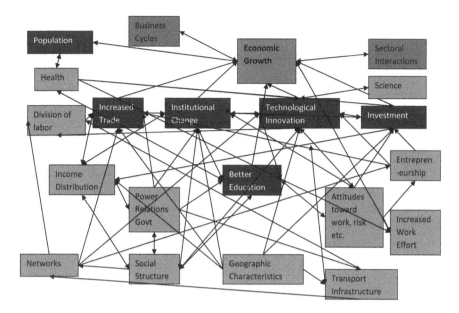

Source: Repko, Szostak, and Buchberger (2020)

FIGURE 2.2   Influences on Economic Growth.

Note: The darker boxes represent the "proximate causes" that economists had tended to emphasize.

operates somewhat independently from the rest of the phenomena in Table 2.1. Indeed, if "attitudes to work" is part of any subsystem, it would be the cultural subsystem studied in other disciplines. We will use phrases like "web of relationships" to describe a set of causal links studied because they shed light on some important question – In this case, what are the main influences on the level of economic output? Such webs are generally focused on understanding the main influences on a particular phenomenon.

You may have noted that Figure 2.2 talks about economic growth, while we have spoken above about levels of economic output. "Economic output" is a phenomenon. "Economic growth," an increase in economic output, is a "realization" of that phenomenon. Our study of causal links asks how a change in the realizations of one phenomenon influences the realizations of another phenomenon.

The reader is now asked to imagine Table 2.1 rendered as a map like Figure 2.1 or 2.2. There will be arrows all over the place. The dozens of phenomena generate thousands of arrows. Some arrows represent very strong influences while others might capture only occasional influences. Nevertheless, the latter cannot be ignored for they may from time to time prove important. We may not always have to worry about the potential impact of epidemics on the economic subsystem but it is best to be prepared for those occasions when we do need to worry.

In Szostak (2017b), I noted that most disciplines investigate a subsystem. These disciplines tend to investigate for the most part sources of stability within these systems: economic stability, cultural stability, and social stability. This stability usually reflects "negative feedback loops": Sets of causal relationships that return the system to stability if shocked away from it (such as the tendency of prices to rise if demand for a product temporarily exceeds supply, discouraging consumption while encouraging production and thus bringing supply and demand back in line). Disciplinary scholars may well recognize that these systems of stability can be shocked from the outside. However, the natural tendency of specialized scholars to emphasize interactions among "their" sets of phenomena means that the sources of stability receive far more attention than the sources of instability. Yet of course, we want our understanding of human science to explain sources of both stability and instability. Indeed, human science understanding may be more important when humans grapple with instability than when they cope with stability. Therefore, we very much need to integrate our understanding of disciplinary subsystems with an enhanced appreciation of the links that connect those subsystems.

We might make special note here of the fact that our map of human science includes sets of both individual-level phenomena and sets of societal-level phenomena. There have been long traditions in human science of both methodological individualism and its converse. Advocates of the former maintain that we can understand everything in terms of individual behavior and that societies are nothing more than a combination of individuals. Advocates of the latter maintain that individuals are merely buffeted by cultural, economic, and political forces beyond their control, and that we should focus our analysis then entirely at the societal level. We will take the sensible middle ground in this book. Individuals are indeed influenced by a host of societal-level forces but in turn make choices that influence societal-level outcomes. This common-sense position accords with how most of us view the world. This need not be correct, we should stress, and human scientists must be ready from time to time to point out that commonplace understandings are misguided. In this case, though, it seems reasonable to conclude that individual humans both influence and are influenced by the societies they inhabit. We will surely encounter multiple examples of influences in both directions in the pages to follow. If methodological individualists were entirely correct then legions of sociologists and anthropologists and others have been simply wasting their time these last decades. If methodological individualists are entirely wrong, then most psychologists and economists could have stayed in bed. We will from time to time in this book question certain research agendas but we would hesitate to suggest that entire disciplines have been completely misguided.[2]

Identifying Phenomena

Let us talk a little bit about the phenomena listed in Table 2.1. These were first identified inductively by reading widely in Szostak (2003). I read hundreds and hundreds of works across all of human science, and identified the key phenomena investigated by these. I have in the time since updated and fleshed out the table for the purposes of library classification (see Chapter 6). Readers can find the expanded schedules of phenomena on the website of my Basic Concepts Classification (Szostak n.d.). Note that these schedules expand what are called third-level phenomena in Table 2.1. I have shown that these schedules do a far better job of capturing the essence of human science literature than do existing systems of library classification. That is, we can through reference to one or a few causal links among the phenomena in Table 2.1 more precisely represent the essence of books and articles in human science than is possible under extant systems of library classification. Moreover, I have performed a few sampling exercises which have found that my classification copes very well with randomly selected literature from across human science. To be sure, on rare occasions I have added the occasional phenomenon to my classification when I came across a book that otherwise I could not classify readily. But I am comfortable in asserting both that my classification can cope with the vast bulk of research in human science, and that small additions can easily be made to cope with the remainder.

The reader can note that the organization of the table bears some resemblance to the disciplinary structure in human science but is not entirely beholden to this. My purpose was to place the diverse literature of human science within some logical structure. Such a logical structure would be impossible if I insisted on merging the two quite distinct activities undertaken by anthropologists, examining the physical remains of hominids and examining modern cultures. Likewise, the distinct efforts of sociologists to study culture, crime, demography, and social structure could not be grouped together logically. The efforts of some scholars in "cultural studies" to subsume wide swathes of political, economic, and social behavior under "culture" would also make a mockery of any attempt at logical structure.

We can attempt simple definitions of our main categories of phenomena. Economy deals with how a society produces goods and services desired for their utility, and then distributes these goods and services among the population. Politics addresses formal mechanisms for making society-wide decisions (that is, formal exercises of power). Social structure looks at how societal subgroups interact. Culture comprises a set of values mainly but also practices that support group identity. Art is distinguished from both culture and economy by examining goods produced primarily for aesthetic appreciation. Health and population is self-evidently a set of phenomena that describe the numbers and health of human populations. Technology and science is equally self-evident. As noted above, in addition to societal-level phenomena we also encompass individual-level phenomena. These are organized in two categories, the first examining the common characteristics of humanity, and the second capturing individual diversity. A final category captures the key elements of the non-human environment with which humans engage.

We will not describe the lower levels of Table 2.1 in detail. We can note that these were derived by a similar combination of induction and deduction: we found a place for everything that scholars talk about within a logical structure. Most lower-level phenomena are "types of" higher-level phenomena, though there are exceptions. We will note in our discussion of terminological clarity below that the fleshing out of Table 2.1 serves to clarify the definition of all terms in the table. Our definition of culture above becomes much clearer if one explores the list of values and cultural expressions it includes, and just as importantly the artistic, economic, and political phenomena that it excludes.

With a small but important minority of the terms in Table 2.1, we have to worry about how our values might shape our definitions of terms. The French philosopher Michel Foucault decades ago warned us that our definitions of "mental illness" and "crime," among other terms, reflected the culture and power relations of the society. The powerful could declare those they disliked to be either criminal or sick and have them removed from society. Homosexuals were one group that were treated in precisely those ways at the time that Foucault was writing. Such horrific practices pose a challenge to our efforts to organize human science understanding. As just one difficulty, we can note that works on homosexuality would have been classified under "mental illness" in our libraries just decades ago, but would now be found within some classification of sexual orientation. Likewise consumption of marijuana was a crime in Canada just a couple of years ago but no longer.

The Foucault challenge is important but not insoluble. First, the reader is invited to interrogate the terminology in Table 2.1: For how many terms do Foucault's concerns seem critical? To be sure, Foucault himself might have viewed such an exercise with suspicion, for he warned us of the dangers of hidden bias. We might have more confidence in some terms than we should have. Yet do we really need to worry about bias in saying that "population" refers to the number of people in a society (at least now that we do not purposely miscount some races or ethnic groups)? For the minority of terms for which bias is a potential problem, we have three strategies. First, we can consciously interrogate our biases.[3] Does our (society's) definition of crime or mental illness go beyond behaviors that are harmful to others or ourselves, to punish people for just being social misfits or having minority perspectives? (see Henry and Howard 2019 for ideas on how to do so). Second, we can appreciate that we may occasionally have to adjust our "map," such as when homosexuality was moved from mental illness to sexual orientation. Third, and most importantly, we can redouble our efforts to investigate particular causal links. Foucault's path-breaking analyses were, after all, a novel exploration of how certain cultural attitudes and power structures influenced our definitions of both crime and mental illness. They do not force us to throw out the very ideas of "crime" and "mental illness" but to recognize that certain realizations of these were misguided and harmful.[4] In particular, we might ask to what extent social categories are defined in particular ways in order to facilitate or justify discrimination? Note that we need to have a fairly clear idea of the phenomena in question in order to investigate biases in their definition.

It may be useful to clarify the meaning of phenomena, realizations, and causal links.[5] We would treat democracy as a phenomenon. We might attach adjectives to this, such as parliamentary democracy. We can agree with Buvke (2019) that phenomena are represented by nouns. The adjectives then represent different realizations of the phenomenon. We can (attempt to) define democracy as a system in which the power to make decisions for society is widely distributed in that society. We can recognize that there are many possible realizations of this (or any other) phenomenon. We can attempt to examine causal links at the level of both phenomena (democracy causes…) or realizations (parliamentary democracy causes…). Buvke (2019) wonders about whether elections or citizen rights are included in our definition of democracy. My preference is to define phenomena narrowly (and generally in functional terms: democracies allow the citizens to influence policy, and this almost necessarily involves some sort of voting) and thus we could treat the influence of rights on democracy as causal links. We agree wholeheartedly with Buvke that authors need to be clear (but often are not) about how they are defining a concept.[6] Buvke argues that western society's definition of family has changed a lot over recent decades.[7] I would suggest instead that we can define the phenomenon of "family" as a group connected by genetics or adoption inhabiting (at least much of the time) the same place. Nuclear families, extended families, and a host of other family types are different realizations of this enduring phenomenon. Again, we can try to seek both a general understanding of the role that families play and more specific understandings of the roles that different family types play. (Buvke then invites us to worry about how closely the data we may employ resemble the phenomena we wish to study; this is a point we will return to later).[8]

The Openness of Subsystems

All subsystems are open. This simply means that the phenomena within any subsystem connect causally to phenomena outside that system (as signaled by Figure 2.1). This is a simple fact of human science.[9] Yet it is a fact regularly forgotten in the daily activity of specialized research. Economists, for example, formulate mathematical models of the economic system and then attempt to estimate the precise mathematical relationships within that system. This is a sensible project for a closed system, for then it might be the case that the system acts with such regularity that precise and enduring relationships can be identified. However, if the phenomena within the model are regularly interacting with phenomena outside the model, the likelihood of identifying a set of stable relationships within the model disappears. Of course, there is a question of degree here. If the strength of relationships within the model is *much* stronger than the set of relationships beyond the model, then one may be able to get some strong sense of how the phenomena within the model interact. Even then, this regularity may be temporary. As noted with the case of pandemics above, a connection to one phenomenon outside the model may lie dormant for years and then strike with devastating effect. The literature on econometric analysis of course recognizes that "unobserved variables" – that is, phenomena not included in the model – can mess up the results of statistical analysis. Moreover, economists are urged to do "robustness checks" to see if their model generates similar results under different conditions. I would not for a minute pretend that all of these efforts at model-building and econometric estimation are useless (though some economic methodologists, notably Tony Lawson in many works, take a far more critical position than I do). Nevertheless, I find it unsurprising that estimations tend to find quite different results when performed on different data sets: choices of country(s) and time period are often crucial. A recognition that we are generally prevented from achieving precision precisely because all subsystems are open would encourage economists to exercise judgment in evaluating the results of their empirical work.

This is our first sign that we will need to interrogate how human scientists develop and employ theories and methods. We will generate below some straightforward suggestions on how human scientists might collectively better exercise judgment in their application of theory and method. At that time, we will also have cause to explore the difference between "phenomenon" and "variable," but can simply note here that scholars can often not directly measure realizations of phenomena but are forced to rely on proxies for these. Judgment is again called for in assessing how well the proxy stands in for the phenomenon in question.[10]

We noted in Chapter 1 that human science differs in important ways from much of natural science. The biggest single difference likely involves the relative openness of systems. Chemists are able to study how a particular pair of chemicals react. They can identify the precise conditions of temperature and pressure under which a certain reaction will occur. They need not worry about the phase of the moon or the brightness of the lights, and certainly not about the cultural attitudes of anyone involved. They can isolate a closed system and study it in detail. Physicists likewise can study atomic structure without worrying about tectonic plates or political institutions. Human scientists *never* have this luxury (We can to be sure sometimes examine one causal link very carefully but still need to place any insights we gain from, say, an experiment in context). It is of course tempting to pretend that we can be as precise as natural scientists, but a scientific project grounded in self-delusion is likely not as productive as one that officially recognizes its limitations.

I should stress that I am definitively *not* calling for an end to the study of subsystems. Quite the contrary. I think that communities of specialized researchers *must* focus on subsystems or smallish sets of causal links. Yet they must appreciate that their subsystems are open. Since communities of specialized researchers focus on a small set of phenomena, they are constantly tempted to forget the openness of their system. That is, they simply do not see the connections to phenomena that they do not study. The only antidote is integrative research that connects the phenomena that different specialized communities study and serves as a constant reminder to them of the influences on and of the phenomena they study.

Natural scientists are able to generate mathematically precise descriptions of a variety of causal relationships. The best that human scientists can aspire to is "contextualized generalizations." These take the following format:

- Phenomenon X exerts influence N on phenomenon Y.
- But only in the presence of realization A of phenomenon Z (W, V, U…).
- And in the absence of realization B of phenomenon T (S, R, Q…).

We may at times substitute for bullet 1 some commentary on a subsystem or other set of causal links:

- This subsystem or set of links exhibits stability, or conversely moves in a particular direction (or cycles).
- But only in the presence of realization A of phenomenon Z (W, V, U…).
- And in the absence of realization B of phenomenon T (S, R, Q…).

Note that once we collectively recognize that contextualized generalizations are our goal then the need for regular interaction between specialized and integrative researchers becomes patently obvious.[11]

No Theory of Everything

We promised above that we would argue against the obvious alternative of developing some "theory of everything" that could encompass all of human science. The human science system is itself not entirely closed since several human science phenomena (economic output, human health) interact powerfully with natural science phenomena, but arguably human science represents a fairly closed system within which we might strive to identify certain regularities.[12] There are myriad reasons to doubt that a unified theory of everything will ever be possible, and even to doubt that it is desirable:

- Human scientists apply a wide variety of different theories to different (sets of) causal links. It is highly unlikely that almost all of them are wrong.
- There is just simply way too much going on to imagine that one big theory could replace hundreds (or more) contextualized generalizations.
- The historical efforts to develop one big theory (or method) of everything have not proven particularly successful, though they have sometimes attracted a cult of followers. (We might consider here the efforts of Rudolph Carnap (1934) and associates in the Unity of Science movement early in the 20th century, or the "transdisciplinarity" of Basarab Nicolescu (2002) and colleagues in more recent decades).[13]
- Natural science has progressed very far without its own theory of everything. Understandings of atomic structure, chemical reactions, biological evolution, and plate tectonics need to be broadly consistent but need not be tied into one tidy bundle in order to be useful.

Most human scientists seem to accept that we should not be striving toward one unified theory. Indeed, Bowen et al. (2021, 1)[14] report a shift in the last decades from the pursuit of grand theories associated with names like Marx or Weber to more focused research:

> The "grand theory" names remain "big" in the twenty-first century, but now we are more likely to define our research in terms of particular problems, specific lines of inquiry, and suitable concepts. In doing so we may well draw from broad-based and far-reaching social theory, but we do so in order to analyze new, specific challenges, from grasping the everyday workings of markets, courtrooms, and clinics, to inscribing the transformations of practice within research disciplines themselves.

As emphasized above, if we accept that a unified theory of everything is impossible, then we must either accept that human science will forever be a congeries of inconsistent blobs of understanding or we can strive for some sort of conceptual unity. Our map of human science allows us to stitch together diverse theoretical understandings of different causal links into a coherent whole (This potential can only be realized with some other innovations to be addressed below, but the map makes it possible). This is feasible because our map itself is stable. Human scientists develop new theories regularly, but the phenomena we study do not change. The realizations of phenomena change to be sure, but the phenomena themselves do not: a new technology is a new realization of "technological innovation."[15] This may be the most important insight of this entire book: that we can develop a map of stable phenomena on which we can place our theoretical understandings of each causal link or subsystem. We can then turn our attention to how to best flesh out this map by clarifying and integrating our understandings of causal links and subsystems. We should stress, though, that our map is able to generate a potential coherence without limiting at all the range of theories or methods that a researcher might choose to apply to the study of any set of phenomena.

Specialization and Integration

Symbiosis[16]

The case for cross-disciplinary integration is commonly made in terms of complex policy issues. We face a set of public policy challenges that involves interactions among phenomena studied in multiple fields: climate change, inner city poverty, and challenges associated with technological innovation among them. We need to integrate the insights of multiple communities of specialized researchers in order to address such problems (We will return to how best to provide public policy advice in Chapter 7). If we rely only on economists to address inner city poverty, we will miss insights about how cultural values, discrimination, and elements of personal psychology encourage a cycle of poverty.

The argument for cross-disciplinary integration goes far beyond complex policy issues. We have seen just above that *all* of the insights of specialized research need to be placed in context, for the simple reason that all systems are open. Moreover, many issues outside of public policy require a broad interdisciplinary investigation, such as how does art move us?[17] In other words, there are a host of causal links among phenomena investigated by different disciplines that tend to receive limited attention by either discipline, and thus require some interdisciplinary attention.

Why even have communities of specialized scholars? Because there are tremendous advantages in communication if a group of scholars share definitions of key terminology and an understanding of how a core set of theories and methods should be employed. Students often think that the books and articles that they are forced to read are acts of individual expression. Yet all of those annoying references should surely signal that scholarship is a conversation in which every contribution is providing answers to questions raised by others or extending the analysis of others or commenting on others. If an author does do something novel they will spend their first paragraphs explaining how their work fits into the conversation. Scholars within a specialized community do not have to waste time defining terms or explaining core theories or methods but can get right on to describing what they are adding to an ongoing conversation. This is a huge advantage, and allows some communities steadily to gain a more refined understanding of their subject matter through time. Yet as with most good things in life, there is a cost: By stressing the study of only some theories, methods, and phenomena they *necessarily* miss insights that might come from alternative theories or methods, or studying interactions with other phenomena.

There is thus a symbiosis between disciplinary and interdisciplinary research. The latter necessarily seeks to integrate insights from the former. In turn, interdisciplinarity can place the work of disciplinary scholars in context:

> Because of the importance of the confrontation of ideas, knowledge produced by the disciplines needs to be tensioned against each other. Considering that the aim of interdisciplinary research is to integrate disciplinary insights to produce an advancement of science, successful interdisciplinary research feeds the disciplines with new concepts, methods, and perspectives. Interdisciplinarity is thus not contradictory to academic disciplines. Rather, it is essential to their evolution and reconfiguration and has a transformative potential for academic institutions, In other words, to be dynamic and thriving, academic disciplines need interdisciplinary research.
>
> *(Wernli and Darbellay 2016, 32)*

We can already see one potential advantage of integration *within* disciplines, to complement both specialized research and integration *across* disciplines. We may be able to link the efforts of scholars employing different theories or methods to study interactions among the same set of phenomena. Can we develop a more comprehensive, more nuanced understanding of how these phenomena interact by integrating the insights of scholars employing different theories and methods? We will argue just below that different methods and theory types have different strengths and weaknesses, and so we are likely to gain a better understanding from a multi-faceted approach.

Yet there is a second reason to encourage integration within disciplines. The scholarly conversations at the heart of specialized communities of researchers tend to be very forgetful. Scholar A makes a point that B builds upon and scholar C critiques. By the time scholar N is commenting on scholar M's contribution to the discourse, the insights of B and C are long forgotten. It is entirely possible for N to make the same point as B without realizing it, or to disagree with B without realizing it. There is usually a paragraph or two at the start of every article that places that article within the scholarly conversation: It is impossible in limited space to pay heed to more than a handful of preceding works (Elman, Gerring, and Mahoney 2020). The occasional survey article in a field may do better, but these are rare and often take a biased approach that emphasizes works that the author finds congenial. There is little scholarly incentive to provide balanced and comprehensive surveys of a field.

The result, then, is that the academy devotes the vast bulk of its attention to specialized research, but makes stunningly little effort to tie individual pieces of specialized research into a larger whole, either within or across disciplines. Yet that specialized research enterprise would clearly benefit from greater efforts at integration. Specialized researchers would become aware of the potential advantages of utilizing different theories or methods or studying a different set of phenomena.[18] Moreover, they would be relieved of the danger of re-inventing the wheel by having access to integrative works that provided unbiased surveys of their fields, seeking to synthesize the full body of research into a coherent whole.[19]

Integrative works serve a further role in identifying which pieces of specialized research contribute the most to our collective understanding of particular causal links.[20] Martinelli (2017) wonders, for example, if works focused on improving our society in any way would ever mention certain types of research in philology. He worries that specialized communities may at times get excited about details that are of limited import beyond that community. On the other hand, integrative works may find great value in particular specialized works that have received limited applause within specialized communities themselves: Such works might fill important gaps in our collective understanding not appreciated by any specialized community.

These integrative tasks are not easy but nor are they unfeasible. They will require a significant effort at integration. Just like specialized research, integrative research is a conversation, and integrative scholars can build upon the work of other integrative scholars. Integrative scholars must also of course build upon the work of specialized scholars (and yes, the same scholar might do both types of work, though the skill set required is somewhat different). We thus see a symbiotic relationship: communities of specialized scholars generate insights on which communities of integrative scholars build, while communities of integrative scholars provide much useful advice on the most profitable directions for further specialized research. A scholarly enterprise that is exclusively specialized is far from being as successful as it could be. A scholarly enterprise that was mostly integrative would lack sufficient insights to build upon and would become an exercise in wild speculation. The ideal balance between specialized and integrative research is hard to estimate at present, but we are clearly far from that ideal balance.

We should stress the novelty of urging integrative work both within and across disciplines. The vast bulk of research on integration has focused on interdisciplinary contexts. Indeed, the two words "integrative" and "interdisciplinary" are often employed as synonyms. Yet we have seen that the two enterprises of integration within and across disciplines serve broadly similar roles. We might also note that interdisciplinary integration will proceed more easily if there is within-field integration: One of the main challenges of interdisciplinary research is gaining a sense of debates within the fields drawn upon. In turn, the insights of interdisciplinary integration can more readily inform communities of specialized scholars via integrative work within those communities. This is a logical place to integrate information about related links, and alternative theories and methods, into the community's discourse.

Standards for Integrative Work

We noted above that specialized research communities share a set of common understandings. These become instantiated in a set of – often unwritten but widely appreciated – standards on how research within a field should be performed. These standards tend to insist on the "proper" application of favored theories and methods. If specialized research dominates a field, then integrative research fails to fit the standards, and will only happen if a journal editor from time to time commissions some sort of survey article. (Handbooks and textbooks are other venues in which integrative work may appear, but authors in these venues will often pursue one narrow theoretical approach to the exclusion of others.)

One critical barrier to the greater pursuit of integrative work, then, is a fear that this work does not somehow meet academic standards. If one defines academic standards as applying theory A and method B correctly, then this will necessarily be true. What, though, if we can identify a set of equally rigorous standards with which to guide integrative research?

I have long worried that interdisciplinary research in particular needs to identify such standards, and issued a manifesto to that end (Szostak 2019). Those who are suspicious of interdisciplinarity can seize upon occasional pieces of superficial interdisciplinary analysis to condemn the entire interdisciplinary enterprise. We can only hope for integrative research to be recognized, appreciated, and drawn upon by specialized researchers if we can show them that it follows its own set of standards (It will also then be necessary to communicate valuable insights as suggested above – but insights alone can easily be ignored if they are generated by suspect investigative techniques).

As the co-author of two textbooks on how to perform interdisciplinary analysis (Repko and Szostak 2020; Repko et al. 2020), I think it is relatively straightforward to identify a set of relevant standards. Both of those books describe a set of steps that are required for successful interdisciplinary analysis, and a set of strategies that scholars have found to be useful for pursuing each of these steps. We can reasonably expect that scholars pursuing integrative analysis will be familiar with strategies that have proven useful in the past. Just as specialized researchers can refer to disciplinary methodologies, without needing to explain these in detail, integrative researchers should be able to employ well-known strategies without needing to justify these to the community of integrative researchers. Only if the researcher wishes to pursue some novel strategy will a detailed explanation and justification be called for – just as specialized researchers need to justify any important deviation from the standard theory or method employed in their field.

In addition to the general invocation to follow recognized strategies, I could outline a set of more precise standards:

- The question under investigation must be clear, unbiased, and jargon-free (or any jargon should be carefully defined). Indeed, clarity should be insisted upon throughout.
- The literature survey for a within-field integrative work should be reasonably exhaustive, detailing contributions from different theories and methods.
- For an integrative work that spans communities of specialized researchers, we need not insist on exhaustiveness but should demand a serious engagement with each field engaged. This will mean at a minimum that the integrative researcher is cognizant of debates in each field around the topic being addressed, and also aware of the general worldview or "disciplinary perspective" of each discipline being drawn upon. We expect the integrative researcher to display both breadth and depth of knowledge, and should be willing to relax our expectations with respect to depth as greater breadth is pursued.
- Integrative works engage in a kind of evaluation that complements the evaluation undertaken within communities of specialized researchers. Those communities will ask whether favored theories and methods were applied correctly. Integrative researchers can ask to what extent results might be biased by disciplinary perspective, and in particular the theories and methods employed. Researchers within a specialized research community rarely if ever will interrogate the favored theories and methods, or overall perspective, of their community.
- Integrative works will clarify the terminology employed in the works they draw upon and create a synthesis in which they express all insights in the same terminology.

- Integrative works will be very clear about which phenomena and causal links are being addressed, and whether different communities of scholars focus on different links. A visual map of these links will be highly recommended. Integrative works will ideally point to how other causal links might potentially interact with those under investigation.
- If examining a subsystem, integrative authors will interrogate whether the links within are indeed stronger than links beyond the subsystem.
- Where many works are surveyed that employ the same method, a meta-analysis should be performed that asks what the results would be if all of the data had been examined together.
- The integrative work should achieve integration. It should be more than a congeries of disparate ideas but produce a more comprehensive understanding that synthesizes at least some of the insights generated by different authors. (We have already discussed a couple of key strategies for this: clarifying terminology and drawing diagrams. There are others outlined in Repko and Szostak (2020).)
- The results should be expressed in a way that addresses the conversations going on within the scholarly communities addressed by the integrative research.

We want to avoid cherry picking, putting together a set of atypical remarks from different fields in a way that supports some pre-determined narrative. We want to insist on a serious engagement with the fields drawn upon, and an unbiased rendering of their insights. Then we want to insist on some actual integration – just as works of specialized research are expected to be novel in some way. Yet of course we should not insist on perfection, just as no work of specialized research is expected to answer key questions forever. These are important standards and a community of integrative researchers could easily monitor them.

The present work is itself an integrative work, though focused on the nature of human science rather than the nature of humanity itself. I have had these standards much in mind as I have written it. I have attempted to be clear throughout, avoiding the temptation to bury my arguments in big words and complex syntax. I will range across virtually all human science communities and thus I might plead for a relaxation of standards regarding depth. Yet I have sought to recognize key debates in the many fields I have drawn upon. I hope that this work is judged primarily on whether the whole is greater than the sum of its parts: Does it make a coherent case for an integrated human science? Note that not every component of my argument need be correct for the whole approach to be accepted. Yet I need to show that there is a credible line of argument justified by respectable lines of argument within diverse fields.

Since our purpose is to develop standards for integrative works that are comparable to the standards for judging specialized research, a direct comparison is valuable. Liao (2020) identifies the key factors that reviewers should engage when deciding if a piece of specialized research is worthy of publication: novelty, appropriate use of methods, internal logic, appropriate references, clarity, validity, identification of alternative explanations, and recognition of potential loopholes in the argument made. Several of these standards can be applied directly to integrative work: novelty, internal logic, appropriate references, and clarity. For appropriate use of methods, we can substitute appropriate use of integrative strategies. Validity means that the results identified apply beyond the particular research product to the world more widely: This standard is important for both specialized and integrative research but may be more easily achieved by works that integrate the results of multiple studies. We have insisted that the integrative researcher report in an unbiased fashion on scholarly debates, and thus they should more than meet the standard of "identifying alternative explanations." Liao notes that the reviewer should have some familiarity with the theory or method or subject matter of the paper in question. We can again substitute interdisciplinary strategy for disciplinary method. We can worry, though, that a specialized researcher may be biased in evaluating an integrative work, for that researcher may have a strong attachment to a particular theory or line of argument. Liao stresses that referees should focus on whether the subject is important, whether the paper adds to our understanding, the novelty of analysis (can a particular method be used elsewhere?), clarity of exposition, and suitability to journal. These can all be translated directly to the case of integrative research (with us yet again substituting integrative strategy for method). One interesting question is whether we need special journals for integrative research or should instead encourage all existing journals to welcome integrative works. It may be that we need new journals for interdisciplinary integration but that within-field integration can be pursued within existing journals. We can only find out for sure in practice.

Liao recognizes a handful of key problems with the present system of peer review. Though papers are expected to reference the literature there is no expectation of exhaustiveness. It is thus easy for a community of scholars to be forgetful, for each scholar only references the bits of prior knowledge necessary to support their results. Moreover, the strong emphasis on novelty limits incentives for any scholar to "replicate" the results of another to ensure their validity. Yet without replication, we can have limited confidence in any piece of research. Refereeing serves as a form of social control, and can easily lead to discrimination against research using theories or methods disfavored by the majority. It is noteworthy that integrative research can alleviate each of these problems. It can be held to a higher standard of exhaustiveness (when performed within fields). It will seek to explore contributions from multiple theories and methods, and thus advertise the value of these to members of the research community. While integrative researchers will not try to replicate individual pieces of research, they will evaluate whether similar pieces of research reach broadly similar conclusions. If they do, we can have increased confidence in this body of research. As we will see below, we can have even greater confidence if different methods point in a similar direction.

Clarifying Terminology

The Costs of Excessive Ambiguity

If we will pursue our goal of integrating both across and within specialized research communities, we will find that one of our first and most important challenges is to clarify terminology. Scholars often use the same word in quite different ways, while conversely they use quite different words for very similar things (Oliver 2010). The strategy of "redefinition" is thus generally the first task of an interdisciplinary scholar seeking to integrate insights from multiple disciplines (Repko and Szostak 2020). Scholars often seem to be disagreeing when one first reads what they have to say about a topic, but this difference turns out after careful (and generally time-consuming) analysis to reflect simply the fact that they defined key terminology differently. The task of integration becomes very difficult when the integrative researcher must carefully distinguish the meanings that authors are attaching to key terms.

Perhaps this is just a cross that we have to bear? We have spoken above about the shared understandings that guide specialized research. Perhaps the interdisciplinary integrator will just have to grapple forever with the fact that different communities establish different definitions that they find to be congenial. Philosophers such as Ludwig Wittgenstein have long noted that individual words take on meaning within a discourse community in which each word is defined in terms of other words, and these reciprocal definitions evolve slowly over time. Yet natural science aspires to and often achieves clear definitions that change little through time and are understood in a similar way across disciplinary boundaries. Geologists and chemists have an idea of what an atom is that is pretty close to what physicists think.[21]

This book aspires to achieving a coherent understanding of human science as a whole. This goal guides us to ask if an understanding within a community of scholars that is only comprehensible within that community is really an understanding. From our perspective at least, we want understandings that can be widely comprehended and then integrated into a larger whole. We have appreciated that specialized communities of scholars can benefit from a shared understanding of key terms. Yet we can now suggest that – if a community sees a need for specialized jargon (a need which itself should be interrogated) – this should be carefully defined. Members of specialized research communities should still find it useful to express their ideas in plain English whenever possible. Even if they will write up jargon-ridden publications, they should draft key passages in plain language to make sure that their argument is both coherent and persuasive.[22]

Despite the fact that specialized communities thrive on shared understandings, we will find that many communities within human science have contested definitions of key terminology. That is, authors disagree about how terms are best defined. Yet authors within these communities often do not bother to indicate carefully how they are defining these terms in their own work. Readers can then have no clear idea of what is being said, or may have to carefully investigate how a word is applied in context in order to discern its meaning. Note the problem here: if an author is claiming that X influences Y in manner N, and our only hope of clarifying how the author defines X is to investigate how the author says it influences Y, then we are forced to define X in a way that the causal argument regarding Y makes sense to us. If the author intends a novel argument, we may miss it simply because we interpret the words in a way that seems reasonable to us. We cannot engage sensibly in the critical scholarly task of evaluating the arguments of others if we cannot figure out what these are in the first place. This limits the cumulative development of specialized research itself, for we can only have productive conversations if we understand what each other is saying.[23]

A comparison with natural science is again useful. Leezenberg and de Vries (2019) list clarity as the first rule of the scientific method: "The first requirement is that, in reporting one's observations one avoids as much as possible any vagueness and/or ambiguity. Hence, researchers are required to report their sensory experience in a plain but detailed manner; accordingly, there is no place in science for rhetorical elegance or eloquence." Natural scientists may not always achieve this ideal, but at least have a recognized standard to which all can aspire. Human scientists may also view clarity as a good thing but many communities of human science scholars have clearly interpreted any commandment to clarity very broadly (we provide examples below).

Unclear terminology can also lead individual researchers astray. That is, not only may others misunderstand them but they may misunderstand themselves. One of the main insights of the last decades of literary discourse is that texts are ambiguous and that authors (especially of fiction but also in non-fiction) can say conflicting things without realizing it. An author should of course weigh conflicting arguments and evidence but should still try to produce some coherent and consistent line of argument. Vague terminology makes it far easier for authors to say different things at different times without realizing it. And let's face it: Authors with weak arguments may be tempted (consciously or subconsciously) to bury these in impenetrable prose where those arguments may seem more impressive than they actually are.

We should also be concerned about communication beyond the scholarly enterprise. Levenson (2018), for example, worries that humanists engage in a discourse of big poorly defined words in a way that cuts them off from the wider public. Humanists are thus no longer able to play a role of inspiring others to the joy of art. They instead send a not-so-subtle message that only devotees of an obscure cult that requires years of mastery of an obscure language can really appreciate art. Similar concerns could be raised in social science that a public in search of advice on important issues of the day will run up against a phalanx of complex terminology.

I promised in Chapter 1 to be constructive in this book, to focus on the things we can do better rather than harp on the things we do wrong. Yet the advantages of terminological clarity are so great that I must break my own rule. It is simply bad scholarship to employ unnecessarily vague terminology. This practice impedes both specialized and integrative conversations. It makes conjectures very hard, if not impossible, to evaluate. And it leaves us with an unnecessarily limited idea of how to actually improve human societies.

Coping with Ambiguity

How much clarity can we achieve? The philosopher Ludwig Wittgenstein decades ago showed us that the goal of defining words precisely in a sentence or two was impossible. He recommended an alternative approach whereby we would instead list as many examples as possible of uses of the word. In defining "game," then we could list soccer, chess, and solitaire, giving users a sense of the breadth of meaning of game. Yet Wittgenstein was, like most philosophers of language, concerned with achieving absolute precision. We as mere humans struggling to understand the world around us can aim for the less lofty goal of "broadly similar understandings" such that scholars using the same term will attach broadly similar meanings to it and can then have productive conversations. With such a goal in mind, we need not completely abandon the idea of attempting a one or two sentence definition – just as dictionaries still do, decades after Wittgenstein's insight. Yet we can hold on to Wittgenstein's insight and hope that by combining the two approaches to definition we can achieve as much clarity as humanly possible. If we had a definition of game that included the idea that games are played for enjoyment, and that each game has a set of rules governing how it is played, and then provided a list of games as well, we could be pretty confident that people could then have a pretty similar understanding of what the word "game" means.

It is useful now to return to Table 2.1. We can see that the table provides a reasonably exhaustive list of the set of values and behaviors subsumed under our definition of the word "culture." This table thus provides a far more precise definition of the word than is common across human science. The same applies to other first and second-level phenomena in the table.[24] Note, importantly, that the table describes not only what sort of things are "culture" but what sorts of things are not. We thus improve on Wittgenstein by not just listing a (reasonably exhaustive) set of components of culture but also a lengthy list of things that are not. Hellemans (2017) may wish to expand "culture" to include visits to the hospital, but our table suggests that this expands the definition too far. We can hardly examine the ways in which culture and economy interact if we define one so loosely that it includes the other. This will especially be so if some scholars include elements of economy or polity in their definitions of culture but others do not. They are unlikely to understand what each other is saying. An argument that culture determines how much we eat may be nonsensical with a narrow definition of culture but perfectly reasonable (if not terribly informative) within an expansive definition of culture.

Note in particular that we have distinguished art from culture, in recognition that humans share a capacity for aesthetic appreciation that spans cultural boundaries. The boundary is fuzzy to be sure: works of art carry cultural messages and cultural expressions have aesthetic elements. Yet we can seek to identify a primary purpose in each case. We can then seek in our scholarship to disentangle the aesthetic and cultural natures of both. We will be far less likely and far less able to do so if we casually jumble art and culture together.

It is worth noting here that Ferdinand de Saussure, often seen as the father of modern linguistics, and of "structural" analysis in many fields, stressed the idea of "difference." He argued that the key to understanding language was not to study (as was previously common) individual words in isolation but to see language as a structure and appreciate the different but complementary roles that different words play within that overall structure (This idea of difference would inspire later "deconstructivist" literary theorists such as Jacques Derrida). Having attempted in this book to develop a structure for human science as a whole, we can applaud de Saussure's insight. The clear implication is that we best understand individual words when we not only examine their components but also differentiate them from other words. Table 2.1 serves both functions.

It is useful here to detail the vagueness with which key terminology is often treated in human science. My purpose here is not to criticize Hellemans (2017), a book that I found quite informative in many ways. In the introductory chapter, Hellemans takes a first pass at defining "culture": this is mostly objects but also ideas. My sense at that point was that she was primarily interested in what I would call "art." She later says that culture is indeed about art, but also gender and queer studies and orientalism. She later suggests that there will always be ambiguity about the definition of culture, but that it is nevertheless a worthy subject of study. Later still in the introductory chapter she asserts that culture is the sum of all representations associated with a society. But even that is not enough; in a later chapter things like paying for a visit to the hospital, buying food, going to the cinema, and even the invention of the paper clip, are all culture (pp. 135–136). Not surprisingly, she then suggests that we can never hope for a rational comprehension of culture but only an intuitive feel for the subject. It is indeed impossible to have a rational understanding of culture if this is defined so broadly as to include almost everything that human scientists study – unless of course we break culture into constituent parts and study these in isolation. I had been confused when in the introductory chapter she said that culture had to be distinguished from nature, but that is apparently the only distinction she is willing to draw.[25]

As mentioned, I nevertheless found the book informative. She provided a very accessible overview of many schools of thought within the field of cultural studies. We will return to this field in the next chapters but it is worth noting that many of these schools (often implicitly to be sure) clearly have a less expansive definition of culture in mind. They each focused on a manageable set of causal links. She deals chronologically with: a school of thought which emphasized the connection between culture and human personality; a linguistic turn which naturally emphasized links emanating from the phenomenon of languages; a Marxist-inspired emphasis on how disadvantaged groups in a society influence and are influenced by elements of culture; a turn to examining how non-western cultures differ from and interact with the western cultures that had been the previous focus of study; and finally an increased concern with how culture affects human lives. It is noteworthy that expansive definitions of culture did not prevent scholars from honing in on a more precise set of causal links, some within culture and some connecting culture to other phenomena (the latter act of course requiring that culture not be defined so broadly as to exclude everything else). Though she at one point opines that the field of cultural studies appears divorced from the search for truth, it appears that different scholars did contribute to our collective understanding. The author urges us to see these different schools as complements rather than substitutes, though each tended to have its period of dominance in the field. Our map allows us to see this complementarity quite clearly as the investigation of different sets of causal links. And it encourages us to believe that the research enterprise could advance human understanding faster and farther if specialized researchers were explicit about which phenomena and causal links they studied, and integrative researchers worked to fit the pieces together.[26]

One tangential question naturally arises here. We have discussed earlier the advantages of specialized research communities: they share a set of understandings about the phenomena studied and the theories and methods applied. Here we have a field of study, "cultural studies" which changes not only its theories but the causal links it focuses on every couple of decades. Could we achieve a more productive scholarly conversation if scholarly communities focused more explicitly upon an identifiable set of causal links?[27] We will return to that question in Chapter 4.

Having above achieved as much clarity as is possible in our definition of phenomena, should we casually throw this clarity away by utilizing terminology such as globalization, patriarchy, or modernization that each encompass a broad set of phenomena and causal relationships? A couple of key questions follow. First, can we identify the precise set of causal relationships subsumed by each? It is notable that scholars employing these words almost never do this. Second, does this set of causal relationships comprise a subsystem such that the linkages among these phenomena are far more powerful than their links to other phenomena? This question also is never posed and thus is hard to answer. But it seems unlikely. We should be concerned that concepts that represent an amorphous mass of causal links will confuse rather than clarify our thinking.

Say that a scholar maintains that globalization causes cultural dislocation. This may well be true. But how can we know, beyond the fact that we may be able to observe some correlation between measures of globalization and measures of cultural dislocation. Note here that if we seek to "measure" globalization then we will need to fall back on measures of its components: foreign investment, trade, migration, watching foreign movies, and so on. Which of these is most important in generating cultural dislocation? If we think cultural dislocation is a problem worth fighting, do we just need to place a tax on foreign movies or do we have to disrupt foreign trade flows too? What is the value of a critique of globalization that is completely dislocated from any sense of how we might address the problem? To be sure, research can be profitably pursued that is not focused on policy issues. However, we should ideally be able to imagine a link from research to our actions in the world. Mewling and crying about some monster named globalization by its nature gives us limited insight into how we might reasonably act in the world.

We can of course find useful insights in the works of scholars writing about globalization[28] or patriarchy or neoliberalism. However, we have to search for them. Then, if we wish to understand the precise mechanisms at work, we have to do a completely different kind of research focused on real phenomena and relationships that can be carefully defined and evaluated. The argument here is not that scholars have been completely wasting their time and producing worthless analyses. They are, after all, guided (much of the time) by a worthy appreciation that the world is complex and that we need to deal with multifaceted events or processes. It is just that we can have a more productive conversation talking about clearly defined phenomena and causal links – and carefully examining the importance of particular causal links rather than assuming this.

It is sometimes maintained that terminological ambiguity may stimulate creativity. Scholars debating the meaning of globalization may be pushed to discover new characteristics or effects of globalization. But what does this mean? It can only mean in practice that they either identify causal links that function within this amorphous blob of causal links called globalization, or they identify novel links that connect some elements of globalization to phenomena beyond the blob. Arguing about vague terminology is a rather tenuous path to understandings that could instead be *explicitly* guided by a search for important causal links between key phenomena such as trade flows or foreign investment and yet other phenomena.

We should note a further characteristic of complex terms such as globalization, patriarchy, or modernization. In addition to referring to an amorphous set of causal links these terms also carry an element of evaluation. Globalization is considered troublesome by most who use the word, patriarchy is generally viewed as evil, and modernization was viewed favorably for a while but is increasingly questioned. Is there some value in weighting single terms with so much meaning? It may serve to bind scholarly communities together and give them a sense of purpose. We have celebrated above the ease of communication within scholarly communities, and can appreciate that saying "I study globalization" can carry a host of information to others about one's research – though not about what causal links one might engage. But is it constructive to perform academic research with terminology that implies an answer to our investigations at the outset? What if – we should not rule this out – globalization is not a complete monster but occasionally does some good (like, say, raising average incomes)? If we aspire to an unbiased scholarly research effort, we should seek unbiased terminology (see Szostak 2016).

Natural science can again provide a useful guide. In the early years of sci-entific investigation of genes, different communities had different definitions of "gene." Yet these definitions were consistent. Scholars seeking to identify the functions of genes developed working definitions that stressed what genes did. Scholars exploring the internal composition of genes developed definitions that emphasized the components of genes. Scholars of evolution focused on how genes might change over time. Over a period of decades, these multiple defini-tions coalesced into a shared understanding of "gene" that could serve diverse communities of researchers.[29] Alternatively, exploration of the term "innateness" never fostered a productive research enterprise because different scholars pursued competing (and often vague) definitions of the term (Griffiths and Stotz 2014). Scholars of globalization might function constructively with different but rea-sonably clear definitions: some might stress economic aspects and others political or cultural aspects. We will only be able to stitch these efforts into a coherent whole if the definitions are clear and compatible. It is noteworthy in this respect that the successful definitional efforts regarding genes focused on things like the components of genes, how these might change through time, and the causal links in which genes are implicated. In the case of globalization, the internal components are themselves causal links. These need to be carefully elicited and examined individually.

In sum, I suggest that these composite terms that embrace a set of phenomena and causal links – and there are many of them, including patriarchy, neoliber-alism, and modernization – likely do more harm than good. It is no bad thing to suggest that there may be some coherence among a set of causal links: that male dominance is instantiated in a mutually supportive set of cultural attitudes and institutions. However, for patriarchy to be more than a catchword, we need to investigate which attitudes and institutions are most important, how they reinforce each other, and how they relate to other phenomena. We might then be able to understand how patriarchy works and how we can change it. Some scholars already do this sort of detailed analysis. They would be better able to proceed if relevant scholarly communities were clear about their purpose and their terminology.

Carefully identifying the phenomena we study is both the easiest and most important definitional task before us. We must also carefully define a set of concepts associated with the dozen scholarly methods employed across human science. Since we will urge methodological flexibility below, we want also to define these concepts in such a way that scholars from different disciplines can share similar understandings. This task also seems to be quite straightforward. We can all have broadly shared understandings of the twelve methods them-selves. Statisticians provide very precise definitions of words such as "multicol-linearity." Humanists who disagree about how to define their subject matter still have broadly shared understandings of techniques of textual analysis. Holosko and Thyer (2011) provide definitions of one or two sentences in length for many dozens of research-related concepts. Undoubtedly, some scholars might quibble about some of these definitions. Oliver (2010) appreciates that different terms are used in different disciplines for the same idea, but is still able to outline how all scholars can share understandings of dozens of key terms employed in human science research. It seems that we can reasonably aspire to shared understandings of concepts associated with human science methods.[30]

The most difficult set of concepts are those that address the mechanisms by which phenomena influence each other, or are employed in the theories we develop to understand how phenomena influence each other. One critical challenge here is that human scientists develop new concepts here with some regularity. Indeed, Brint (2017) found that the most-cited works in five human science disciplines were celebrated for developing new concepts of this type (a slightly larger number of highly cited articles, but not books, addressed methodological issues). There is clearly a potentially large scholarly payoff for developing new terminology. Yet our discussion above of the ambiguity with which certain phenomena are treated leads us to worry that authors need not always define new concepts very carefully. Indeed, it seems likely that some of the citations garnered involve efforts to clarify or perhaps re-define these new terms. If scholars have not achieved consensus around what "culture" means after centuries of research on the subject, we can suspect that different scholars will often understand new terms in quite different ways. Unfortunately, such ambiguity serves to decrease the likelihood that scholars will find a new term to be unhelpful: If we do not agree on what it means how can we show that it does not aid our understanding of any causal linkage?

We noted above that Table 2.1 serves to clarify the meaning of each phenomenon within it. In so doing, we have also identified a set of criteria that can potentially be applied to any concept employed within theories and methods: What is it?; What is it not? What are some key components or examples of its use? In the case of concepts connected to mechanisms and/or theories, we can also insist on efforts to identify the range of applicability: To which set of causal links is the concept to be applied? Note that we can then seek to test how useful the concept is in each case. There is a natural and healthy tendency for concepts to be applied more broadly through time. Scholars naturally wonder if a mechanism observed along one causal link can also be observed elsewhere. Care must be taken, though, that we not simply assume this result. Brint indeed warns us of the danger of misguided analogies. We need carefully to test each potential application. We should strive to endow our definition of the concept with a detailed understanding of where it can be usefully applied, but expect that the range of applicability will be clarified by future research.

The temptations to define new concepts carelessly are large. As a scholarly community, though, we can insist on careful definition. In particular, we can insist on careful analysis of range of applicability.

I should in closing return to a point made at the start of this discussion: Perfect clarity is beyond human capability. As we have seen in preceding paragraphs, clarity is harder to achieve in some endeavors than in others. We should be careful of criticizing activities that face particular challenges in achieving clarity. We should be aware that on the frontiers of human understanding greater clarity may be achieved slowly through time.[31] Yet we should each pursue as much clarity as possible, and urge others to do the same. In particular, we can achieve great clarity in describing the (vast majority of) things we study, and the methods used to study them, and can do much to reduce ambiguity in our theories.

The Style and Substance of Argument

We have pointed out above that integrative research integrates the insights generated by specialized research. This is, of course, only possible if it is clear what those insights are. Unfortunately, it is not always clear what point human scientists are trying to make in their published work. One problem is excessive jargon. Jargon is at times unavoidable: We have seen after all that one of the key strengths of specialized research is a shared understanding of key terminology. From time to time, specialized research communities will adopt new terminology. Far more often, researchers propose new jargon that does not catch on widely. Such jargon likely does more harm than good. Yet it serves the researcher's selfish interest in making their ideas appear more innovative than they might appear if expressed in plain English. We cannot have a blanket prohibition on the creation of new jargon (since this is occasionally useful) but we can insist in our refereeing that authors nevertheless state their key argument in a jargon-free manner at some point, ideally in both introduction and conclusion. This will make it easier for all readers to appreciate readily what the author is saying, and will make it much easier to spot specious lines of argument that only appear worthwhile when obscured.[32]

A second problem, particularly notable in the humanities, is an emphasis on style over substance in presentation. It is not my intention here to urge a dull form of presentation but to encourage authors to make a clear point, at least in introduction and conclusion. If a work has no clear point – if it is, say, a series of impressions of a particular work of art – it should say so.[33] Novels are to be appreciated in their entirety. Scholarly works about novels are not themselves novels: They are contributions to an academic conversation, and may contribute only a little understanding to that broader conversation. We may admire a novel for its style more than its substance. A work of scholarship should be valued more for what it says than how it says it. To be sure, the scholarly conversation involves multiple interacting acts of persuasion: We do not just make a point but try to convince others of its value. Style of presentation can be invaluable to efforts at persuasion.[34] Yet style without substance means that you are not actually persuading the audience of anything in particular.

Hayot (2014) provides detailed guidance on how to write in the humanities.[35] He does often stress clarity. The introduction should give the reader a clear idea of how the research fits into the academic conversation. It should engage the reader, tell them why the research matters, and tell them what they need to know to proceed further (for example, it should place the works of art discussed in historical context). He urges authors in an article introduction to describe what is to come. Yet while some of his exemplary examples outline the key questions to be addressed, others do not (he does applaud one author for clearly indicating what is novel in the work). He stresses the value of a key anecdote at the start. He devotes a lot of attention to style of presentation, urging the author to grab the reader's attention with style of expression. At least one of his exemplary openings caught the reader's attention with what struck me as vague terminology. When talking about an introduction to a book, he urges the author to say what the key questions are and why they matter, but leave some room for the reader to be surprised along the way. Indeed, Hayot strongly urges authors not to explain their whole argument at the outset. He wants authors to tantalize the reader and surprise them later. He wants us to raise the questions but not give the answers (but recall that not all of his exemplary examples even did the former). He wants us to use telling and hiding strategically.

One might hope that the tantalized reader will eventually encounter the truth. Yet, amazingly, Hayot says that the closing remarks should absolutely *not* summarize the argument, for that would be anticlimactic. Instead, the conclusion should raise new possibilities. You might start the conclusion with a summary, he admits, but only to show how you have created something new. Half of the books he surveyed had no concluding chapter at all. His review of endings focuses at least as much on style as substance. He urges authors to leave the reader pensive.

This would all be fine if we were playing a game for pleasure and never really hoped to get anywhere. However, if we are actually engaged in a productive conversation, we need to be clear about our contribution. It is notable that Hayot does *not* argue that it is not possible for humanists to explain carefully where they are going in the introduction and where they have been in the conclusion. These are clearly options that an author might consider, but that he advises them to reject. He urges authors to sacrifice a clarity *that they can readily achieve* in the interests of tantalizing the audience. There are heaps of good advice in Hayot (2014), and many places where he urges clarity. Yet it is shocking that a leading text on how to write urges authors purposely to avoid clarity. We have a duty as human scientists to try to advance human understanding, and this duty should easily dominate our desire to entertain each other.[36]

Hayot (2014) must be a far more patient reader than I am. He advises the author to assume that the reader intends to read the entire article or book. Yet surely many readers will set aside a work if they have no clear idea where it is going. Those readers may leap ahead to the conclusion to see if there is a point worth pursuing. If they find nothing noteworthy in either introduction or conclusion, why read the rest? They might find a particular chapter of interest, but Hayot urges authors *not* to describe chapters in any detail in either introduction or conclusion. There is no shortage of things to read in this world. If readers clearly indicate a preference for works that make style the servant of substance, they will guide authors away from Hayot's advice toward encouraging a more productive scholarly conversation.

Unnecessary jargon, and lack of clarity in expression, have an important further cost: They make it far more difficult than it need be for the public to read academic works. This cost is likely highest in the humanities where there is a potential audience for analyses of particular works of art. Levenson (2018) thus urges scholars of the humanities to pursue an accessible expertise that allows for an easy exchange with the amateur humanists in the real world. He notes in particular that humanists should see amateur historians and genealogists as collaborators rather than completely excluding them from academic conversations.[37]

Theories and Methods

We shall see in this section that each of the dozen methods employed across human science has strengths and weaknesses. Some are better suited to some questions than to others. Yet we shall argue that each method may have something useful to say about any causal relationship. Moreover, we will make an epistemological observation below that, since science can neither prove nor disprove any hypothesis, we should seek to amass and carefully evaluate diverse sorts of evidence concerning any hypothesis. It follows logically that we can be most confident in a hypothesis when evidence from different methods supports it, and that we will need to employ our collective judgment (and integrative strategies) when different methods point in different directions. Why then, is human science characterized by different communities of researchers each loyal to just one or two methods? We have recognized above the advantages to specialized research communities of shared methods and terminology. But can we not achieve the benefits of specialization without tossing away the potential advantages of employing multiple methods? We will argue that we can – and thus should. We will make a broadly similar argument about theory types.

We have urged above a coherent approach to the study of causal links, in which we appreciate the openness of subsystems and accept the simple fact that all human science phenomena interact. Within such a coherent approach, it makes little sense to study some causal relationships with some methods and other causal relationships with others. If a method proves useful in some places, sound scholarship demands that we ask if it might be useful elsewhere. Our approach to methods (and theories), then, flows from and reinforces our desire to achieve a coherent human science.

Identifying Methods

From afar, it may seem that human scientists employ a bewildering array of research strategies. Yet there are only a dozen methods, broadly defined, that scholars employ across all of human science. We can list these here without much need for detailed description:

- Classification
- Experiment
- Intuition/Experience[38]
- Mathematical modeling
- Statistical analysis
- Physical traces (as in archaeology)
- Textual analysis
- Interview
- Survey
- Observation
- Hermeneutics (the study of symbols)[39]
- Mapmaking

This list, I should stress, was derived inductively by reading widely across human science. It is thus possible that other methods might exist or be developed. It is certainly true, though, that the vast bulk of research in human science employs one or more of these methods. The reader may have noted that we have not yet defined the word "method." In accord with our advice on defining terminology above, we can define a method as a means by which we obtain evidence of how the world functions, and proffer the dozen methods listed above as Wittgensteinian exemplars of what we mean by method.

There are a wide array of more precise techniques for pursuing each of these methods: different ways to perform statistical analysis, interview, or read a text. The argument that all methods have strengths and weaknesses necessarily applies also to particular techniques: these are each neither perfect nor useless.

Strengths and Weaknesses of Different Methods and Theory Types

It is now common, though far from universal, to recognize the value of employing multiple methods. Indeed, works on research design such as Buvke (2019) and Gorard (2017) take for granted that different methods have different strengths and often recommend combining methods. Bastow Dunleavy, and Tinkler (2014, 281) celebrate how "the pooling of methods across the social sciences has similarly progressed a lot further in recent years." They report that experiments, statistical analysis (often of big data), mathematical modeling, textual analysis, and the systematic use of various qualitative methods are each employed in fields that used to shun these. Greener (2013, 20) is thus hopeful "for researchers from different perspectives to gain an understanding of how their approaches differ, and for this to promote dialogue rather than conflict. Social researchers will disagree about the best way to do social research, but understanding our differences gives us a better chance of learning from them and of doing better research in the future as a result."

Nevertheless, there have been naysayers. I can recall in my own discipline how economists harshly criticized the first efforts at employing experiments or surveys in the field, and know that a healthy suspicion remains in certain circles. Across human science, the main divide occurs between those who favor quantitative methods and those who favor qualitative methods. The former view the latter as subjective and the latter view the former as simplistic. Tuckett (2018), for example, claims that human science is in crisis because it has different methodologies that do not cohere. He urges us to appreciate that there are many life-worlds, and ignore methodologies that assume there is only one. That is, he embraces certain qualitative approaches that grapple with multiple perspectives while totally rejecting quantitative approaches that assume there is one right way to view the world. Such a view is less popular than it once was. "Yet constructivist critiques have shifted character in all the social sciences in the last decade, only infrequently now decrying the use of organized empirical evidence. Instead they emphasize the need for multiple sources of evidence, multiple methods of study, a focus on holistic phenomena, close attention to meanings as well as behaviours, and frequent triangulation of different kinds of evidential information." (Bastow et al. 2014).

We noted above that all human science subsystems are open. Williams (2020, 66) recognizes that open systems create real problems in inferring causality from statistical models of closed systems. These models are necessarily imprecise because they exclude causal relationships with phenomena outside the subsystem. Williams appreciates that some methodologists such as Roy Bhaskar and Tony Lawson had argued on this basis that there was no place for quantitative methods in human science. Williams takes a more typical view: We need to interpret the results of quantitative analysis carefully. Qualitative analysis can increase our confidence in quantitative results. Moreover, qualitative analysis may be able to flesh out the causal mechanism that generates quantitative results – while perhaps identifying further hypotheses to be investigated quantitatively (Williams 2020, 169–181).[40]

A growing community of scholars advocates the pursuit of mixed methods (Hesse-Biber and Johnson 2015). That is, they urge the use of multiple methods within particular research studies. Though they can advocate the mixture of any methods, they focus on the advantages of blending quantitative and qualitative methods. There are two broad types of approach. In one, the different methods are employed to answer the same question, and the results are compared. In the other, different methods are applied sequentially, as when a qualitative method is employed to flesh out the mechanism behind a quantitative result.[41]

It is useful at this point to seek to identify the key strengths and weaknesses of the dozen methods employed in human sciences. In Szostak (2004), I employed the simplest classificatory approach of all by asking the Who, What, Where, When, and Why questions of each of the dozen methods:

- Who is the (causal) agent being examined? Is it an intentional agent such as an individual or group or an unintentional agent such as an institution? How many agents can the method examine?
- What is studied? The big distinction here is between studying actions (which might just be passive reactions) and studying attitudes.
- Why does a certain causal relationship unfold? Does the method establish a clear correlation between cause and effect? Does it establish that cause precedes effect? Does it identify the mechanism between cause and effect? Does it rule out alternative explanations?[42]
- Where does a certain causal relationship unfold? This question can be interpreted literally as whether we can follow agents as they move through space. It can be interpreted figuratively as how generalizable is the causal process that is observed.
- When is a certain causal process observed? Do we examine phenomena at one point in time, several points in time, or continuously through time? Can we identify trends in a particular direction, cycles, return to equilibrium, or stochastic (unpredictable) trajectories?

Table 2.2 shows how the first ten methods listed above fare with respect to ten questions derived from the above. The detailed derivation of the table is explained in Szostak (2004, chapter 4). Yet for our present purposes the obvious point is that different methods do different things particularly well. Some are particularly good at grappling with intentional agents while others are better with nonintentional agents. Some can encompass thousands of agents while others give a detailed description of a few. Some are good at describing actions while others are better suited to discussing attitudes. Some can serve particular tasks in establishing a causal relationship while others cannot. Only some can tell us much about how humans made particular decisions. Only some have inductive potential: That is they can generate hypotheses rather than just test hypotheses. Some are better than others at following agents through time or space. Some are well suited to generalization while others are better suited to examining specificity. [43]

We can ask of any possible causal relationship in our map of human science above a set of questions: What kind of agents are involved? Do we need to know details about a few agents or the general tendencies of lots of agents, or both? Are we concerned with actions or attitudes, or both? Are we seeking a generalization or to understand an exception to a generalization (note that our task of identifying contextualized generalizations requires both)? Do we need to follow agents through time and/or space? Are we hypothesizing a cycle, trend, equilibrium, or stochastic process (we will likely want to test for each)? We will for any link undoubtedly find that some methods are better suited than others, no method is

TABLE 2.2 Typology of Strengths and Limitations of Methods

Criteria	Classification	Experiment	Interview	Intuition/Experience	Mathematical modeling
Type of agent	All	All; but group only in natural experiment	Intentional individuals; relationships Indirect	Intentional individuals; others indirect	All
Number investigated	All	Few	Few	One	All
Type of Causation	Action (evolutionary)	Passive, Action	Attitude; acts indirectly	Attitude	All
Criteria for identifying a causal relationship	Aids each, but limited	Potentially all four	Might provide insight on each	Some insight on correlation, temporality	All; limited with respect to intermediate, alternatives
Decision-making Process	Indirect insight	No	Some insight; biased	Yes; may mislead	Some insight
Induction?	Little	Some	If open	Yes; bias	Little
Generalizability	Both	Both	Idiographic	Idiographic	Both
Spatiality	Some	Constrained	From memory	From memory	Difficult to model
Time path	No insight	Little insight	Little insight	Little insight	Emphasize equilibrium
Temporality	Some	Constrained	From memory	From memory	Simplifies

Criteria	Participant observation	Physical traces	Statistical analysis	Survey	Textual analysis
Type of agent	Intentional individual; Relationships groups?	All; groups and relationship indirect	All; groups and relationship indirect	Intentional individuals; groups indirect	Intentional individuals; others indirect
Number	Few; one group	Few	Many/All	Many	One/few
Type of causation	Action (attitude)	Passive, Action	Action, Attitude	Attitude; acts indirectly	Attitude, Action
Criteria for identifying a causal relationship	All, but rarely done	Some insight to all four	Correlation and temporality well; others maybe	Some insight on correlation	Some insight on all
Decision-making process	All	No	No	Little	Some insight; Biased
Induction?	Much	Much	Some	Very little	Much
Generalizability	Idiographic; nomothetic from many studies	Idiographic; nomothetic from many studies	Both	Both	Idiographic; nomothetic. from many studies
Spatiality	Very good; some limits	Possibly infer	Limited	Rarely	Possible
Time path	Some insight	Some insight	Emphasize equilibrium	Little insight	Some insight
Temporality	Very good up to months	Possibly infer	Static, often frequent	Longitudinal somewhat	Possible

Source: Szostak (2004, 138–139).

Note: The "criteria" reflect the questions addressed in the text above.

perfect, we should employ multiple methods, and we might well identify some purpose for each of the dozen methods.

The Who, What, Where, When, and Why questions were also applied to theory in Szostak (2004, chapter 3). This allowed us to identify a large but finite set of theory types reflecting the answers given to each question (for example, rational choice theory is of a type that focuses on individuals, actions, rational decision-making, generalizable results, and tends to predict equilibrium outcomes). As with methods, different theory types have different strengths and weaknesses. As with methods, we will then find for any causal relationship that no theory type is perfect but that many theory types may prove useful. [44]

We waited to define "method" above until after identifying the dozen methods employed across human science. We can take a similar approach to the vexed question of defining the word "theory."[45] Our definition of "theory" is thus "an attempt to specify in a logically consistent manner agency, action, decision-making processes, location, and time path with respect to any posited causal relationship(s)." The various theory types that accord to different sets of answers to each of the questions posited just above serve as examples of theories. Note that a theory should be explicit about answers to each question, and also about which causal relationships it can be applied to. Sadly, many human science theories are not clear about either (and are thus hard to classify or apply or test).

Note also that what we are defining here is "scientific theory" about how the world works. We should carefully distinguish this from a set of philosophical theories that address "how the world should work" (ethics), "how scholars should study the world" (epistemology), and "what is the meaning of life?" (metaphysics). In practice, though, many human scientists (Marx leaps to mind) blend scientific hypotheses with ethical, epistemological, or metaphysical arguments. A coherent human science enterprise should clearly distinguish scientific from philosophical theorizing. It should in particular appreciate that we must evaluate these in different ways: Scientific theories are evaluated through applications of the dozen methods identified above, whereas philosophical theories for the most part are judged by argument alone (see Chapter 4). This does not mean that there is no place for philosophical theorizing in human science – far from it – but just that we should be clear about when we are doing it. If we are positing a particular implication of a philosophical theory for a scientific theory, we should be transparent that we are doing so.

Having defined theory and method, we are also in a position to define science: Science is the effort to understand causal links (as defined above) among phenomena (as defined above) through the application and integration of theories (as defined above) and their evaluation by methods (as defined above) and integrative strategies. Human science, the subject of this book, is the study of the set of causal links involving the phenomena in Table 2.1. Though these basic definitions of science and human science are valuable, it is useful to add one further clarification: Science exercises judgment in the evaluation of evidence from all methods and seeks to identify and transcend possible biases. It is useful to evaluate any piece of human science research to see if it accords with this simple yet important definition of human science.

The Value of Employing Multiple Methods and Theories

We have already identified some critically important reasons for employing multiple theories and methods along every causal relationship. These deserve repeating:

- Every theory (type) and every method (or technique) has strengths and weaknesses.
- We can thus have the greatest confidence in a hypothesis when it is supported by multiple methods.
- Our best understanding of any causal link will likely involve the integration of multiple theories.

There are other advantages. First, what do we do if different methods point in different directions? Then we use our understanding of the strengths and weaknesses of different methods to "triangulate" between the predictions of different methods. Statistical analysis justifies a belief that humans act rationally. Experiments suggest that they behave non-rationally. For any particular decision that humans make we can evaluate how non-rational people may be: in choosing to go to university hopefully fairly rational, in choosing who to date perhaps not. Note that in triangulating there is a necessary exercise of judgment. This is best exercised openly and communally rather than individually and implicitly. While some may regret the need for judgment, we should stress that triangulation promises a superior understanding than reliance on any one method.

By asking the same questions of both (scientific) theories and methods, Szostak (2004) could establish empirically that disciplines choose theories and methods that provide similar answers to the Who, What, Where, When, and Why questions.[46] Economists have long favored rational choice theory. Not coincidentally, they have also long preferred methods that are well suited to individuals, actions, generalizability, and equilibria. Moreover, one of the beauties of assuming rationality is that the researcher need not mess with internal thought processes or cultural attitudes. If we know the agent's goals (we can conveniently assume much of the time that they want to maximize income or minimize costs), and the options they face, we know what decision they will make. Rational choice, unlike any other decision-making process, lends itself to mathematical modeling and statistical analysis, whereas other types of decision-making invite the use of interviews or observation.

It may seem innocuous that disciplines choose compatible theories and methods. Yet this joint choice introduces a powerful bias. Mathematical modeling and statistical analysis tended to reinforce economists' belief in rational choice theory. Experiments have suggested that humans do not make decisions rationally (in a host of important situations). Other methods not yet common in economics, such as interviews or observation, might likewise suggest important deviations from rationality.[47] The same is true of any discipline or field in human science: Favoring one or two methods will bias that community of scholars toward certain theories. We need to test those theories with alternative methods if we hope to have confidence in those theories (while appreciating their limitations).[48]

How strong is a causal relationship?[49] Standard statistical techniques often evaluate "statistical significance." Yet this only tells us that there is likely an observed correlation between two variables. It does not tell us at all whether this correlation is large or important. We can again apply our judgment in looking at the statistical results: How much of the change in Y is due to a change in X? Yet a complete understanding of the strength of a causal relationship will only come from a more nuanced understanding of how X affects Y. What exactly happens when X changes, and why does Y change as a result? Statistical analysis will not tell us this but interviews, observation, or experiments might.

One of my favorite books is Rule (1997). He (and others since; see Elman et al. 2020) worried about the tendency of human scientists to focus on testing theories rather than explaining processes. When a particular theory falls out of favor, all of the efforts to test it tend to be forgotten. Human science is not then as cumulative as it could be. If we focus our attention on causal links, and strive to integrate across theories toward a more comprehensive understanding, we will be far less forgetful. We will not hold theories to an unachievable standard of perfection but will instead be willing to recognize that each theory might have some element of insight within it.

We started this section with three important reasons for employing multiple theories and methods. We can now add:

- To triangulate when methods point in different directions
- To counter the bias introduced when disciplines choose methods that support favored theories
- To establish the importance of causal relationships
- To salvage the best parts of theoretical explanations and integrate these

Responding to Postmodern Critiques

We are now at a place where we can address a series of critiques of human science that decades ago went under the title "postmodernism," but have now diffused into many corners of human science. Some postmodernists doubted the very possibility of advances in (natural or) human science understanding: We should just give up and make arguments that we found congenial as forcefully as possible. Yet others felt that while postmodernists raised valid concerns *that needed to be taken into account in the pursuit of human science research*, we could and thus should seek to transcend these in pursuit of superior human science understandings.

Rosenau (1992) thus recommended an "affirmative postmodernism" which took the concerns seriously but sought to address each in turn. We can very much endorse this position.

We have already dealt with some postmodern concerns above. One of these was ambiguity. If humans are severely limited in their ability to understand each other, because there is unavoidable ambiguity in language, then productive scholarly conversations are impossible. We have recognized above that ambiguity is indeed a problem but have suggested some simple strategies for dramatically reducing ambiguity in our use of language. We have also encouraged clarity in expression to reduce the ambiguity of texts.[50] Postmodernists also worried about subjectivity. We may not be able to achieve consensus around any scientific hypothesis because different people have different perspectives on any issue. We have suggested above that we can and thus should integrate across different perspectives. That is, we should seek to identify why people disagree and then synthesize their analyses into a coherent whole. We may never achieve perfect consensus but we can hope slowly to expand areas of consensus through time.

Postmodernists naturally built upon a growing recognition by philosophers of science that absolute proof or disproof of any hypothesis is impossible. It is always possible to sketch some alternative explanation for the results of any piece of scholarly research. This is simply a fact that we must accept. Positivist philosophy of science had decades ago argued that science advanced by disproving alternative hypotheses until only one remained standing. This cannot be. Even in natural science, we could sketch alternative understandings of observations that the earth orbits the sun, chemicals react in a certain way, or earthquakes reflect tectonic shifts. Yet natural scientists have managed to amass compelling bodies of argument and evidence that allow us to have great confidence in certain explanations of certain natural processes. We have argued above that human scientists can best do the same by integrating across perspectives and especially through the application of different theories and methods. Some postmodernists worried that there were no standards by which to evaluate research, but we have outlined clear standards above.

Postmodernists worried that in a world without proof, scholarly biases could influence research results. However, unless *all* scholars have the exact same bias, the simple act of integration should expose these biases. The integrative researcher will evaluate why different researchers achieve different results, and should then recognize the biases driving some researchers. The process is not perfect, of course, and we cannot expect every integrative researcher to spot every bias. Nevertheless, we can hope that over time most biases will be exposed and that scholarly understanding can then transcend these biases. Note that we are most likely to spot bias when we integrate across diverse perspectives. Interdisciplinary integration is thus critical for transcending disciplinary biases. A diverse body of human science researchers will be the best defense against bias rooted in gender or ethnicity or sexual orientation (Gross and Robertson 2020). Interacting with the wider community that we perform research on – and actively involving them in the design of research projects – is a further strategy for identifying bias. This latter practice will be particularly important if certain biases are common across human science.

Some postmodernists doubt the very existence of a fixed external reality for (especially human) scientists to study. As we discussed with respect to Foucault above, humans invest at least some phenomena with meaning. The telephone was introduced in the late 19th century as an instrument of business communication. Phones were placed in homes so that business*men* could tell their wives that they would be late for dinner. Telephone companies were *shocked* when homemakers overwhelmed their exchanges in order to talk to other homemakers. The telephone may seem like a physical object but homemakers gave it a new meaning as a mechanism of social contact. If different people will see a different reality, then we can have no hope of shared understandings of a shared reality. Note, though, that homemakers and telephone companies were disagreeing not about the internal mechanisms of the telephone but about causal links: one sees it as facilitating social interaction while the other sees it as facilitating business deals. They may fight about how to allocate precious resources at telephone interchanges, but the human scientist can readily appreciate a shared reality of multiple causal links.

Some postmodernists appreciated the problem of open systems. They noted that it was impossible to identify firm regularities within open systems. We can concur that this simple fact deserves wider recognition. Some postmodernists went further and argued that we cannot understand causality at all in a world where all phenomena influence all other phenomena. Yet we have argued above that we can sensibly pursue contextualized generalizations. These may not be as emotionally satisfying as unachievable iron laws of human behavior, but we can carefully amass arguments and evidence in support of contextualized generalizations.[51]

Postmodernists – especially Jacques Lyotard – were highly suspicious of efforts to comprehend the complexity of human science in its entirety. Lyotard spoke against what he termed "meta-narratives," which might be ideologies or grand theories that aspired to explain many causal links simultaneously. The world was simply too complex for this to be feasible, and meta-narratives were thus simplistic and erroneous in important respects. We can endorse this suspicion of meta-narrative here, and indeed doubted the possibility of a theory of everything ourselves above. Yet we need not go as far as Lyotard in doubting that we can ever synthesize our investigations of particular causal links into a broader understanding. He was right to be suspicious of grand theory but did not consider the possibility that we might organize distinct theoretical understandings of causal links or subsystems into a coherent understanding of human society.

Postmodernists worried both that there was no perfect method and that human scientists were overly ambitious in their theorizing. We have suggested a powerful answer to these concerns above. We should first recognize the strengths and weaknesses of different theories and methods, and then integrate across research employing different theories and methods.

One of my favorite books is Collins (1998) who provides a wonderful sociological take on how scholarly communities operate (with a focus on ancient Greek philosophy). Along the way, he compares the ancient Greek skeptics and contemporary postmodernists. He suggests that both of these schools of thought were reactions to the proliferation of alternative theories in their times. Lacking a simple way of choosing among alternatives, they gave up and doubted the very possibility of human understanding.[52] We have suggested a set of strategies for bringing coherence to human science and integrating across alternative explanations. In addition to having responses to each individual concern raised by postmodernists, then, we also address their overarching (if generally implicit) concern that human science research is too messy and conflicted to comprehend.[53]

A false belief that humans cannot grapple with complexity can cripple the scholarly enterprise. It encourages scholars to argue for congenial beliefs, rather than let the evidence guide them. It discourages us from trying to understand those we disagree with. It discourages integration. It guides us away from mutual respect and a shared pursuit of collective understanding. It encourages skeptics to exaggerate the degree of ambiguity or subjectivity that we must engage, and dismiss strategies for addressing these challenges. We have argued above that the scholarly enterprise needs to exercise judgment in its evaluation of evidence from multiple methods. This evaluative conversation is unnecessarily difficult if some scholars dismiss *any* evidence. While it is useful to have some skeptics around to spot biases and weaknesses in human science research, a large body of scholars who dismiss the very possibility of advancing human science understanding likely does more harm than good. If we do not believe as a scholarly community that we can collectively advance human understanding, we will severely limit our ability to do so.

The Culture Wars

It is decidedly *not* a primary purpose of this book to enter into the so-called "culture wars": a discourse about (at least in part) whether human science research is heavily influenced by extreme ideological positions.[54] Yet since the issue is important, this book touches upon (some aspects of) the culture wars at least tangentially in many places, and the culture wars might interfere with the reforms recommended in this book, it is worthwhile to make a few brief comments. I am not naïve enough to imagine that anything I say here will impress those outside the academy who find it congenial to argue that most/all human scientists are ideologues (where ideologue can be understood broadly as arguing from any preconceived beliefs rather than evidence). Yet I think over the longer term the human science enterprise can take certain steps – advocated above for other reasons – that would reduce the scope for ideological posturing or bias within academia.

Most importantly, integration serves naturally to transcend biases of any type, including the ideological. It encourages us to actively seek out different points of view, and integrate across these, and thus works against excluding any view-points from an academic conversation.

We have mentioned more than once that scholarship advances by amassing argument and evidence. An integrative effort will soon recognize that some works leap directly from ideological assumptions to ideological conclusions without much intervening argument or evidence. Recall that efforts at integration involve a critical evaluative step so that we will later end up integrating the best parts of the insights of different authors. Works of ideology will have little to contribute to integrative overviews of a field.

There is of course a danger that ideologues will attempt integrative work themselves. Yet these efforts will surely conflict with the standards such as inclusiveness and unbiasedness by which integrative work should be evaluated. Of course, the journals that allow ideological diatribes to pass as specialized research may do so for supposedly integrative research as well. Yet journals that aspire to a reputation for quality integrative work will not.

I am confident that human science can grapple with complexity.[55] Yet I can appreciate that others might reasonably doubt our collective ability to master the complex set of relationships with which human science must engage. They might then urge us to humility in both our theorizing and policy-making. Conservative figures such as Friedrich Hayek and Edmund Burke indeed used complexity as a reason to be suspicious of both grand theories and policy interventions (Epstein 2015). We can aspire to have intelligent conversations about whether we understand certain sets of relationships well enough to intervene. That is, we can move beyond an ideological belief that the world is too complex for human intervention toward reasoned debates regarding whether particular interventions might do more harm than good. Such conversations would ideally combine theory and empirics. Moreover, they should appreciate that "not acting" is also a decision that has repercussions.

As noted in Chapter 1, this book has some loose synergies with my *Making Sense of the Future* (2022). This book can encourage research that informs the pragmatic search for policies for human betterment *that can be widely appreciated* pursued in that book. Ideologues (especially of the left) are likely encouraged in their activities by an awareness of the flaws in existing societies. If we were making greater progress in addressing societal ills, some of those who at present produce ideological tracts might be inspired instead to provide detailed arguments and evidence in favor of particular policies. They might find it both professionally advantageous and personally fulfilling to produce research worthy of being included in integrative analyses of a field that might in turn inform public policy. The reforms advocated in this book should thus make the pursuit of quality research more attractive and ideological posturing less appealing. (While I largely favored a series of moderate-sized changes to public policy in that other book, I did recognize that there might be a need for more dramatic changes. There is an important place in human science for some to imagine major transformations in human society.)

We noted above that this book allows us to recognize a range of postmodern critiques while seeking to transcend these. Postmodernism was particularly popular in its heyday among disenchanted socialists. The decline and fall of the Soviet Union dashed ideological aspirations and encouraged nihilism. Many welcomed an extreme postmodernist indictment that human science could not progress and thus one should just argue for points of view that one found congenial. Postmodernist attitudes have now dispersed across human science but are particularly common in areas such as globalization studies and cultural studies. Globalization can then be treated as capitalism once was, as an evil to be fought on all fronts. Culture can take the place of armed struggle as a mechanism for achieving social change.[56] Such attitudes, we should stress, do not characterize all scholarship in those fields. Yet we can recognize the dangers of a toxic combination of ideology and postmodernism that assumes away the possibility of – and thus denies the responsibility of – careful engagement in a respectful conversation about arguments and evidence. We need to alter these self-reinforcing beliefs and practices toward beliefs and practices that encourage a coherent human science effort to inform improvements in public policy.

One unfortunate irony is that if academic research is perceived to be ideological then it cannot play a role in guiding careful public policy. Nor can academia then play a critical role in supporting democracy by providing a trusted arms-length analysis of public policy.[57] Only a trustworthy academic enterprise can support democracy and encourage improvements in public policy by carefully evaluating alternatives.

If we can achieve a more coherent and cumulative human science, and especially if this can (be seen to) usefully inform valuable public policies, then ideological posturing will be much less alluring. In turn, a decrease in ideological posturing will make it easier for the academy to pursue integration and methodological flexibility, for both of those enterprises require the exercise of careful and collective judgment. Judgment is more easily exercised in a community firmly devoted to being guided by the strength of argument and evidence.[58]

Summary

- We can and should develop a "map" of human science, consisting of a large but manageable set of phenomena and the causal relationships among these. We carefully defined phenomena, realizations of phenomena, causal links, and subsystems.
- It is possible for scholars to share broadly similar understandings of the phenomena on our map.
- All subsystems in human science are open. That is, the phenomena within the subsystem relate causally to phenomena outside the subsystem.
- As a result, human scientists cannot identify causal regularities. They can, though, seek contextualized generalizations whereby the existence of a

particular realization of X increases the likelihood of a particular realization of Y when there are particular realizations of other phenomena.

- For various reasons, a unified theory of all of human science is highly unlikely if not impossible.
- Communities of specialized researchers can be very productive because of shared understandings. Yet those shared understandings limit what those communities investigate.
- There is thus a need for integrative work within fields to compare different approaches to the subject matter. This will also tie disparate pieces of research together, and militate against important insights being forgotten.
- There is a symbiotic relationship between specialized and integrative research (both within and across fields). Integrative research inevitably builds upon specialized research. In turn, integrative research informs specialized researchers of what they are missing and how their research fits within a broader whole.
- Specialized researchers are sometimes suspicious of integrative research. It is possible to develop a set of guidelines for integrative research that are comparable to the standards used to evaluate specialized research. We developed such a set.
- There are huge costs of miscommunication and misunderstanding if scholars cannot share understandings of key terminology.
- Our map of human science clarifies the meaning of terminology by listing what sorts of thing a phenomenon is and what sorts of things it is not.
- Terminology that refers to a vaguely defined set of causal links encourages misunderstanding. It is generally best to specify which causal links one is investigating.
- We can and should achieve shared understandings of terminology associated with theories and methods.
- We can and should insist on clarity of expression.
- Each of the dozen methods (or theory types) employed in human science has strengths and weaknesses. These were summarized briefly.
- We can have the greatest confidence in a hypothesis that is supported by evidence from multiple methods (or theories). If methods point in different directions, we can triangulate.
- Our best understanding of any causal link will likely involve the integration of multiple theories.
- The use of multiple theories and methods also better allows us to establish the strength and importance and nature of a causal relationship.
- Focusing on causal links rather than theory testing renders human science better able to develop more comprehensive understandings.
- We were able to provide definitions of phenomena, causal link, theory, method, science, and human science.
- Postmodernists raised a set of valuable concerns about ambiguity, objectivity, reality, and a host of other issues. Yet there are strategies for addressing

(imperfectly) all of these concerns and thus aspiring to enhanced human science understanding. We collectively should seek to judge the evidence and arguments regarding particular hypotheses, and should aspire toward consensus.

• The strategies outlined in this chapter, and especially integration, reduce the scope for ideological posturing within human science.

Notes

1 In Szostak (2003), I detailed hundreds of such links proceeding to and from cultural phenomena. In Szostak (2001), I outlined dozens more connected to elements of social structure. Szostak (2003) also describes how Table 2.1 was first derived. Scholars of interdisciplinarity emphasize the need to identify a "common ground" that allows the integration of insights from different disciplines (Repko and Szostak 2020). A map that indicates how the phenomena studied in one discipline interact with phenomena studied in other disciplines is an important type of common ground.
2 We can thus welcome Guerin's (2020) urging that psychologists pay more attention to the social influences on human behavior while worrying that he leaves too little scope for individual action. We can welcome Boero (2015, 1): "The main assumption of this book is that individual behavior and social phenomena are somehow connected and that the investigation of that connection is central for all social sciences." Boero explores how emerging methods of big data analysis can be applied.
3 Ásta (2018) advocates a "conferral" approach in which social categories including race and gender are conferred on people by others. That is, categories are created, and people placed within them, by others. Nevertheless, she appreciates that social categories are generally grounded in physical characteristics such as genitalia. Most importantly, she appreciates that we can still have a shared conversation about (causal links such as) oppression of women even if there is some fuzziness regarding who will be included in the category of "women."
4 Martinelli (2017, 67) is harshly critical of a stream of humanities scholarship that focused on contesting the definitions of particular terms. The goal was not to clarify but to criticize. He argues that such research contributes little to a progressive scholarly conversation. I would concur that we should recognize ambiguity but seek to transcend this.
5 Buvke (2019, 41–43) speaks of different "levels" of phenomena. We think a distinction between phenomena and realizations is more useful (and easier to comprehend).
6 In the Basic Concepts Classification, democracies are indicated as governments that hold elections. It is appreciated explicitly that healthy democracies likely depend on other factors that will be captured by causal links. See the schedule on Politics, PI2g. Note that this detailed classification of phenomena can spare us from endless confusion regarding the nature of democracy or any other phenomenon.
7 Fusari (2014) also raises the problem of historical processes. Natural scientists can seek general laws because their phenomena change slowly or not at all. But social scientists must deal with changes in [realizations of] phenomena due to innovation and path dependence. Fusari appreciates that this is more of a problem for some phenomena than others. There is an important point here: If change in some phenomena was not so rapid, we might have had better luck establishing regularities in certain causal relationships *because the context would have remained stable.* We would have been too confident in those results and too easily surprised if the context then changed, but could have operated with confidence in an unchanging world.

8 "Social phenomena involve the interactions of large (but still finite) numbers of heterogeneous entities, the behaviors of which unfold over time and manifest themselves on multiple scales. It is hard to understand, for example, why even a single organization behaves the way it does without considering (a) the individuals who work in it; (b) the other organizations with which it competes, cooperates and compares itself to; (c) the institutional and regulatory structure within which it operates; and (d) the interactions between all these components. To draw an analogy with physics, one must solve the equivalent of quantum mechanics, general relativity and the multi-body problem at the same time — even string theorists don't have it that bad!" (Watts 2007). We can agree with the general thrust of Watts, and applaud his recognition of this important difference with natural science. We can clarify his argument by recognizing that he is referring to a set of causal links that jointly influence an organization. We can note that the term "heterogeneous" just means that for some phenomena we need also to worry about internal structure.

9 Sayer (2010) discusses the severe requirements for a closed system to exist. He argues that philosophers have focused on a few cases in physics and chemistry where closed systems can be achieved, and thus exaggerated the role that iron laws or regularities should play in scientific explanation.

10 6 and Bellamy (2011, 6) argue that "Making warranted inferences is the whole point and the only point of doing social research." Their book is devoted to identifying methodological practices that can increase our confidence in interpretations of any kind of evidence. Notably, they argue for the unity of social science in their concluding chapter on the basis that the same guidelines for good research apply everywhere.

11 Chambers (2017, 49) recognizes that hypotheses are usually clarified as science proceeds. Our idea of contextualized generalizations fits with a sense of how science proceeds through clarification. One scholar may boldly hypothesize a connection between X and Y, and other scholars then identify circumstances in which the relationship appears to hold and circumstances in which it does not.

12 The European Union's SHAPE-ID project addressed what human science has to contribute to research projects grounded in natural science such as climate change: place these in human context, shape research questions, understand human complexity, provide historical or ethical perspective; reflect on terminology and narratives, identify side effects of proposed interventions, and communicate to diverse audiences (Shape-ID, 2021a). An integrated human science will be better placed to do most of these things.

13 Contemporary references to a theory of everything generally refer to the field of physics and do not pretend to address human science. White (2014) uses the phrase in his title but provides a set of guidelines for social inquiry rather than an overarching theory.

14 I confess that I have concerns about the vagueness of some of the terminology that research now focuses on (and that chapters in the Bowen book are organized around). Yet I can see great potential in some of these, such as the comparative analysis of how humans justify actions after the fact.

15 Each realization may have its own causal effects. We can have a general understanding of the effects of technological innovation, and particular understandings of the effects of particular innovations. It will be obvious in both cases where they fit on our map of phenomena. As noted above, we may rarely also tweak our definitions of phenomena themselves but this no more problematic than when a cartographer needs to recognize the formation or disappearance of a town: Such changes do not erase the value of maps.

16 "I can see no other escape from this dilemma (lest our true aim be lost forever) than that some of us should venture to embark on a synthesis of facts and theories, albeit with second-hand and incomplete knowledge of some of them—and at the risk of making fools of ourselves" (Schrödinger, 1944, cited in Renn, 2020, ix).

17 This question should likely be more important than it is in public policy circles.

18 Barry and Born (2014) indeed applaud interdisciplinarity for generating new ideas that disciplinary scholars might pursue.

19 Despite decades of advocacy of interdisciplinarity by university presidents and granting agencies, some specialized researchers remain suspicious. This suspicion can be attenuated through time by advertising the symbiosis identified in this section and by encouraging rigorous standards for integrative research. We will address the latter concern below. In Chapter 8, we will talk about how to institutionalize integration in universities that tend to be governed by specialized researchers.

20 The British Academy (2016) argued that interdisciplinarity enhances the "rigor" with which scholars understand their own discipline. They reached this conclusion from an extensive survey of scholars.

21 Ramadanovic (2021, 14) favorably cites the philosopher of biology Bertolaso (2011, 246) that the "challenge is to confront concepts and vocabulary to make our discourse understandable and useful for different disciplines."

22 Schaffer (2015) argues that while "positivists" view concepts as representing an objective reality, interpretivists see both everyday concepts and scholarly concepts as developed intersubjectively. Still, he appreciates that even interpretivist scholars need to have agreed-upon concepts with which they perform and communicate research. He thus urges us to strive for shared understandings while subjecting these to scrutiny. We should seek to understand why different groups attach different meanings to the same term. We should also be alert to how concepts may embody cultural biases or power relationships.

23 Bracken and Oughton (2006) explored the necessity of shared understandings both for research within the field of geography and for interdisciplinary understandings.

24 Barrow (2019) doubts that human science concepts can be defined as precisely as natural science concepts. Two of her three examples, "depression" and "middle class" are implied in Table 2.1. Depression would be a psychological disorder as defined by the American Psychiatric Association's *Diagnostic and Statistical Manual of Mental Disorders*. The APA changes its definitions over time, but we can still have a shared understanding at any point in time (and authors suggesting a change can be clear that they are doing so). Middle class can be defined in terms of a precise set of occupations (authors preferring a cultural definition should be clear that they are talking about something else). Her third example, "imaginative" is not a term that needs careful definition beyond what dictionaries provide. Her main point is that there is a critical role for philosophy in clarifying concepts.

25 Stjernfelt (2017) lists sixteen distinct broad definitions of culture, and appreciates that his list is not exhaustive. He recognizes this is problematic, but does not call for clarification. His list is instructive. Some differences reflect disagreements about the internal workings of culture: "internal process of refinement" versus externalized; unchanging versus constantly evolving; monolithic versus particularistic. Many reflect questions of at what level we should investigate culture: elite versus popular; universal versus group-specific or subgroup-specific; location-specific or not. And of course some differences reflect disagreements about causal links: whether culture is determined by socio-economic circumstances or not. Note that these are *all* things (most of them sets of causal links) that deserve to be investigated rather than assumed implicitly within a definition.

26 Klein (2005, 104) identified concerns that the rise of cultural studies threatened the viability of traditional fields such as art history. The academy would benefit from a clearer understanding of who studies what and how those efforts are related.

27 Hayot (2014) estimates that introductions take up about a quarter of the space in humanities articles. This seems to me much longer than is the case in the social sciences. Some of this difference may be inevitable: one task of the introduction is to introduce the works that are to be discussed (at least if these are not particularly well

known). Yet Huyot stresses that the main task of the introduction is to situate the work in the wider literature. This appears to be much harder to do in the humanities than in social science.

28 A subset of scholars of globalization investigate the links between economic, political, and cultural types of globalization, while appreciating that yet other phenomena may be causally important. Such an enterprise has much merit, though care must still be taken not to assume that there are always tight causal links between economic, political, and cultural processes.

29 Brigandt (2020) notes that even though scholarly understanding of concepts such as "genes" and "species" have evolved over time, these shared concepts nevertheless guided scientific exploration and encouraged scholarly understanding. He appreciates that concepts cannot be defined in just a couple of sentences and must be understood in relation to other concepts. He urges scholars of science to devote more attention to concepts rather than just focusing on theories and disciplines. He stresses the important fact that concepts can carry similar meanings across disciplines and theories, and can survive the decline of a theory with which they were once associated.

30 O'Leary (2007) surveys a broad range of concepts: some are phenomena, some are methodological, and others are theoretical. In each case, she provides a brief definition but also about a page of discussion. Though the discussion indicates that some terms (such as culture) are contested it is notable that she is able to provide an overview of these debates about meaning in just a page. Note that methodology embraces some general terminology (such as objectivity and reflexivity) that can be applied to many methods: We will seek to show in later chapters that these terms can also be carefully defined.

31 We will urge in chapter 3 a broadening of publication venues so that it is easier to publish new hypotheses or identify stylized facts or note anomalies or disagreements. We will appreciate that we may wish to hold such publications to less stringent requirements. Authors should still strive toward clarity.

32 Hayot (2014), who we discuss below, appreciates that some authors use big words and fancy prose in their conclusions to cover their inability to say something new. So does Greener (2013, 2): "Nobody likes jargon. It's depressing to sit in lectures or meetings and to simply not understand what anyone is talking about because they seem intent in stringing together sentences that are based on obscure terms and acronyms that seem designed to obscure rather than improve understanding. Any author therefore has a duty to try and minimise their use of terms …" Human scientists could benefit from the idea of plain language abstracts (and sometimes introductions and conclusions) that emerged in legal and medical fields and is spreading in the natural sciences: the idea is to communicate main results in a manner that a general audience will understand. See for an example https://www.agu.org/Share-and-Advocate/Share/Community/Plain-language-summary

33 Recall our argument above that we can integrate across diverse perspectives. These perspectives should be stated clearly to facilitate this integration.

34 Chambers (2017, 175) recognizes that his success came not just from producing good research results but tying these to a great story.

35 He recognizes at one point that he is both European and idiosyncratic in approach. Yet his advice surely resonates widely.

36 Other humanists are more insistent on clarity. Newman (2021), President and Director of the National Humanities Center in the United States, sees the future of the humanities "engaging in multidisciplinary collaborations that address pressing problems." In doing so, humanists should apply "the methodologies fundamental to humanities study: problem solving, imaginative bridging, argumentative clarity, evidence-based analysis, among others."

37 We could for example do a meta-analysis of family trees to examine rates of intermarriage across various social divides (Levenson 2018). I should salute here the growing practice of "Public Humanities" which seeks to engage the wider public in conversations around heritage, art, and culture. See Smulyan (2020).

38 The intuitive method involves introspection, and often drawing upon one's lived experience. Often employed explicitly in the humanities, it may be viewed with suspicion in social science as being both subjective and not subject to replication. We shall see that all methods are at least somewhat subjective, and that replication is rare in human science. We might also note that this method is widely employed implicitly: We believe results that strike us as intuitively plausible and question results from any method that strike us as implausible.

39 After a few pages discussing hermeneutics as the study of the meanings humans attach to words or acts, Buvke (2019, 63) notes that some scholars are suspicious of hermeneutics. Yet he suggests that hermeneutics can usefully suggest generalizations that can be investigated with other methods.

40 Roseneil and Frosh (2012) observe that the "cultural turn" in social science has led to the pursuit of a broader range of methods in an effort to grapple more fully with symbolism and not just the structure of societies. They appreciate that there was more of a turn in some fields than others. Many of the authors in their volume worry that qualitative methods have squeezed out quantitative methods rather than being employed in concert. We aspire in this book to a less faddish, more balanced and coherent human science enterprise.

41 6 and Bellamy (2013, especially ch. 17) discuss how mixing methods can enhance our confidence in our interpretations of results. Smith (2008) provides numerous examples of successful mixed methods research.

42 We will return to a discussion of the nature of causality in Chapter 3. We can follow Buvke (2019) here in thinking of a mechanism as placing a causal relationship in context and identifying intervening variables.

43 It should be clear that human science employs some methods that will be of limited or no use in the natural sciences. Yet Peterson (2020) nevertheless notes that biology makes use of several distinct methods (he mentions experiments, mathematical modeling, statistical analysis, observation, and physical traces, though not always by these names). He notes that different methods have different strengths. Some are inductive while others are deductive. Some observe organisms in the wild while others observe them in a laboratory. Some interfere with organisms while others do not. Both of these latter distinctions capture important elements of our questions about whether we can follow agents through time and space. Some look at wholes while others look at parts. This last distinction captures some of our "How many?" question, but also to what extent we examine an agent within a system.

44 Our approach to theories bears a close resemblance to Robert Merton's advocacy of "middle range theory" in the 1960s. He advocated a middle ground between theories that attempted to explain everything and the simple hypotheses that guide particular pieces of research. Such theories would attempt to generalize across a small set of causal links. While such theories may be limited in scope, they can be combined to generate broader understandings. See Williams (2020, 97), Smith (2008). Merton, it might be noted, appreciated that most middle range theories would be limited in scope. It is thus important to establish under what circumstances they apply.

45 This is one of my favorite quotes: "Trying to give a basic comprehensive account of the concept of a 'theory' is an invigorating but fruitless walkabout in metaphysics" (Ziman 2000, 117). Ziman later asserts that scholars generally know a theory when they see one. Our definition allows us to criticize some alleged theories for being incomplete. Our definition is consonant with but a bit more precise than this from Buvke (2019, 43) "While concepts in the social sciences define social phenomena and facts, theories deal with the relationships between phenomena. Said differently, theories are concept structures … because they focus on how various scientific concepts relate to each other."

46 Similarly, Greener (2013, 12–17) shows how different methods are associated with different epistemologies and ways of seeing the world.

47 Many economists, if aware of a study that employed interviews to question rationality, would be tempted to disdain the result and attribute it to a malign combination of bad theory and bad method. The belief that only some (that is, our) methods are useful prevents us from seeing the potential advantages of integrating across the results of multiple methods.

48 We should also test theories against other theories. "New knowledge occurs when we have presented a more convincing explanation of the phenomenon or connections we observed. Thus, scientific work has to do with assessing rivalling theories and hypotheses against each other and not only with falsifying or verifying individual hypotheses" (Buvke 2019, 54).

49 The economist and philosopher Deirdre McCloskey has referred to this in many publications as "oomph." She is very critical of the common practice of thinking that empirical analysis is complete when statistical significance is reported.

50 Postmodernists tended to celebrate ambiguity rather than strive to reduce it. "A brief glance at many of these postmodern writings would indeed invite the conclusion that they fetishised language and obscurity. This was deliberate. Post-modernism, in rejecting science, also rejected the clarity of scientific language…" (Williams 2020,32)

51 Mattick (2020, 1) favorably quotes Tom Bottimore: "one powerful argument against the scientific character of the social sciences has been that they have not in fact produced anything resembling a natural law." He observes that some think this inevitable while others see laws as a goal toward which we are tending. We would be better served by abandoning the pretense that we can do the impossible.

52 Skepticism may be further encouraged by the likelihood that the average contribution of researchers has declined as the number of professors has exploded in recent decades. It is thus more difficult for individual researchers to feel that they are adding much to human understanding (Smith 2021). Smith suggests that the best solution involves identifying new research questions, and approaching existing questions with new methods. We will encourage both strategies in this book, but can also note that integration and the pursuit of contextualized generalizations both have potential to allow more voices to be reflected in scholarly understanding.

53 Martinelli (2017, 67–72) criticizes postmodernism for having distracted the humanities from studying reality and proposing strategies for improving the world.

54 The Culture Wars had more specific manifestations, such as the debate about whether multiculturalism was squeezing out an understanding of Western Civilization, or whether literary theory was replacing longstanding approaches to humanities research (Klein 2005). More recently, there has been a debate regarding how racism is and should be addressed within the academy. These issues are touched upon in Chapters 4 and 5.

55 It is noteworthy that ideologues of both right and left are often simple thinkers while those in between are more likely to embrace complexity (Simonton 1990).

56 When factory workers did not organize themselves as Marx had predicted, scholars sought a cultural explanation. They found social explanations inadequate, and turned to symbols, rituals, and social practices as explanatory variables (Hellemans 2017). "The growth of 'culture' in the humanities rather gained speed during the demise of Marxism in the 1980s when many humanities scholars began to see themselves as studying culture…" (Stjernfelt 2017).

57 I wholeheartedly endorse the argument of Daniels (2021) that universities have a critical role(s) to play in supporting democracy. He recognizes that universities naturally threaten autocracy: "The authoritarian allergy to universities is no mystery. Everything that universities embody is inimical to the autocrat's interest in the untrammeled exercise of arbitrary public power. They are institutions committed to freedom of inquiry, to the contestation of ideas through conversation and debate, to the formation of communities that gather and celebrate a diverse array of experiences

and thought, and to individual flourishing achieved through diligent study. They rest upon a foundation of reliable knowledge and facts, which are antidotes to the uncertainty and dissimulation peddled by authoritarian regimes." Yet he appreciates that universities can only support democracy if university research is both trusted and accessible (his Chapter 3), and if university scholars model respectful discourse (his Chapter 4). We return to both arguments in later chapters.

58 Marks (2021) provides a spirited defense of a Liberal Arts education from a conservative standpoint. He recognizes that scholarly discourse requires the exercise of judgment. He urges scholars to employ reasonableness in their interactions.

3

CONNECTING TO OTHER SUGGESTIONS FOR REFORM IN THE HUMAN SCIENCES

Scholarship is a conversation, and it is critical that we place the arguments in this book in the context of other works that suggest improvements to human science. We will find in general that this work recognizes similar problems and makes recommendations that are compatible with the recommendations of others. Yet our focus on the big picture allows us to make novel recommendations that enhance the analysis and reforms suggested by others. In sum, our investigations in this chapter will force us to clarify and extend our recommendations in the preceding chapter, while appreciating further advantages of these recommendations.

We should be clear about our goals in this chapter. Our goal is *not* to provide a detailed philosophical justification for the arguments made in the previous chapter. This would surely be possible: Philosophers disagree enough about epistemological questions that one could sketch a philosophical justification for any reasonable methodological proposal.[1] It is not our wish to take sides in important philosophical debates. Rather, we will survey several recent works that address methodological issues in the social sciences and humanities, some written by practitioners and some by philosophers. Our purpose is threefold. First, we will naturally celebrate the many instances where our analysis and proposals align with the analysis and proposals of others. We mentioned in the last chapter that we could have the greatest confidence in any hypothesis when multiple types of argument and evidence support it. It is thus invaluable that we can find authors from diverse perspectives urging the same sorts of practices that we do. Second, and importantly, we will identify situations in which the arguments of others force us to clarify our thinking. Scholarship is a conversation, and we should avail ourselves of the wisdom of others in fleshing out our approach. Third, we will point to many cases where the arguments of this book provide clarifications to the arguments of others, answers to questions raised by others, and solutions to problems recognized by others. This activity further advances the scholarly

DOI: 10.4324/9781003275237-3

conversation while providing evidence of the value of our approach. Note that we can achieve these three purposes by focusing here on the key arguments of the works addressed. We have neither the space nor inclination to reprise the detailed justifications provided by each author for their main conclusions (though I have mastered these enough, I hope, to speak knowledgeably about each work). We are here as elsewhere purposely choosing breadth over depth of coverage, and delving into each work only so far as required to meet our three objectives.

Our mapping of human science guides us to treat the humanities and social sciences together. This is a very rare approach.[2] We must deal in this chapter, then, with distinct works that address either social science or humanities. In both cases, we have faced a choice between organizing our discussion around authors or topics. Since there are advantages to both approaches, we have tried to blend the two. The chapter is thus structured around topics, but one or two authors are emphasized under each topic, and we feel free to engage related issues engaged by a particular author.

Reforming Social Science

Comprehensive Appraisal

On the social science side, we can turn first to the excellent Elman, Gerring, and Mahoney (2020), which draws together several scholars to suggest reforms that would encourage a more productive social science enterprise. The editors identify three key challenges in the introductory chapter. The first is that there is little explicit reproduction of research results. We can thus have only limited confidence in any author's claims.[3] The second is that theories rise and fall in most social sciences without necessarily generating any net advance in our collective understanding. The third is worth quoting: "Finally, the bits and pieces of truth that we feel fairly confident about do not fall neatly into place within a larger theoretical scaffolding. Cumulation is not easy." All of these challenges can be addressed, at least in part, by integrative analyses focused on particular causal links or subsystems. These can somewhat substitute for the lack of direct reproduction by evaluating whether studies on somewhat similar topics point in the same direction. By comparing and integrating what different theories tell us about a particular link, integrative works insulate us from losing the insights a theory might generate when that theory passes out of fashion. And of course, integrative analysis places the little bits of understanding within a broader context. Here we might stress the reciprocal relationship between integrative exercises on a particular causal link and those which seek to connect literatures on different links.

The editors make this observation in the introductory chapter (p. 6):

> It is understandable to find confusion and ambiguity in research focused on the decisional behavior of human beings, where outcomes are subject to

myriad causes and to contextual variation (including variation over time), where questions of theoretical interest cannot always be studied experimentally, where categories may depend on collective agreement for their meaning and where the results of any study are available to the subjects of interest and may shape their future behavior. Social science is hard. In this light, the nonprogressive features of social science are endemic to the enterprise.

This is a sage observation, but this otherwise excellent book does not follow up on a couple of obvious implications. They do not anywhere address the need for clarity in terminology. Though they recognize the pressing need for integration, they focus mainly on improving the practice of specialized research. They thus do not explore as we have the need for integrative research to identify contextualized generalizations.

The most intriguing proposal in the Elman et al. (2020) book is the idea of comprehensive appraisals of the literature (Gerring 2020). They characterize the social science literature as a large set of focused research projects. Each starts with a paragraph or two that places the project within the context of a few other works. There is also the occasional survey article that attempts to summarize a particular field of inquiry. Yet these are often idiosyncratic in coverage. The result is that we have many intriguing bits of analysis but no concerted effort to tie them into a larger whole. One negative side effect is that we often waste time re-inventing the wheel, making "discoveries" that have often been made before. The solution proposed is the occasional (maybe once a decade) comprehensive appraisal of a field. This should, among other things, evaluate the contributions made by different methods, and suggest new methods that might be applied. It should also compare the results found by different authors and seek to explain differences. It should identify possible sources of bias. It should identify areas of consensus and disagreement, and suggest future research avenues. How should this comprehensive appraisal be performed? The best way might involve one author doing most of the work but reporting to a diverse committee that could ensure exhaustiveness in coverage and police against bias in analysis.[4] I naturally am in total agreement with their analysis of the problem, but think that the proposed solution is misguided. We cannot right the balance between specialized and integrative research with one effort toward the latter every decade, no matter how detailed and dedicated that appraisal may be. Integrative research is itself a conversation, and one that requires a community of integrative scholars building on each other's insights. We need an entire sub-literature of integration, which builds on itself and seeks to identify novel connections among the specialized research that it embraces.

There have been some steps in this direction in recent years. "Systematic reviews" identify a well-defined research question, and the criteria for inclusion in the review, and then perform a broad literature search (which should be reproducible). They summarize and suggest future research. They are still rare but are becoming more common. Though there had been some efforts at systematic review decades ago in human science, it is generally thought that human scientists are borrowing the idea from the health sciences where systematic reviews are now common. The Campbell Collaboration was launched in 2001 to encourage and support systematic reviews in human science, following the example of the Cochrane Collaboration in health science. The Preferred Reporting Items for Systematic Reviews and Meta-Analysis (PRISMA) from 2009 provides a set of guidelines for performing systematic reviews. Yet when Chapman (2021) surveys dozens of systematic reviews in human science, she finds that only about a quarter of them reference any set of guidelines. Many of the systematic reviews she found make serious errors such as not carefully defining their inclusion criteria, not clearly outlining how the literature search was performed, not following up on citations from included works in order to identify similar works, and relying only on one database. There is thus considerable scope for improving the quality of systematic reviews. There is even greater scope for increasing their quantity: They have only been performed to date on a minute subset of the causal relationships that might be surveyed, and generally within rather than across disciplines. The sorts of problems that Chapman identifies highlights the value of a community of integrative scholars who can maintain quality in systematic reviews, but such a community is only possible if such reviews become much more common.

Novelty

As noted above, the Elman et al. book largely focuses on specialized rather than integrative research. Yet it nevertheless provides useful insights to both the practice and value of integrative research.

In the concluding chapter, the editors stress the tension between the scholarly pursuit of novelty and the collective pursuit of understanding (they say "truth"). They recognize an ideal research cycle that advances from the identification of stylized facts about the world, the formation of hypotheses to explain these, the testing of these hypotheses, and further refinement. The emphasis on novelty means that the scholarly enterprise puts more emphasis on developing hypotheses than on either identifying the state of the world or testing and clarifying.[5] They sensibly recommend that we find a place for different types of publication that can better serve the other stages in the research cycle. In particular, they think it should be far easier to publish exploratory research that reports on underappreciated stylized facts without necessarily forming a firm hypothesis to explain them.[6]

I concur that it is important to support these other types of publication. Yet we must also appreciate that we then need to tie them into the academic conversation. Integrative works could summarize all types of publication. They could report, that is, on the state of the world as uncovered in exploratory research, and the questions that remain unanswered across all types of research. Integrative research can then serve as a critical generator of research questions.[7] We can achieve a healthy dynamic in which integrative research summarizes what we know and what we do not know, and specialized (and some kinds of integrative) research chips away at the latter without unnecessarily re-establishing the former.

The editors bemoan the lack of replication in social science. Whereas researchers in natural science will attempt to replicate the key discoveries of other researchers,[8] this almost never happens in social science. Yet the authors appreciate that a number of studies that ask similar questions but in slightly different ways may serve the purpose of replication. Indeed this practice is superior in one important way for it potentially establishes "robustness": that a similar result holds with different data sets or slightly different methods.[9] Integrative works can play a critical role here in summarizing across what range of circumstances similar results are found, and also when different results are found. (Chambers 2017, 15–16 warns of an important danger in this kind of replication; that we will attribute any differences in results to differences in research design rather than questioning whether the ideas they share may be mistaken; an integrative work should keep this potential bias in mind.)

In an earlier chapter on Research Cycles, Lieberman (2020, 63) worries: "And here is the fundamental rub: If we cannot be convinced that the treatment variable is truly exogenous – if we are always left wondering whether some omitted variable has confounded the results – can we really believe that the research output is significant and worthy of publication in a top journal or is the basis for professional recognition?" He goes on to urge that more careful estimation be performed at later stages of the research cycle. I can applaud the analysis and recommendation while suggesting that it is incomplete. After all, he is raising the challenge of open systems. As we have argued before, we cannot be confident of our understanding of any one causal link unless we understand how the phenomena involved in that causal link relate to yet other phenomena. Lieberman's challenge, then, is best addressed by investigating those causal links that might confound the results in question to determine how important they are and how that importance may vary due to yet other causal links. That is, we need carefully to identify contextualized generalizations.

The editors also recommend a separate review of the importance of a work before assessing its quality. We should be willing to accept somewhat weaker evidence for a truly novel hypothesis than we require for a trivial hypothesis. The former, after all, may encourage further investigation by other researchers. The task of assessing novelty will be easier if there is a strong integrative tradition. Is the hypothesis something that has been mooted before? Does it have the potential to shed light on unanswered questions? Referees and journal editors should not have to do a massive literature survey in order to answer such questions.

The editors encourage both group (class, race, and so on) and ideological diversity so that we will focus on the issues that society cares about and have spirited debates. The obvious danger is that different groups will engage in separate conversations rather than one shared conversation. Integrative works must seek to integrate across different perspectives (We will address below the concerns of some humanists that this is not possible). Integrative works can then serve not just to highlight differences but show how these might be transcended.

It is almost too easy to see a key role for integrative research in abetting many of the recommendations made by Elman et al (2020). Their laudable pursuit of diversity may lead to fragmentation rather than healthy discourse without integration. Lieberman's concern can never be fully addressed without integration. Integration provides an important source of research questions (and our map will generate more in the next chapter). Integration facilitates the estimation of the importance of a piece of specialized research. Integration serves at least some of the purpose of replication.

Cumulative Inquiry

One work cited favorably by Elman et al. (2020) is Smith (2008). Smith worries that we pursue novelty at the expense of cumulative research programs. A cumulative research program would move between theory and empirics, using empirical evidence to revise theoretical conjectures. Yet in many fields (he mentions sociology and political science in particular), theorists and empiricists interact little. He notes that natural scientists have a narrower definition of "novelty" than human scientists have and are thus able to embrace novelty within cumulative research programs. He urges human scientists to focus together on a set of shared questions – our suggestions in the next chapter of key questions that deserve greater attention may prove helpful here. He, like us, urges a kind of theorizing that focuses on a small set of causal relationships. He applauds theories that make a small number of explicit assumptions and lend themselves to empirical examination. He recognizes the value of both quantitative and qualitative empirical analysis and urges mixed method analysis.

We can entirely embrace Smith's emphasis on cumulative research, and the importance for this of theories that look at one or a few related causal links. We can also applaud his celebration of mixed methods research. Smith stresses one kind of integrative research: meta-analysis. He discusses how meta-analysis might give different weights to different pieces of research in terms of whether the right concepts are addressed, how well these are operationalized, the generalizability of results, the quality of the methods employed, and the degree to which the research controlled for contaminating variables (2008, 136–139). We can see in these criteria a desire to clarify what we have called contextualized generalizations. We would recommend a broader range of integrative research, but with this same goal in mind.[10] Most importantly of all, we would stress that a cumulative research program will be encouraged and facilitated by integrative research that examines the interplay between theory and empirics, evaluates all evidence, and identifies challenges and questions.

Confirmation Bias

Chambers (2017) worries that social science may embrace a variety of hypotheses more strongly than it should. This is a very worrisome suggestion. We have been urging in this book the pursuit of sound argument and evidence in the hopes of achieving scholarly consensus. Chambers points to the uncomfortable fact that we may often achieve consensus without good reason. One reason is psychological. Both experiments and observations confirm that people look for evidence that confirms their ideas rather than conflicts with these. If a scholarly community finds a certain hypothesis congenial, it may only look for evidence that supports it. This is, Chambers appreciates, an odd attitude since disconfirming evidence is far more powerful than confirming evidence: If we believe X, evidence of X is unsurprising but evidence against X should grab our attention. Psychologists debate why this "confirmation bias" exists: It may be that confirmation is easier, or that we naturally go with ideas we can retrieve easily from memory (and thus do not have to think about), or that we are trained culturally to win arguments and not engage counter-arguments.[11] Yet psychologists have little doubt that such a bias exists.

Scholarly practice in human science reinforces the confirmation bias. We have noted above that there is little replication. Replication becomes difficult when journals do not require authors to publish the data they employed. Journals in human science also very rarely publish "negative" results: results suggesting that a posited causal relationship does not hold. Say there is a hypothesis that X exerts influence N on Y. Studies that find the relationship get published. Studies that search for but do not find the relationship are not published. (Scholars then sometimes develop alternative hypotheses that the data might justify rather than reporting the negative result of the hypothesis they set out to investigate.) The scholarly community thus gains a mistaken impression that the hypothesis is more powerful than it actually is. In psychology, over 90 percent of published papers provide positive findings (Chambers 2017, 9).[12] We cannot know the precise number of unpublished studies that did not generate positive results but it is surely large. Our ability to determine which causal links are most important, and under what circumstances, is severely compromised if the scholarly community regularly exaggerates the importance of all causal relationships.

Journals in most social sciences expect a 5 percent confidence interval. That is, it should be that the statistical results could only happen by chance 1 time in 20 for the results to be publishable. Yet scholars have many ways of gaming the system. A weak relationship may become statistically significant if the sample size increases: A scholar that falls a bit short of the 5 percent target can collect more data until successful. Alternatively, the scholar may look for excuses to toss away some of their data. It is clear that scholars engage in these strategies: They admit to this when surveyed, and results just inside the 5 percent target occur five times more often than they should. Note that our ability to identify the conditions under which certain causal relationships hold is weakened if authors throw away inconvenient data points without explaining why they did so. Note also that the fact that scholars game the system means that chance outcomes are misinterpreted as causal relationships far more often than 1 time in 20. Integrative studies should view with suspicion results that barely clear the 5 percent hurdle.

Integration can yet again be invaluable – but can be far better if negative results are published somewhere.[13] One solution urged by Chambers (and also Elman et al. 2020) is to have journals accept papers on the basis of guiding hypothesis and research design, and then publish these whatever results are found. They thus evaluate good science rather than good results. Chambers also urges journals to commission replications of articles they publish.

Chambers recognizes an alternative danger: that small but robust causal relationships may be missed. They will not be seen as statistically significant in studies with small or moderate sample sizes. Yet if such results were published, an integrative study could potentially recognize the relationship. Integration effectively increases the sample size by noting that many studies found a particular small effect.

Causality

Lebow (2020) provides an intriguing history of the concept of causality. He argues that our understanding of causation has varied through history and deserves to be interrogated. Notably, given our stress on complexity in this book, he finds that scholars become more concerned about the nature of causality when the world appears to be increasing in complexity – but then we have trouble grappling with it. There is then a temptation to think we understand more than we do. This has led to some regrettable strategies, such as privileging one (set of) phenomenon as a causal agent (as in Social Darwinism or some versions of Marxism) or denying the complexity of the world (he harshly criticizes rational choice theory for oversimplifying a harsh reality). Though Lebow at times appears to reject causation entirely, this is because he treats the term narrowly. He does not proffer a definition of causality, since philosophers have failed to achieve consensus over the centuries. He instead focuses on distinguishing good strategies from bad. The strategies he recommends appreciate complexity: that causation operates in multiple directions. He recognizes that every causal relationship is shaped by context, and criticizes those who seek stronger regularities than it is possible to find. He urges us to evaluate our hypotheses empirically. He applauds those who investigate both emergence and non-linear relationships, and are open to indeterminacy and randomness in outcomes. These are all characteristics of causal analysis as it is treated in this book. Lebow's own approach in his previous book on international relations was to pursue multiple interacting chains of causation. Moreover, he used history, counterfactuals, and comparisons as evidence. We can applaud both the approach to causation and recourse to diverse types of evidence.

"In the social sciences, agent-based models are the most prominent non-causal approaches to knowledge. In contrast to much research in the social sciences that is confined to one level of analysis, these models probe interactions across levels. Outcomes at the system level are the result of behavior at lower levels of aggregation. Many agent-based models seek to account for these outcomes in terms of rules that govern the aggregation of actor behavior. If discovered, these rules cannot be characterized as causes as that term is understood by Weber or most contemporary philosophers" (Lebow 2020, 306). This passage voices a conclusion we will reach below that we need to understand how individuals influence societal-level phenomena (and vice versa), but somehow doubts that this qualifies as causal analysis. Lebow goes on to worry that the models are unrealistic because they abstract away from context. We can embrace such a concern without abandoning hope of identifying contextualized generalizations. Indeed our definition of contextualized generalization would embrace an approach that recognizes that some realizations of individual beliefs or behaviors increase the likelihood of some societal outcome through a clearly specified mechanism.

We should not be surprised that Lebow objects to the word "causal" while welcoming arguments that seem causal. Gorard (2017, 60) notes that authors who object to the word causation often use words like impact, influence, reduce, cure, impact, and even effect. He urges us to be more open about causal arguments, and recognize that science only progresses through articulating and testing causal arguments.[14] Yet at the same time, he is critical of researchers who make causal assertions with limited evidence or analysis.

What is my definition of causation? I would join Williams (2020) on two key points. First, he concurs with Lebow that philosophers have yet to agree on such a definition.[15] Second, he urges us to see causation in social science in probabilistic terms. There may be some relationships in natural science that are deterministic (if X then Y always follows), but this is simply never the case in social science – though sometimes probabilities are close to one. The best we can do is claim that the occurrence of X increases the likelihood of Y.[16] This may be because we do not understand deterministic relationships, but is more likely because the social world is in fact indeterministic. I would add that we can seek to identify the circumstances (that is, realizations of other phenomena) under which Y is more likely to follow X. I would also stress that we should seek to explain why X increases the likelihood of Y by describing a causal mechanism between X and Y.[17] Williams appreciates that our knowledge of reality is imprecise and thus that we cannot leap from evidence of a statistical correlation to a conclusion of causation. We must use our judgment as to whether there is a plausible mechanism of causation.

Williams also invests a wide variety of phenomena with causal power. Our individual beliefs and capabilities have causal powers because they influence the probabilities of various outcomes. Social objects like cultural attitudes and institutions are real even though constructed, and thus have causal power. Indeed, their causal power makes them real. Yet different types of phenomena will exert different types of causation, and thus we will need to approach them with different theories and perhaps methods. This is exactly the point of view taken in this book.

How then can we establish probabilistic causality in practice (in both specialized and integrative research)? Gorard, building on the sage advice of John Stuart Mill over a century before, suggests several useful criteria (which I have tweaked to emphasize probabilistic causation):

- X increases the likelihood of Y in different studies, with different researchers, using different methods and differing populations.
- X occurs before the increased likelihood of Y.
- The lack of change (or perhaps removal of) X decreases the likelihood of Y.
- "There is a coherent, plausible, workable agreed mechanism for X to influence Y that is consistent with prior knowledge" (Gorard, 66).
- We should be able to dismiss alternate explanations of the connection between X and Y.

Pearl and Mackenzie (2017) celebrate an increased interest in causation across many fields in both human and natural science in recent decades. Their main concern is with "confounding," or the interference with causal relationships by other phenomena (they couch their argument in terms of variables). They note that there has been much scholarly misunderstanding about the nature of confounding. They strongly urge the drawing of flowcharts (or perhaps mathematical models, though they prefer flowcharts) that detail how different phenomena are related.[18] Then we can see how we can address confounding. We want, for example, to account for a phenomenon Z which might exert an influence on the phenomenon X that we are concerned with, but if Z is also an intervening variable between X and Y we cannot seek to hold Z constant without interfering with our understanding of how X affects Y. Their goal is effectively to identify contextualized generalizations of a particular type: "X has a particular effect on Y if we hold Z (maybe many of these) constant." Their book thus gives much practical advice on how to establish contextualized generalizations. I would stress again that in each application Pearl and Mackenzie begin with a drawing of how key phenomena interact. I would note, though, that their examples generally involve interactions among only a handful of phenomena. We need to adjust these strategies for the common case in human science where a dozen or more phenomena interact.

Pearl and Mackenzie recognize that our data may at times suggest false correlations. If we study people in hospital, we might think that two diseases are correlated because we often observe them together, when all that is happening is that neither disease on its own is usually serious enough to merit hospitalization. The two diseases appear correlated because they jointly cause hospitalization. Yet Pearl and Mackenzie still argue that statisticians are misguided in proclaiming "correlation does not mean causation." To be sure, a correlation between X and Y need not mean that one causes the other, but there is likely some causal mechanism at work such as another phenomenon jointly causing X and Y. We thus have a general strategy for identifying contextualized generalizations: identify correlations and then seek to identify the causal relationship at work by studying a set of related phenomena.

Representation (Variables versus Phenomena) and Reflexivity

Williams (2020) argues that social scientists cannot measure phenomena the way some chemists and physicists can. Our measurements are always imperfect.[19] Yet this is a far greater problem for some phenomena (he mentions attitudes) than for others (I might mention population and prices as among the phenomena we can often measure well). He uses homelessness as an example, recognizing that there are many different kinds of homelessness. This, of course, is a challenge of realizations: We must be clear which kinds of homelessness we are embracing in a particular study. Then we will face challenges in measuring this: at times people claim homelessness for political reasons and at other times the homeless avoid being surveyed. People with a permanent home in a shelter may not see themselves as homeless. He had argued in previous publications that homelessness might not be a thing in itself but just a symptom of other things like addiction, mental illness, or migration. This seems an unfortunate confusion of phenomena and causal links: Even if we think that homelessness is a result of addiction we need to recognize both addiction and homelessness as phenomena and study the link between them.[20] Happily, Williams himself seems to appreciate this point – arguing later that there are many causes and effects of homelessness.

One strategy for addressing the measurement problem is "operationalization" whereby we define a phenomenon by how we measure it. We might, for example, define happiness as what people say when asked how happy they are. Yet Williams recognizes several problems with this approach. It limits the kind of research we can do: There are other ways that we can try to measure happiness. It confounds our understanding with measurement problems: Different ethnic groups may give different answers to a survey about happiness, and we should seek to understand why. It guides us away from reflecting on any biases there may be in how we measure things. We would join Williams in urging scholars to avoid conflating what they want to study with what they can measure. They must of necessity then engage in an act of interpretation: how well does what they measure reflect what they are hoping to study?

One of the great insights of Kahneman's (2011) survey of how humans make decisions is this: Faced with a question that we do not know the answer to we seamlessly substitute a question that we do know how to answer. Humans do not like admitting ignorance, and will leap to a (subconscious) belief that the answer they can provide is actually related to the original question. It is only, human, then, for scholars to focus on what they know how to do – examine relationships among variables – and simply ignore the additional steps necessary to translate such an understanding into arguments regarding (sets of) causal links. These additional steps *necessarily* involve the exercise of judgment, precisely because we cannot directly measure phenomena themselves.

Just as we must interpret our measurement of phenomena, we must interpret our measurement of causal links. Williams speaks of an empirical finding that being Welsh is associated with several undesirable health outcomes. He warns us not to conclude that Welshness makes one ill. Instead, we are guided to search for some mechanism(s) that operate between ethnicity and health outcomes. Williams describes the variable "Welsh" in this example as a "variate trace": it is not directly signaling a causal relationship but merely indicating a causal mechanism that needs to be uncovered. Though Williams urges us carefully to identify causal mechanisms, he doubts that we can ever be completely successful here for the simple reason that causal mechanisms interact and leave limited traces of their operation (ch. 8).[21]

Williams is suspicious when researchers react to disconfirming evidence by tweaking their original hypothesis to explain away the evidence (2020, 118). This is another situation where we need to exercise our collective judgment. Williams himself has argued that we can only speak of probabilistic causation. He later (p. 134) accepts that theories more often get amended than rejected. We need then to be open to explanations of cases where a particular hypothesis does not hold. How else can we identify contextualized generalizations if we do not pursue a hypothesis across different cases, carefully identifying when it holds and when it does not? We have no recourse then but to ask whether the researcher's tweaking of the original hypothesis is reasonable.[22] Williams is right to worry that we may protect incorrect hypotheses from disconfirmation by such a practice. Yet if those hypotheses are often confirmed, we need to ask why they work sometimes and need to be adjusted in others.

Williams notes that communities of scholars abandon certain research programs over time. He hopes that this is because these came to be viewed as a poor fit for the data. Disconfirming evidence thus does take a toll in the end. Yet Williams cannot entirely dismiss an alternative possibility that research programs were abandoned for reasons of taste or academic faddishness. Moreover, he recognizes that abandoned research programs are often reborn. This may reflect the fact that the abandoned program had some merit, or perhaps that its problems have been forgotten. Integrative research should try to avoid faddishness. It should survey more than just the last couple of years of research, and compare the insights of different research programs. It should be focused on contextualized generalizations, and thus not shy away from complex integrations of the sort X has effect N on Y but only in the presence of A, B, C, D, and E and absence of F, G, H, and J. Faddishness in human science may reflect, at least in part, an unattainable search for law-like regularities. We can be both less wasteful and more precise if we integrate the best parts of diverse research programs.

Since human science necessarily involves the exercise of judgment, Williams urges an open-ended reflexivity. We cannot be sure what sort of biases might creep into a particular research project, and thus should regularly interrogate our practices. He appreciates that reflection is both an individual and collective pursuit. We should be reflective about our own practices but also those of others. I would agree with Williams that we should encourage all researchers toward reflexivity. I would stress, though, that integrative work, by seeking to understand why different researchers achieve different results, will often uncover biases of which individual researchers were unaware. Integrative work will be less likely to identify biases shared by all researchers, and so will do a better job of policing bias when the research community is diverse.

Lumsden (2019) explores reflexivity in detail. There is now widespread recognition that authors of social research should be reflexive: about personal biases, biases in the methods and theories they pursue, and biases in their disciplines. Reflexivity has become increasingly important with the rise of interdisciplinarity. Lumsden urges researchers to be more open about their reflections in their publications: What biases did they worry about and how did they try to grapple with these? Yet Lumsden recognizes some problems in the literature on reflexivity. Reflexivity has become a buzzword, and may thus be asserted without being actively embraced. It has been employed most often to date for commentary on how gender identity has influenced research; we must be wary that reflexivity not privilege some groups over others. In the hands of some authors, reflexivity can mean an excessive navel-gazing in which the author's views become more important than the research subjects themselves. Some scholars have embraced a "messy" presentation where authorial reflections are interspersed throughout a research report. I would share Lumsden's desire to see all authors engage in some reflexivity, but also her fears that this can come to overshadow the research itself.[23] The best balance here may involve a brief reflective commentary in the introduction or in an appendix. I cringe at the thought of celebrating messiness as a good thing. We want the research results to be clearly stated.

Lumsden, like Williams, argues that there is no simple checklist for a researcher to engage in pursuing reflection. Like Williams, she appreciates that reflexivity is both a personal and collective responsibility. While I concur with Williams and Lumsden that we cannot prescribe a clear checklist, I would proffer the list of reflections suggested in Repko and Szostak (2020, 358–364) as a very good starting point. The author should reflect on their results (are they reasonable and important?), their methods or integrative processes (did they miss or downplay any steps?), their theoretical and epistemological approach (what biases might they possess?), their disciplinary biases, and a set of possible personal biases (why was I interested in this topic, what results did I hope for, did I bring appropriate expertise, did I prefer approaches and evidence that I agreed with or was familiar with?).[24] I would also stress that while individual reflexivity is important, it is even more critical that reflexivity be pursued at the community level, and thus it is especially important in integrative works. Integrative researchers can communicate reflexive insights to specialized researchers and will hopefully influence specialized research practice.[25]

Given that this book attempts (among other things) to link the social sciences and humanities, we should close here with Ramadanovic's (2021) argument that humanists, and literary scholars in particular, have an important role to play across the scholarly enterprise in addressing bias and interpreting results. Humanists have expertise in the close reading of texts and the interpretation of the (often hidden) meanings of texts. Humanists have most often applied these skills to works of art but can apply them to works of science. Though Ramadanovic discusses epistemology often, and at times speaks favorably of objectivity, it was not clear to me whether he imagines that humanists would identify multiple conflicting meanings in scientific texts as they often do in works of fiction, or whether humanists would aid in the pursuit of scholarly consensus. He does recognize that it is possible to integrate across different interpretations.[26] Moreover, he does share the vision of this book of tying islands of specialized research into a consistent whole – though he speaks of shared narrative(s) rather than a shared conceptual map.

Structure

Heyck (2015) argues that an emphasis on systems – on interactions among a set of variables (he sometimes uses the phrase "organization" instead of system) – came to dominate all social sciences in the decades after 1955. The system itself, defined by relationships, processes, or mechanisms, was viewed as being more important than the components of the system. He performed an analysis of top journals in all disciplines, searching for words like system, structure, function, and modeling. He found a dramatic increase in the use of such words across the social sciences after 1955. Anthropologists decided that their purpose was the study of culture as a whole, and political scientists came to study the state as a complex system (they had previously compared democracy to monarchy or studied particular policies).[27] He argues that this emphasis on systems within social science both encouraged and reflected the development of large systems within government and business. Yet by the late 1970s, there was growing skepticism about our collective ability to understand complex systems, encouraged by the economic dislocations of the 1970s.[28] It is useful to view this history through the lens of our discussion of the rise and fall of research programs above. Why might social science have lost interest in systems? This can hardly be because systems are unimportant in our world. Therefore, it must be because we had collective difficulty in comprehending these. One obvious explanation for this would be that we studied open systems as if they were closed systems. Another would be that we devoted insufficient attention to how individuals influence society-level phenomena. This generally led to unsatisfactory results. Heyck does not appreciate that the system-oriented research program remained stronger in Economics than elsewhere. This may be because the economy subsystem is more closed than others are, or because economists became more attached to mathematical modeling. In any case, we can see one purpose of this present book as resuscitating an emphasis on systems that has been somewhat dormant in at least some social sciences. Yet we wish not to duplicate the research program of 1960 but take that which was good in it – the desire to understand subsystems – and improve on this by placing these subsystems in the context of the broader human science system. It was wasteful and unnecessary to move away from the study of subsystems. We should strive to incorporate the insights gained from those investigations into an understanding of how the subsystems that were studied in different disciplines interact which each other and with phenomena ignored in these subsystems.

Individuals and Societies

Epstein (2015, 6) helpfully diagnoses five broad challenges we face in understanding the role of both individuals and groups in society:

1. *Our models of the individual are inadequate.* He claims here that we often make simplifying assumptions of rationality, homogeneity, perfect information, and independence.
2. *We have a poor understanding of the "emergence" of group properties out of aggregates of individuals.* He notes that, "A brain has different properties than individual neurons, an ant colony has different properties than the individual ants, and likewise a society has properties that cannot easily be predicted from the properties of individuals."
3. *We are building models in the wrong style.* Some scholars disdain mathematical models while others want more math.
4. *We are building models at the wrong level.* Some favor models at the individual level, while others think we should only model societal-level variables. More recently, some have suggested internal models at the level of neuroscience.
5. *"Grand theorizing" is out of our reach altogether.* "In recent years, many social scientists have grown suspicious of theories that intend to model societies or economies as a whole. ... Other theorists are devoting their energies to small models that test hypotheses about very narrow parts of the economy."

We have ourselves argued against the possibility of grand theory, and can welcome Epstein's skepticism on that point. As for his other concerns, these can be addressed in turn by integrative works that explore how different assumptions affect results, exploration of causal links between individual-level phenomena and societal-level phenomena, and appreciation of the strengths and weaknesses of different methods.

The role of integrative works in addressing simplistic assumptions deserves emphasis. Specialized researchers will make a variety of assumptions – some explicit, others common to a field of inquiry and thus generally implicit.

Integrative works within a field should naturally explore how different assumptions generate different results. We can hope that integrative works can give space to works within a field that query common assumptions in a field. Integrative works that span fields will be expected to explore the hidden assumptions that characterize those fields, and the effects that these have on results.

Sadly, Epstein concludes that the big problem is that we exaggerate the importance of individuals within society. He is entirely correct, of course, that groups and organizations (quite different phenomena that he treats together) operate in ways that cannot be explained simply in terms of the personalities of their members. This, though, is an argument for examining group processes, not ignoring individuals. The precise importance of individuals within human science needs to be established carefully across a wide variety of causal links, and can reasonably be expected to vary considerably across links.

Epstein stresses in the first part of his book that we need to carefully distinguish the internal structure of a phenomenon from the forces that act upon it. We have made the precise same argument ourselves. The second part shows that groups are more than the sum of the individuals within the group. We cannot understand the United States Supreme Court as just the sum of nine people. Rather, we also need to appreciate the set of rules that govern its powers, who gets appointed, terms of office, precedents it has set and much more. While we can agree with Epstein's main point, we can quibble with key parts of his analysis. First, it would have been helpful if he had distinguished a formal institution such as the Supreme Court from less formal groupings. His concerns about characteristics like terms of appointment matter only for formal institutions. There is a more general lesson here: that referring explicitly to the phenomena in Table 2.1 can spare all scholars from careless generalizations. Second, it is helpful to distinguish the phenomenon of "courts," which have existed for thousands of years across myriad societies, from the particular realization of "United States Supreme Court." That realization reflects a variety of causal links (such as from the executive and legislature that together appoint the justices) and internal dynamics (such as the precedents set over time). Note that causal links to a particular realization can be unique and not apply to the phenomenon more generally. The same is true of causal links leading away from a realization: The Supreme Court makes diverse decisions and thus has myriad effects.[29] Again, there is a general lesson: Authors should carefully distinguish phenomena from realizations of phenomena. Third, and perhaps most importantly, Epstein shows that the court is much more than the nine judges, but cannot show that they do not matter. Indeed the intense debates and spectacle that have surrounded the appointment of Supreme Court justices in recent years would be hard to fathom if those nine people were not in fact an important component of the realization of the Supreme Court at a point in time. Legal scholars and journalists agonize over the effect that a particular judge may have on the court's functioning. Epstein is quite right that the nine justices are constrained, but this hardly renders them unimportant. As noted above, we should embrace the study of group processes while not ignoring the role of individuals. A general lesson here is that we should not casually assume away the importance of any phenomenon.

Epstein does usefully identify common errors in the treatment of groups. Some have theorized that we can understand groups as expressing the (average) attitudes of members. Epstein notes both that groups face constraints and that some group members may be more influential than others. Other theorists have suggested that groups have their identities thrust upon them by external forces. Epstein urges a sensible middle ground, that we can endorse, whereby we study both the internal dynamics of group decision-making and the external forces (that is, causal links) acting upon the group.

Consensus

Martini and Boumans (2014) begin by noting that science aspires to be objective and unified. By the latter, they mean that scholars strive to achieve consensus over time. However, there is no clear methodology for achieving either objectivity[30] or consensus. They recommend an approach that is identical to what we have advocated:

> Acknowledging a wide variety of sources of evidence and methods in social science, different kinds of "triangulation" have been developed to reach convergence. The strategy of triangulation requires that more than one method, or more than one source of evidence, should be used to validate an observation. The rationale for this practice is that we can have more confidence in a certain result when different methods or sources of evidence are found to be congruent and yield comparable data.
>
> *(2014, 4).*

Triangulation is a term borrowed from surveying: Surveyors can identify a precise location by taking readings from different locales and seeing where those readings intersect. Note, then, that we do not need each method or research project to point in precisely the same direction. If they are in broad agreement, and we can identify reasons for any disagreements, we can still be confident. Martini and Boumans appreciate, as we have above, that synthesizing across diverse studies is similar to replicating particular results. They recognize, though, that there are challenges in synthesizing evidence from diverse methods. They argue that theoretical and methodological plurality is often advocated for encouraging creativity; they urge researchers to see it also as a path toward consensus. Recall that Elman et al. (2020) above worried about a potential conflict between the pursuit of novelty and the pursuit of understanding. Here we see that the use of multiple methods and theories might support both goals.

Denscombe (2010) argues that there is indeed a fair bit of consensus about how to perform good social research – despite disagreement about which methods to use. He identifies twelve characteristics of good research. Most of these we have encouraged above: "have clearly stated aims and questions" (see Chapter 2), "relate to existing knowledge and ideas" (we worried in Chapter 2 that most literature surveys are too limited in scope), "be open-minded and self- reflective" (see above), "contribute something new to knowledge" (we have stressed adding to our understanding and contributing to ongoing conversations at many points), and "be cautious about their claims" (we have recognized that no research is perfect at many points). A couple more refer to particular types of reflection: "Be aware of underlying assumptions" and "apply to other situations." The rest deal with questions of research ethics or the details of research design that are beyond the scope of this volume – but reinforce the idea that no piece of research can be perfect.

Debates in the Humanities

The literature on reforming the humanities is far more diffuse. There is a widespread concern that the humanities are not advancing our collective understanding but rather stumble from one big theory to another. Yet there is a paucity of confident proposals for transformation – beyond the promulgation of new grand theories that might be better in some way than the old. Leezenberg and de Vries (2019) note that philosophers once proposed strategies for making the humanities progressive like natural science, but are now content to describe how the humanities operate. We can comment here on some of the key challenges recognized in the literature on the humanities. I might stress that these are challenges identified by humanists themselves.[31]

Martinelli (2017) is an exception who does provide a manifesto for a new approach to the humanities. He urges humanists to look inside the humanist community for the source of at least some problems. While he urges a conversation among humanists, and is thus sometimes vague about the direction in which the humanities should move, he provides several clear pieces of advice. Most of these we can wholeheartedly embrace. He is clear about encouraging interdisciplinarity in general, and especially connecting the study of the human with the study of the social.[32] He encourages an openness to applying the methods of natural and social science as appropriate. He urges an empirical approach that moves beyond speculation to seek evidence of diverse sorts. He advocates clarity and logical argumentation. He urges humanists to be clear in particular about what they are studying, and to what cases any hypotheses might apply.[33] He is very critical of extreme postmodern views.[34]

Martinelli urges reflection on the purposes of the humanities. These have an important role to play in treasuring the great thinkers of the past. (I concur, though I think we should appreciate that the great thinkers of the past generally understood some causal links better than others, and we should thus be wary of celebrating their entire systems of thought.) Humanists can encourage us to appreciate creativity, beauty, quality of life, dignity of life, empathy, tolerance, culture, and reflection (The first of these are obvious; the role of the humanities in encouraging empathy or tolerance needs to be established rather than assumed.) Yet he urges the humanities to be forward looking, willing to question inherited traditions and values, and willing to value rather than fear new technologies (he lauds the digital humanities). I applaud Martinelli for seeking to identify how the humanities "add value" to the scholarly enterprise. Yet I think that this value can be more clearly expressed by simply explicating the set of causal links that are its focus: the links to and from art and cultural expressions. Humanists may interact with other scholars along any of these links, but humanists will engage most profoundly with questions of how and why art moves us. [Humanists may also usefully apply skills in the close reading of texts to texts in any field, and may thus contribute to interdisciplinary endeavors far distant from art.]

One of Martinelli's key proposals for reform is for a "meta-humanities" that would reflect on the nature of research. He, like us, worries that independent research may not be as productive as it should be. He thinks it invaluable for the community as a whole to reflect on where research is heading and how it is best performed. These are, of course, among the purposes of the integrative research that I have lauded in this book. Integrative research will spot gaps in our understanding, and identify which sorts of research have added the most to our collective understanding of key questions. While some integration may occur at a broad level, much of it will focus on particular causal links, and will thus encourage the sort of well-defined research that Martinelli advocates.

Defining the Humanities

There is an ongoing debate over how to define the humanities. This may be insoluble. The task of philosophy is quite different from the task of the rest of the humanities. We will discuss the role of philosophy in more detail in the next chapter but can merely note here that its function is quite different from the task of exploring particular causal links or subsystems that we could attribute to the other disciplines in the humanities. Therefore, if we try to define the humanities in terms of purpose, the best we can do is "The humanities, with the exception of philosophy, are concerned with the investigation of a set of causal links and subsystems concerned largely with art and cultural expressions."[35] From the perspective of this book, it is important to appreciate that such a definition also indicates what the humanities is not: detailed analysis of economy or polity or society more broadly. Yet many humanists aspire to speak of such matters, a point we return to below. If definition in terms of purpose is problematic, we might essay a definition of method: The humanities involve the study of texts (including visual and musical texts). However, we have seen in the preceding chapter that all methods have uses across the human sciences. There is now a wide range of methods employed in the humanities (Emmeche, Pedersen, and Stjernfelt 2017). The best that we might say here is that textual analysis is particularly important in the humanities.

I would boldly suggest that the humanities is hard to define precisely because it is an integral component of the broader project of human science, and is best understand as inextricably intertwined with social science. Yet I would also note that the dry exposition above about exploring causal links involving art or cultural expressions subsumes something transcendental: trying to understand how art moves people, and arguably encourages empathy, raises consciousness, and teaches us about life. This is a noble and important task, and deserves appreciation for both what it is and what it is not.[36]

The Aesthetic versus the Cultural

Some humanists celebrate the aesthetic: the elements of human appreciation of art that allow humans from different times and places to appreciate works of art (including literature) created in quite different times and places. What is it that allows us all to appreciate Chinese landscapes, Renaissance portraits, and Egyptian temples? Other humanists emphasize the cultural: That any work of art inevitably reflects the cultural milieu in which it was created. What should the humanities be: a study of the universal or the particular? The seemingly obvious answer is *both*. We need to understand both how a work can appeal broadly but also how it can carry particular meaning for some. This simple observation has a critical methodological implication: We will best be able to disentangle these affects by comparative analysis of works from different cultures. What do they share and how do they differ? The natural tendency of humanists to specialize limits their ability to compare. They inevitably know more about works from some societies than from others. Here again there is an important task for integrative scholarship. Comparison is, after all, a kind of integration. Integrative scholars can survey a vast array of analyses of works from different times and places, seeking to identify the similarities and differences.

A Few Causal Links or Many?

Most humanists focus on art and/or cultural expressions. Some, though, seek to theorize about much broader sets of causal links. They are guided to do so by the fact that the texts they investigate grapple with complexity. Indeed, it is often argued that one of the main attractions of the novel is that it allows us to submerse ourselves in the experiences of others as these cope with the interwoven challenges of life. Humanists can therefore do much for us by discussing how (works of art show us how) people grapple with complexity. Yet it is less obvious that they can tell us much about the nature of that complexity itself. A novel can describe in detail how an individual responds to poverty, but need not tell us much about why poverty exists.[37]

What is it that makes a successful artist? It seems likely that artists have some intuitive feel for the subject matter and are able then to paint or write in a way that carries a message that would be difficult to consciously articulate (This supposition deserves to be investigated but we will accept it for now). We might then imagine that when an author writes about economic or social matters that they have some intuitive understanding of economic or social subsystems. Yet this hardly seems necessary. The author's gift lies in showing us how individuals react to social and economic circumstances. The author can portray enslaved people without understanding the causes of slavery. The author needs to have an understanding of the choices the slave faces and the psychological trauma they endure, but need not understand why slavery was profitable. My skepticism that successful authors need be excellent economists or sociologists can itself be subject to investigation – but unless we have good reason to believe that I am wrong, humanists (like all scholars) should be wary of commenting on causal links that lie distant from the study of art based on their interpretations of works of art.

We can criticize the humanities for trying to develop big theories of everything, and instead urge a more focused look at particular causal links. It is not surprising that big theories rise and fall – this itself is a subject of much concern in the humanities – since they are inevitably wrong in some respects and fall out of favor as criticisms mount. Yet they keep innumerable scholars busy in the meantime. Maybe some shreds of insight remain. These should not die when the grand theory dies but should be captured within integrative research. This last part is important. Only by carefully evaluating and integrating at the level of individual causal links can we hope to maintain the good parts of every research program. If we insist instead on only evaluating each grand theory in its entirety – Foucault or Bourdieu or Habermas (or Marx or Keynes or Weber for that matter) are either completely right or wrong – then we will throw out the baby with the bathwater. Just because these great thinkers imagined that their analysis of one link was wedded tightly to their analysis of others does not mean that we cannot and should not seek to disentangle these – and then see what supporting argument and evidence is provided for each distinct argument made. [This is, we might note, the approach taken in this chapter: We deal with what authors say about matters important to our project but have not felt it necessary to describe the entire edifice of each author's thoughts.]

The novelty of this argument deserves emphasis. Some humanists devote much effort to reinterpreting the great thinkers of the past. Yet they tend to do this in a holistic fashion. They seek to identify through close reading consistencies or inconsistencies within the great thinker's work. I suggest a more focused and more useful inquiry in which we break each thinker's ideas into their constituent parts. What did they say about particular causal links and why? A good starting assumption is that every great thinker probably grasped some links better than others. Rather than seeking to reify or damn a particular author, we should be seeking to integrate the best ideas from multiple authors.

Explanation versus Interpretation

It is often argued that humanists cannot or should not attempt explanation but should focus on the subjective meanings attached by observers to works of art. In such a view, any interpretation is as valid as any other, and there is no hope of integrating toward a more comprehensive understanding. Leezenberg and de Vries (2019), for example, suggest that whereas scientists pursue truth claims, humanists pursue meaning, and it is quite possible for different authors to find different meanings in the same text. Martinelli (2017, 37) agrees that the humanities pursue meaning while scientists pursue causal understanding. Yet the example he provides as justification is informative: "while sciences have given us the most precious information that it was that virus to cause that disease (plus additional important information on how it was formed, what was its chemical composition, what could be the cure, etc.), the humanities complement that part of the story by analyzing the conditions and impacts of the disease (e.g., it is the result of a given psychological/existential condition of the subject, it affects certain layers of society, it generates forms of social discrimination, it is not properly faced by institutions, etc.), adding significance to meaning." These are, of course, just a different set of causal links (not necessarily those that humanists should study, but certainly causal links from a particular virus to a set of individual or societal practices).

It is quite possible, then, for a scholar to emphasize interpretation, or the pursuit of meaning, and yet simultaneously urge the understanding of particular causal links. How can this be? We are trying – or at least should be – as scholars to understand how and why art moves us. We can then explore what any interpretation of any artwork tells us about that question. Was the viewer/reader moved emotionally, did they find the work educative, was it cathartic, or indeed did they react in some completely unexpected way? Given the ubiquity of art in human societies, it is likely the case that art moves us in multiple ways – and that different people value particular works of art in different ways. Moreover, different works of art likely move us in different ways. Only through comparisons across both works and individuals can we hope to identify or understand such differences. There is thus no conflict between appreciating individual acts of interpretation of individual works of art and yet seeking to integrate across these in order to identify multiple ways in which art works.

Steinberg (2014) appreciates this point. He suggests that we get a better understanding by integrating different perspectives. He uses the analogy of several people dispersed around the edges of a room describing a person standing in the middle of a room. We will obviously gain a more complete picture of the person in the middle by integrating the different perspectives. In doing so, we will wish to know where each observer was standing. Likewise, we should always query the basis for different perspectives. In doing so, we are not trying to decide that one perspective is better than another, but rather appreciating what each perspective has to offer to a more comprehensive understanding.[38]

It might be useful to return here to Martinelli's concern that we identify clear purposes for the humanities. What is the value of interpreting thousands of works if we are not ever going to attempt to integrate across all of these interpretations in order to achieve some greater understanding? To be sure, there is an audience for individual interpretations: fans of Shakespeare may enjoy reading an interpretation of his plays, and connoisseurs of Botticelli may likewise enjoy an interpretation of his paintings. Yet as a scholarly enterprise, we surely hope for something more than a congeries of isolated and incomparable bits of interpretation? Do we wish to concede that some key causal links within human science are simply beyond human understanding, or should we at least try to integrate our way to a better understanding of how and why art moves us? I think the choice is clear.

High Art versus Popular Culture

One important development in humanities research in recent decades has been the expansion of the canon of works studied. No longer do humanists just study masterpieces. Rather it has become increasingly common to study "popular art" of the sort that typical humans might listen to, read, or hang on their walls. Naturally, this change has been controversial. Yet if we accept that we are collectively trying to comprehend how and why art moves us, it seems only logical that we would wish to study the role that art plays in everyday lives. Art is not something that humans only encounter on occasional trips to a museum but something that can be found in almost every home and office – and increasingly on urban murals. We are unlikely to understand fully the role of art in our lives if we limit our attention to a small minority of artworks that most people rarely if ever encounter.

Perhaps inevitably, the expansion of the canon has led to questioning of the very idea of the masterpiece. Are there really some works that are significantly superior to other works in some way? Or is art just art? These are, of course, the sort of conjectures that need to be investigated rather than assumed. If we appreciate, though, that humans have a shared aesthetic sense, then it is quite possible to imagine that some works may strike a chord with humanity (on average) better than other works.[39] The empirical fact that some works are widely esteemed might be attributed to the influence of a few art connoisseurs on public tastes, but might also reflect the fact that these works really are very good (or a bit of both). Comparisons of how people react to masterpieces with how they react to other works of art may inform our judgment of whether masterpieces really are superior. Such comparisons can be usefully informed, we might note, by our understanding of how and why art moves us: It could be that some works are better at achieving catharsis while others are educative and still others encourage empathy. We can only have a limited understanding of why any particular work of art is valued unless we have a solid understanding of how art in general affects us. In turn, though, a comparative understanding of why particular works move us can inform our more general understanding of why art moves us.

The Humanities No Longer Inspire

We have recognized above that art serves an important role in human societies. Yet the work of scholars in the humanities hardly serves to inspire the general population to appreciate art. Jargon-ridden books and articles are not inspiring, except perhaps to a precious few willing to devote years to mastering a particular discourse. Yet if the purpose of humanities scholarship is to understand how and why art moves us, then a two-way communication between academics and the public seems advisable (Levenson 2018). Steinberg (2014) concurs that reading great literature should be enjoyable. He worries not only that humanities research is impenetrable but also that the way we teach literature to students often sucks the joy out of reading. If students do not enjoy reading, they will avoid it and then not be able to learn from it. Integrative work will necessarily transcend the jargon of particular theoretical discourses and thus should be more accessible than the works it integrates across. We will return to questions of teaching in Chapter 5 but can usefully note here that an integrative understanding of why art moves us might encourage students to enjoy art more rather than less.

Coherence

Leezenberg and de Vries (2019) are among many who worry about a lost sense of coherence within the humanities (see also Ramadanovic 2021). They worry that the humanities have fragmented into various fields and specialties, and these communicate little with each other. There is little possibility of consensus. In every discipline within the humanities, there have been concerns that they have lost their way. "And has the increasing specialization in the literary and cultural disciplines not degenerated into an exaggerated focus on highly theoretical questions formulated in esoteric jargon, replacing attention for the works of culture themselves, that is, the novels, poetry, visual art, and music that are their original objects of interest?" (Leezenberg and de Vries 2019, 33). In this book, we have been advocating an even greater coherence across human science as a whole. The recipe is clear. We need integrative works within fields to combat unnecessary jargon and integrate across interpretations. We need fields to focus on a manageable set of causal links. We need integrative works across fields to show how the insights of different fields are connected, and together give us a sense of the role that art plays in human societies.

The Value of the Humanities

Small (2013) outlines five broad arguments that are employed to argue for continued funding of the humanities.[40] The first is that "they study the meaning-making practices of the culture, focusing on interpretation and evaluation with an indispensable element of subjectivity." She clarifies this rather vague statement with a reference to subject matter – cultural practices, including art – and an emphasis on the need for judgment in evaluation. She appreciates that she has so far provided just a description of what humanists do rather than why this might be valuable. She then notes that humanists often contest the meanings of key terminology: While some see this as a laudatory critical facility, she appreciates that it can be taken to extremes in which productive dialogue becomes impossible. She applauds an emphasis on the particular rather than a search for generalizability. She also applauds an emphasis on stylistic expression. She then speaks favorably of the role of the humanities in encouraging critical thinking, worried only that other fields can also claim this. She seems unaware that an emphasis on style, and disinterest in generalization, both detract from the demonstration of critical thinking. She later applauds an emphasis on qualitative analysis and on interpretivism. It is hard to see how any of these arguments would persuade someone outside the humanities of their value. Several of them fly in the face of our arguments in favor of integrating across perspectives, pursuing multiple methods, and engaging with social and natural scientists.

Second, she looks at arguments for utility. Some have celebrated the deliberate impracticality of the humanities, arguing (correctly) that humans are much more than just economic beings. Others, though, have sought to identify practical outcomes. She concludes that the humanities can serve practical purposes but nevertheless should emphasize its impractical role. I would argue from the ubiquity of art in human societies that art must play important roles in human society. Explicating that role is thus not impractical. Society would benefit from better understanding how and why arts moves us: This would, I hope, allow us to better integrate art into contemporary society. I think there is a huge danger in thinking that the study of art is impractical. And I suspect that this feeling that it is impractical plays no small role in the celebration of interpretation, specificity, and style of scholarly presentation that so limit our pursuit of understanding of how and why art moves us.

Third, the humanities may add to human happiness. This may happen directly through the joy some people may find in works of artistic criticism. We have seen above, though, that contemporary scholarship is generally inaccessible to the public.[41] We might also worry about hoping that scholarship will entertain. Small is more interested in any case with a secondary claim that the humanities teach us about the nature of happiness. She asserts that it can do so better than psychology or economics. We will discuss briefly in the next chapter the interdisciplinary field of happiness studies. There is undoubtedly some scope for humanists to inform this field – but primarily by better understanding how art itself makes us happy. Novelists may have a better understanding of human happiness than of economic theory but we should still be wary of grounding our understanding of human happiness too much in how novelists (or other artists) depict it.

A fourth argument is that the humanities teach the intellectual skills necessary for successful democracy.[42] Small is willing to give some credence to the importance of teaching students how to engage in constructive analysis and debate, though she is cognizant that non-humanists may also do this. I think this is one of those questions where trying to argue at the level of the humanities as a whole leads us far astray. We will argue in Chapter 5 for some particular types of teaching – ethics, rhetoric – that have a critical role to play in supporting democracy, and draw heavily (but not exclusively) on philosophy. Teaching the history of countries that have slid from democracy into authoritarianism, or reading novels of life in authoritarian states, might do much to educate our students on the importance of maintaining a healthy democracy. Yet perhaps most of all we need to model constructive arguments grounded in argument, evidence, and respect for opposing points of view. This an integrative human science would do but a humanities that celebrates postmodern excess or stylistic expression will not.

Fifth, Small examines the "intrinsic value" of the humanities – or perhaps of the works that humanists study. On the latter, I can reassert that art plays an important role in human lives and we should essay to understand this better. On the former, then, I would say that the humanities are inherently valuable in so far as they provide enhanced understanding of why art is so important. In this light, the priorities asserted by Small appear misplaced: "If, as Chapter 1 explored, interpretation, judgement, and the performance of the scholar's own style are often deemed to be of more importance, these activities nevertheless supervene on, and would be impossible without, underlying disciplinary knowledge." She appreciates, that is, that the humanities do in fact generate some sorts of understanding, but thinks that this is not their primary purpose. I would assert in contrast that we should pursue enhanced understanding of art as we do other subjects. This is a far more valuable enterprise than an endless parade of idiosyncratic perspectives.

Summary

- It is valuable to engage other works concerned with the state of the humanities and social sciences. These often agree with us, and thus provide justification for our arguments. They occasionally guide us to clarify those arguments. Most importantly, perhaps, they often raise concerns that we can provide answers to. This serves to establish the value of our approach. (We focus on the second and third of these purposes in the chapter.)
- Frequent efforts at integrative research are the best means of combining individual pieces of specialized research into a coherent whole, and not forgetting and then re-inventing the wheel.
- Integrative research also could take account of stylized facts that have not yet been theorized.
- Integrative research compensates for the lack of replication in human science.
- Integrative work can suggest new research questions.
- We can only fully appreciate any one causal link in the context of related links.
- Integrative work can synthesize diverse perspectives.
- Integrative works can identify situations in which misguided or simplistic assumptions drive results.

- We need to appreciate – and not confuse – internal dynamics within a phenomenon, and causal links involving the phenomenon.
- Integration can combat confirmation bias, especially if negative results are published somewhere.
- Integration can allow us to identify effects that are found to be statistically insignificant in many studies.
- Scholars who are suspicious of causation nevertheless employ causal analysis. We can apply causal analysis to all of our phenomena. Though a formal definition is elusive, we can understand causation as when a particular realization of one phenomenon increases the likelihood of a particular realization of another phenomenon.
- We can seek multiple kinds of evidence for causation. We should look for the effect (that is, a correlation between a posited influence and effect) to be found in diverse studies. We should seek evidence for some mechanism that explains the effect. We should seek evidence that the cause precedes the effect. In some cases, it is valuable to find that removal of the cause decreases the likelihood of the effect. We should compile evidence against alternative explanations.
- Scholars need to exercise judgment, because our data do not perfectly reflect our phenomena. Judgment is also called for when we adjust our hypothesis after examining our data: This may be a form of research trickery but may be essential in identifying contextualized generalizations.
- We should thus be reflective. We encouraged individual researchers to engage in several types of reflection. We also appreciated that integrative researchers are forced to reflect on why different researchers reached different conclusions.
- Integration, and the search for contextualized generalizations, should act together to reduce the faddishness of some fields in human science. We should retain insights from discontinued research programs.
- The historical recognition that systems analysis fell out of favor in some fields from the 1970s is best understood – and addressed – by a recognition that systems are open.
- We can have greatest confidence in a hypothesis justified by different methods. When different methods point in somewhat different directions, we can triangulate to the most likely explanation.
- Integration can serve to evaluate how productive a field is, and suggest changes.
- We can best understand the humanities (excluding philosophy) as studying a set of causal links involving art and cultural expressions.
- Comparative research, a kind of integration, is the best way of distinguishing the aesthetic from cultural effects of art.
- Although humanists study works of art that embrace complexity, humanists in their research should avoid the temptation to address myriad causal links far from art or cultural expressions. We should not assume that artists understand economic or social theory. Humanists can also, of course, engage in integrative research (drawing in particular perhaps on great thinkers of the past).

- There is no conflict between the goals of interpretation and understanding. We can integrate across interpretations in the pursuit of understanding.
- An integrative understanding of why art moves us might encourage students to enjoy art more rather than less.
- Integration naturally combats a sense that the humanities are no longer coherent.

Notes

1 This is not intended as a criticism. I find much of value in a range of approaches to epistemology (with a particular attraction to critical realism and pragmatism). I think it useful to draw on as many of these as possible rather than declaring a favorite (an argument I make at length in Szostak 2011). In the next chapter, I will urge more integrative work among philosophers to identify pieces of methodological advice that accord with different epistemological approaches.
2 Tuckett (2018, 2) is one of the few that appreciate that the division of social sciences from humanities is an administrative convenience more than anything else.
3 Daniels (2021, ch. 3) argues that the reputation of science as a whole suffers because results are not replicated. The public needs to trust scholarly practices.
4 "Comprehensive appraisal begins by paying close attention to the chosen theory or theoretical issue, in all its formulations. The research question might be fairly well developed, or it might be more open-ended. An example of the latter is modernization theory, according to which development (variously understood) affects democracy (variously understood) through a set of mechanisms (variously understood). If there are outstanding debates or ambiguities with respect to the nature of the theory, this will require a good deal of work. Confusion notwithstanding, the writer's job is to bring diverse work on a topic together into a coherent whole. In doing so, she will need to consider the measurement of key variables, scope-conditions, as well as background factors (contextual/interaction effects) that may be at work. She will also need to consider the position of that theory within the firmament of other theories and theoretical frameworks, eliminating ad hoc and idiosyncratic elements wherever possible so that theoretical unification is enhanced. A comprehensive appraisal involves active theorizing. Indeed, the primary contribution of an appraisal may be theoretical rather than empirical" (Gerring, 355–356). Again, I applaud the general thrust. I would prefer focusing on causal links rather than theories. And I wish Gerring had commented on the disadvantages of vague theories and terminology.
5 Chambers (2017, 12) shares this concern. We can only be confident of a result if it is found in multiple studies, but the constant pursuit of novelty militates against this.
6 6 and Bellamy (2013, 9) concur: "It is very difficult to go on to do anything more ambitious in social research if you have not got the descriptive inferences right. It is true that the most prestigious journals do not publish articles that offer only descriptive inferences. But the articles that they do publish rely, in a vital part of their overall argument, on the soundness of descriptive inferences, even if those parts of their workings are not shown."
7 Gorard (2017) talks about how different research designs are called for at different stages of the research process. He sees integrative work – identifying what we know and do not know about a particular topic – as the first step in a research cycle. He later warns that a limited literature search can lead to biases in research. He worries that most research in social science is based on only a cursory literature survey. He also worries that we rarely proceed to the rigorous testing of a theory or policy proposal.

8 Chambers (2017, 47) reports how a claim that neutrinos move faster than light in 2011 led to falsification soon after and discovery that the original result was due to a loose cable. In human science, such a mistake could easily go un-noticed. He notes that social scientists act with horror if someone attempts to replicate their results, whereas natural scientists take this as a compliment (52–53). In Chapter 5, he discusses how the failure to replicate encourages academic fraud.

9 6 and Bellamy (2013) appreciate that different researchers make different tradeoffs between virtues such as parsimony, precision, or generality. They urge authors to be explicit about their choice. They then urge integration across different approaches.

10 Smith also urges an exercise whereby we (teach students to) dissect research articles, identifying key arguments, claims for which authors provide no evidence, and more. We have urged clarity in expression in Chapter 2 and will urge a similar teaching practice in Chapter 5.

11 Lebow (2020) raises an alternative possibility: that we seek order in a complex world, and thus want to believe that we understand it better than we do.

12 He also finds that this is true of 70 percent of papers in space science. The natural sciences appear to be better but far from perfect.

13 The journal *Plos One* does publish both replications and negative results, but is very unusual in both respects.

14 He appreciates that some have argued that the world is essentially random and that we only imagine that we can detect causation. But then social science is impossible.

15 Williams repeatedly warns his readers that he is not attempting a contribution to philosophy of science but to practical methodology of social science. I, like him, try to ground practical arguments in philosophy but think it is often possible to make strong practical arguments despite philosophical disagreement.

16 Williams appreciates that a probabilistic approach to causation makes it impossible for a hypothesis to be disproven: It is entirely possible that a given correlation will not be found in a particular study. We have argued above that falsification is impossible even for deterministic causation, but can appreciate that it is "even more impossible" for probabilistic causation.

17 "The central problem for causality is that whilst very often A will lead to B, this is not always the case and whilst C rarely leads to D it might do so and whether A is followed by B, or D follows C is dependent on a lot more antecedent relationships. In a closed, or relatively closed system, the possibility of all trajectories can be modelled" (Williams, 2020, 58).

18 Morgan (2014) stresses the importance of causal analysis in human science (though recognizing a place for descriptive analysis). Morgan also emphasizes the value of drawing diagrams of the causal chain, including confounding factors (that is, he recommends drawing contextualized generalizations). He also stresses the value of counterfactual analysis: what if X did not happen?

19 "Realists do not deny the existence of unobservables, and indeed it is an article of faith that there is more to the world than we can sense or measure. So, it follows from that, that what we measure or understand, is rarely the thing in itself, but a representation of the thing in itself" (Williams 2020, 202).

20 "But what of mechanisms? Let me be candid: there is no sharp divide between social objects and mechanisms. Both are merely linguistic placeholders, for the "real." But mechanisms certainly imply something bigger and a connectivity, or coalescence, between social objects" (Williams 2020, 201). We will not progress very far in human science if we cannot distinguish phenomena from causal mechanisms. [I should note here that BCC captures homelessness synthetically as "people without homes."]

21 Pearl and Mackenzie (2018) also stress the identification of mechanisms. While the recognition that consumption of citrus fruits prevented scurvy was critical in saving sailor's lives in the nineteenth century, the failure to appreciate that the mechanism by which this worked was vitamin C meant that explorers of both Arctic and

Antarctic died of scurvy in the early twentieth century. The identification of mechanisms can aid us in identifying contextualized generalizations: we can examine the effect of citrus fruits on vitamin C absorption, and vitamin C on scurvy, and gain a good sense of the link between citrus fruits and scurvy even if there are other phenomena that confound estimates of the relationship between citrus fruits and scurvy.

22 Development economists have hypothesized that poor countries should grow faster than rich countries because they can import both capital and technology from those richer countries. Faced with evidence that some poor countries have grown faster than others while others have languished, the hypothesis was tweaked to suggest that faster growth only occurs if the country has the capability to import capital or technology. Some scholars worry that it is too easy to explain any instance of sluggish growth by pointing to some limit in capability (all poor countries have some questionable institutions and gaps in infrastructure) but the general consensus has been that this is a sensible tweak.

23 I would note that Lumsden takes an interpretivist perspective, doubts the possibility of objectivity, and argues that all concepts are contested. Though I am more epistemologically optimistic than Lumsden, we can agree on both the importance and pitfalls of reflexivity. I can also agree with her concerns that both pressures to publish, and to perform policy-relevant work, can detract from a researcher's time and inclination to reflect.

24 Jungmeister (2016) also provides a lengthy list of reflective questions.

25 Schmidt (2022) urges an even stronger form of critical/reflective practice, and argues that the best sorts of interdisciplinarity question the core elements of scholarly investigation.

26 He also argues that deconstruction is no longer a priority as a method of critical analysis and has in many fields including politics gone too far (2021, 12).

27 Natural scientists also came to focus on structures at the time: atomic, molecular, organisms, ecosystems.

28 Heyck sees his book as a prequel to Rodgers' *Age of Fracture* (2011) which describes the splintering of social thought after the 1970s, the rise of discourses around feminism and globalization, and an increased emphasis on personal choice. Heyck likely exaggerates the difference between the network analysis that came after the 1970s and the systems analysis he studies: Both can be seen as efforts to grapple with complexity.

29 It is beyond our scope to explore Epstein's argument in excruciating detail. I think the distinction drawn here between phenomena, realizations, and causal links is more easily grasped than the distinction Epstein attempts to draw between grounds and anchors.

30 Williams (2020) addresses objectivity. Ontologically we can speak of objectivity by asserting that there is a reality to be investigated. Epistemologically, we pursue objectivity when we apply methods thought to be the least biased but remain willing to interrogate our methods. Our theories may reflect our values but once they are out there in the world, they have an objective reality that we can examine. I would add that we can be even more objective by integrating across different theories and methods. Denscombe (2010, 93–94) usefully compares the researcher's quest for objectivity with the chef or surgeon seeking hygiene: We know that perfection is impossible but strive to get as close as possible.

31 Enrolments have fallen across the humanities in recent decades. This may in part simply reflect the fact that female students now pursue a wider range of academic programs. Yet it also likely reflects a concern that humanities degrees do not guarantee successful careers. This concern may be exaggerated. We will suggest in this and later chapters some reforms that may attract more students to the humanities.

32 Martinelli (2017, 79) appreciates that "interdisciplinarity" is often claimed by humanists when engaging only superficially with another discipline (perhaps borrowing some political terminology, say). He would instead encourage sustained engagement with disciplines where there is a shared interest, and a willingness to borrow theories

and methods. Ramadanovic (2021) shares a concern that literary theorists in particular engage in very limited forms of interdisciplinarity.

33 Sadly, Martinelli later in his book applauds a list of roles for the humanities generated by Martha Nussbaum that includes elements like "evaluating political leaders and policies" that seem far from the expertise of the humanities– though there is some scope for the close reading of political texts by humanists.

34 He wonders if postmodernists can see any value in their work. Does it add anything to our understanding of the world? He says that postmodernists should not be surprised if nobody wishes to fund their research (2019, 38–9).

35 We will address the study of languages, and of history, in Chapter 4.

36 "Today we might think that the humanities consist of all those fields of study and activities that teach us what it means to be human; in ways both bad and good. The humanities present us with numerous alternatives for behavior and the basis for choosing among them" (Steinberg 2014). This quote captures some of the majesty of the humanities. Yet in its vagueness it encourages humanists to expound on almost any subject, and raises questions about how exactly the humanities encourage ethical consciousness. This needs to be shown, not assumed.

37 Madjesberg (2017) takes a more expansive view. He argues that the purpose of humans (relative to Artificial Intelligence) is to "make meaning" and that we do this through holistic understandings. The humanities can provide us, he argues, with holistic understandings of different times, places, and situations. His emphasis is on intuitive thought processes rather than grand theorizing.

38 Buvke (2019) suggests that interpretations can serve an important inductive role in suggesting hypotheses that we can test with other methods.

39 There is, of course, much scope for differences in taste within our common aesthetic sense. I often find works hidden in corners of museums that I find more striking than the works the curators stress.

40 Ramadanovic (2021) treats Small (2013) as emblematic of a larger literature that takes a similar approach to the challenges facing the humanities.

41 An obvious exception occurs when literary scholars translate a work from another language.

42 Bate (2011) asserts that the paramount value of humanities research comes in informing teaching. This may be truer for the humanities than other fields. Watt (2011) argues that the practice of law depends on the close reading of texts, a skill fostered in the humanities.

4

RESEARCH IN HUMAN SCIENCE FIELDS

Specialization by Phenomena or Subsystem

The subject matter of the human sciences is vast. How might we best divide the pursuit of understanding into manageable segments so that we can gain the advantages of specialized research? There are two broad possibilities: scholars might specialize around a particular subsystem or set of causal links, or scholars might specialize around a particular method or theory. Human science has for the most part chosen the first possibility but with a heavy dose of the second. Disciplines tend to be defined around the phenomena they study. For example, Economics is generally defined as the study of the production and distribution of wealth. Yet we have seen that it is harder to define some other disciplines – anthropology, sociology, some of the humanities – in terms of a clearly delineated set of phenomena. In practice, most disciplines are also closely identified with one or two methods. Most economists perform mathematical modeling and/or statistical analysis. Most humanists engage in the close reading of texts. Anthropologists have tended to immerse themselves in traditional societies or engage in archaeological digs. In some disciplines, notably economics, there is also a preference for one kind of theory.

There are good reasons for specialization around both phenomena and method. We have seen in Chapter 2 that we need to define phenomena carefully. It is important that scholars share some common understanding of the phenomena they study in order to engage in fruitful conversations. We have and will see that some disciplines do a far better job of clarifying terminology than others, but we can appreciate that clarity around the definition of phenomena is highly desirable. For every method employed in human science, scholars that employ that method have developed over decades guidelines for employing that method properly. Those guidelines are critically important in judging the quality

DOI: 10.4324/9781003275237-4

of research. Researchers with a similar understanding of such guidelines can readily communicate regarding their research.

We have seen in Chapter 2 that no method is perfect, and that we can have the greatest confidence in a hypothesis supported by evidence from multiple methods. Specialization of disciplines by both phenomena and method is therefore troubling, for it means that certain causal links or subsystems are only investigated with a small number of methods. Yet scholarly communities are large enough that we can potentially specialize primarily around phenomena but still have experts in multiple methods study those phenomena. Economics has found room in recent decades for research that employs experiments (sometimes surveys, occasionally some textual analysis). Some quantitative methods are employed in the humanities. Yet experimental economists have had to battle hard for recognition. It should not be so hard for advocates of alternative methods to gain a hearing, or for communities of scholars interested in applying a new method to a particular causal link to emerge. We need a change in worldview among human scientists where they stop mistakenly seeing one method as superior and appreciate the simple but powerful insight that we should seek evidence from multiple methods.

We will in what follows, then, urge specialization around sets of phenomena. We will seek to identify logical sets of phenomena to study – and note when disciplinary boundaries do not reflect this division. We will seek, that is, sets of phenomena that interact powerfully with each other. We will ask in each case to what extent these internal links appear much stronger than external links to phenomena studied in other disciplines. Yet we will appreciate that no discipline deals with an entirely closed subsystem.

We will then ask what sorts of questions scholars of particular sets of phenomena might explore that would be of particular interest to scholars of other sets of phenomena.[1] That is, we will ask in what ways each smaller field of study can best inform the larger human science project. We will also discuss the methods to which these communities might devote more attention. This simple project of examining each field from the perspective of human science as a whole is quite novel. It will yield recommendations that contrast with standard practices in most fields.

It is worth stressing here that we are guided not to organize our discussion around the present structure of disciplines but rather the logical identification of categories in Table 2.1. The subheadings in this chapter will seem jarring to anyone expecting a unified discussion of Sociology. Yet our goal of a discussion of logical subsections of our map of human science forces us to deviate in important ways from existing disciplinary boundaries.

Note that we will often reference the works of others in this chapter. When we do so we have the same purposes as in the previous chapter: to appreciate areas of agreement, to clarify our thinking, and to suggest responses to challenges identified in the works of others.

Particular Subsystems or Sets of Causal Links

Economy

Economists are blessed with one of the more closed systems in all of human science (see Figure 4.1). At the level of individual goods and services, economists can examine how costs of production interact with the characteristics of consumer demand to determine prices and output. At the aggregate level, they can examine how investment, consumption, and money supply interact to determine output and employment levels. Yet, of course, non-economic phenomena influence all of these economic phenomena. Consumer demand reflects cultural attitudes. Climate, labor laws, and a host of other phenomena affect costs of production. Economists have only come in recent decades to recognize that economic institutions, which are in turn generated by political processes, shape economic activities. Though economists have an advantage in the rather powerful relationships that exist among economic phenomena, this can and has easily lulled them into a false sense that they can treat the economic subsystem as if it were closed.

Non-economists might expect that economists would spend much of their time worrying about economic growth, and trying to understand why some regions of the world have far higher incomes than other regions (and why some individuals have higher incomes than others do). Differences in incomes across people and regions interact powerfully with politics and social structure and culture and art and more, and thus are a subject of inherent interest to non-economists. Yet economic growth is a minority pursuit within Economics. There are occasional bursts of interest when a new generation of mathematical

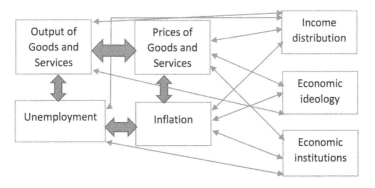

FIGURE 4.1 The Economic Subsystem.

Note: Economists have the pleasure of studying a subsystem of output and prices (at both the level of individual goods and services, and the aggregate economy) and unemployment and inflation, that is relatively closed. Nevertheless, all of these phenomena are influenced by non-economic phenomena. The links to other economic phenomena such as economic institutions, income distribution, and economic ideology are weaker, and the links from these to non-economic phenomena likely stronger.

models of growth or empirical methods for comparing countries (or examining growth in one country through time) comes along. Yet these models and estimations do not take us very far in understanding why some countries grow faster than others (or the incomes of some groups grow faster than others). To answer that question, we need to ask why some countries have better institutions, more technological innovation, more entrepreneurship, better education, better infrastructure, and cultural attitudes that better encourage investment or work effort. This calls for both an interdisciplinary investigation, and openness to multiple methods (Szostak 2009). We cannot fully comprehend economic growth without understanding a host of causal links among economic and non-economic phenomena (see Figure 2.1). Understanding growth also requires that we look over a longer time period than is embraced by most economics research projects; Economic growth does not happen overnight, and there is much evidence that economic success today depends importantly on political circumstances centuries ago. Since quantitative data become thinner as we go back in time, we need to supplement quantitative analysis with historical judgment. Returning to the present, economists in their statistical regressions throw in international survey results as measures of cultural attitudes, but these give a very limited understanding of cultural differences and no indication at all of why such differences might exist. There may be no substitute for actually talking to people.

Economists have tended to shun asking economic actors why they behave as they do. Rational choice theory tells us how agents should behave. If we ask them why they act as they do, and they give a non-rational explanation, they are just wrong. Yet as experiments (and an associated increased interaction with psychologists) have shown us that people behave non-rationally in a host of circumstances, our excuse for not asking people how they make decisions disappears. So we should see a place for interviews, open-ended surveys, and the careful reading of texts in our understanding of economic behavior. Amazingly, it is common for theorists studying the aggregate economy to invoke changes in "expectations" to explain changes in economic activity that they cannot explain in any other way, but they do not actually investigate what those expectations are or were. (I find it unconvincing to attribute the Great Depression to people feeling bad, but this is a popular approach; Szostak 2005a).

As an economist who will suggest transformations in other disciplines below, it is valuable that I can make broadly similar arguments here about my own discipline. Economics gives us many important insights into how the economy functions. Yet its focus on one theory and two methods, and its tendency to ignore all non-economic phenomena, has often led us astray. In the aftermath of the financial crisis of 2008, many leading economists urged theoretical and methodological flexibility and interdisciplinarity.[2] There are clear but slow changes in these directions within the profession. The fact that economists spend relatively little time studying economic growth can be attributed to the facts that its dominant theory and methods have cast little light on this, and that non-economic phenomena are clearly important. We can hope that economic growth will receive greater and more diverse attention in future (perhaps encouraged by the challenges associated with the COVID pandemic).

These ideas may surprise contemporary economists but would have seemed innocuous to earlier generations in the field. Martini and Boumans (2014, 3) cite Alfred Marshall, widely seen as a/the founder of modern economics: "The laws of economics are to be compared with the laws of the tides, rather than with the simple and exact law of gravitation. For the actions of men are so various and uncertain, that the best statement of tendencies, which we can make in a science of human conduct, must needs be inexact and faulty" (Marshall 1920, p. 32). They then explain Marshall's reasoning: "The key to Marshall's view lies in his claim that economic mechanisms work out their influences against a messy background of complicated factors, so that the most we can expect of economic analysis is that it capture the "tendencies" induced by changes in this or that factor." This is precisely our point: that economic activities need to be understood in a broader context.

Polity

Political scientists are less fortunate than economists. They can and do of course analyze how the different components of governance – executive, legislature, judiciary, bureaucracy – interact. Yet it is obvious that social, economic, cultural, and other phenomena powerfully influence political decisions. Political scientists may be tempted to exaggerate the degree to which public opinion translates into public policy, in large part because they have access to lots of public opinion data (Mahoney and Thelen 2015). They need also to understand both how public opinion is generated and how those who are economically or socially privileged can achieve their ends at the expense of broader societal wishes.

Just as we might expect more economists to study the sources of economic growth, we might expect political scientists to devote lots of attention to the sources of stable democracy.[3] Even more so, perhaps, than with economic growth, this requires a long-term perspective. The most stable democracies have been around for centuries, and often emerged slowly as kingly powers declined. Democracies established suddenly by revolution often prove short-lived. What, then, are the reasons why democracy has prospered in some places rather than others? What sorts of characteristics (say, constitutional protections) and causal links (press freedom, cultural respect for diversity) are most important for the maintenance of democracy? These sorts of big questions are explored in the field of comparative political history, but do not lend themselves to the trendier methods of experiment or big data analysis that increasingly characterize political science (Mahoney and Thelen 2015). They thus receive far less attention in the discipline of political science as a whole than they should. At a point in history where democracy is threatened in many parts of the world, we could know far more than we do about what factors are most important for maintaining democratic stability.[4]

Mahoney and Thelen (2015) urge an approach to political analysis that fits well with the approach recommended in this book. They are suspicious of slavish adherence to one or two methods.[5] They appreciate that the historical analysis they encourage often raises questions that other methods can address. They note in particular a synergy with regression analysis: historical study can explain why certain cases deviated from average trends identified by regressions. Historical analysis can also identify the mechanisms that may drive a causal relationship suggested by statistical analysis. Mahoney and Thelen also laud historical analysis for seeking to understand causal relations in context. That is, scholars seek to show how particular causal relationships influence other causal links. They worry that scholars employing other methods often oversimplify their analysis by excluding phenomena that are actually important to the results they are seeking to explain.[6] They thus embrace both the idea of contextualized generalizations and the value of multiple methods in identifying these.

Social Structure

There is much interest these days by human scientists in "intersectionality," the intersection of social divisions by gender, ethnicity, class, sexual orientation, and class/occupation.[7] We may not have needed another piece of terminology but it is good to see this enhanced recognition of the interactions among different elements of what we call social structure. After all, each individual has multiple identities, and we need to appreciate how gender, race, and other characteristics combine to shape identity and behavior. The key insight of the literature on intersectionality may well be that the experience of being a black woman cannot be understood by simply adding our understandings of blacks and women. It is also useful to appreciate that the cultural acceptance of one kind of discrimination may encourage cultural acceptance of other types (though this needs to be shown rather than assumed). Note that scholars of intersectionality often investigate internal and external links simultaneously, examining how discrimination works against combinations of gender, race, and other characteristics. That being said, each element of social structure would seem to have very strong linkages to diverse cultural values and economic and political phenomena (and more; the relationship between biological sex and cultural gender is much studied). The upshot is that scholars of social structure need to strike a careful balance between studying the internal dynamics and the external linkages. Social structure is a very open subsystem (if indeed it qualifies as a subsystem) and we will not get very far in understanding it without investigating the links to many non-social phenomena. In particular, we will not be able to understand how to reduce discrimination without understanding how social structure is embedded in a very broad set of causal linkages. The big question that should animate (much of) the study of social structure is this: What are the political institutions, cultural attitudes, and economic relationships that need to be altered in order to reduce discrimination in human societies (and what role can art and technology play in this transformation)? [We should also care very much, of course, about the effects of discrimination on both democracy and economic prosperity.][8]

Social structure has traditionally been one of the core areas of concern in sociology departments. In recent decades, gender studies and other programs have emerged to look at particular elements of social structure. The rise of intersectionality suggests a widely perceived need to integrate our understandings of different elements of social structure. It has also drawn numerous humanists into the conversation. It seems unlikely that the best way to organize our understandings of social structure is to have several distinct scholarly communities studying different aspects of this. On the other hand, there can be little doubt that the study of social structure benefits from an interdisciplinary approach: This has characterized gender and ethnic studies programs more than sociology departments.

Health and Population

To the extent that there is a subsystem here, it tends to be studied in the health sciences rather than human science. Yet medical professionals have a natural tendency to focus on how they can treat disease rather than on the broader social determinants of health outcomes (though some research of the latter type certainly occurs).[9] Within human science, the study of population and health is very fragmented. Demography tends to be concentrated in sociology departments, but there are a smattering of demographers in economics departments. There is a field of health economics. Psychologists, as we will see below, have often focused on mental illness rather than on the determinants of human happiness. Some sociologists, political scientists, and a few anthropologists explore health outcomes. A growing number of humanists explore the impact of art on health. There is thus no one specialized research community in human science that explores human health. There is the potential for an integrated interdisciplinary conversation that could look at how economic, political, cultural, social, artistic, and other phenomena interact in generating health outcomes.

Bardosh et al. (2020) note that each pandemic reinvigorates calls for the integration of human science understandings of pandemic response, to facilitate the better application of these understandings to public policy. They suggest that integration is critical to other health issues also, including the social determinants of health (see also Gavens et al. 2018).[10] They argue that integrated human science understandings would exert a greater influence on biomedical researchers who at present dominate the study of human health. There have been some successes in developing interdisciplinary research centers. "However, critical institutional, cultural, and political gaps exist that prevent social science insights on issues ranging from (mis) trust, (mis/dis) information, the acceptability of laws and mandates, human behavior and social norms, stigma and discrimination, the impact of geopolitics, and the unintended consequences of interventions, as currently seen in the COVID-19 pandemic, from being mainstreamed into epidemic response" (Bardosh et al. 2020, 2). The fragmented study of health across human science limits the ability of humanity to identify the best policies for encouraging public health.

Culture

There is surely a cultural subsystem (see Figure 4.2). The values of a particular society must largely cohere. If it values fairness, it must also encourage honesty. The stories that a society tells – especially to its children – will tend to support its system of values. Likewise, its religion will tend to support and reflect its values. The connection to cultural expressions may be less strong. It may be important that a society dances but not that it dance in a particular way. Dances and cuisine may have a tenuous connection to any of the society's values. Such a connection certainly needs to be established rather than assumed.

It is now widely appreciated by scholars in many fields that cultures are not "monolithic": different people within a society may disagree regarding key cultural values or practices, and there may be some degree of inconsistency between cultural values. A society may have egalitarian impulses but nevertheless value human ambition, and then needs to negotiate situations in which ambition leads to inequality. It is also now widely appreciated that cultures change through time. Some members of a society develop new attitudes or practices and these spread through the society. The ideas of diversity and change are mutually supportive: it is hard to understand how cultures would change unless members of society occasionally disagreed, and a society that never changed might view disagreement more harshly. Neither idea – change or diversity – is particularly remarkable. Yet there have been longstanding traditions in different parts of human science that conflicted with one or both of them. Anthropologists long

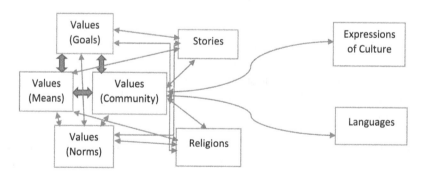

FIGURE 4.2 The Cultural Subsystem.

Note: We can expect (but need to establish) strong links among key goals, and weaker links to everyday norms, stories, and religions. Though expressions of culture and languages may be the most visible markers of a society, the strength of the links to other elements of a society's culture are often assumed rather than shown. There may well be much stronger links to non-cultural phenomena. These are not shown on our diagram.

tended to view the traditional societies that they mostly studied as unchanging –
at least until these societies came in contact with more technologically
advanced societies. Those who have rejected methodological individualism in
many fields have treated (implicitly or explicitly) individuals as mere cultural
creations lacking the autonomy to reject the values and practices into which
they were born.[11]

It is thus of critical importance that we explicitly examine the links among
particular values. It is likely that our values regarding equality and ambition may
conflict a little but not too much. How much conflict among values do we see
in different societies? How much can humans cope with? Do such conflicts loom
larger in cultures that are changing rapidly? We have criticized scholars of other
subsystems above – especially the economic subsystem – for focusing too much
on the internal workings of that subsystem and downplaying its external linkages.
In the case of the cultural subsystem we can bemoan a common tendency to
assume that cultures cohere and not investigate to what extent they actually do so.

We can of course only sensibly explore such questions within a community
that agrees that culture comprises a finite set of values and practices. This we
do not have. There are literally thousands of definitions of culture employed in
human science. Many of these are vague. Many would subsume what we call
art within culture – leading to problems also in our study of art (as we shall see
below). Some are so broad as to embrace almost all of the phenomena in Table 2.1
(see Chapter 2). Despite the breadth and vagueness of definitions of culture,
many scholars make causal claims about culture: that "culture" affects political,
economic, or social outcomes. It is of course very difficult to investigate such
claims without some consensus on what culture is or how it operates. Once we
have appreciated that some of the links among cultural phenomena may be weak,
we are guided to be careful in using the aggregate "culture" as a causal agent in
our analyses. It may make sense to say that culture as a whole gives us guidance
on how to live our lives. However, more precise influences are best traced to
particular elements of culture. If we get angry when a co-worker or friend is late
for an appointment, this will mostly reflect cultural attitudes toward punctuality,
tempered by cultural attitudes toward displays of anger (mediated by our own
personality and whether we are having a good day, I might add).

Note that our understanding of links beyond culture will inform our evaluation of links within culture. That is, our understanding of the internal workings
of culture is intertwined inextricably with our understanding of the role that
culture plays in human lives. Though these external links also require investigation, a good starting assumption would seem to be that the main purpose of
human cultures is to facilitate human interaction. We saw in Chapter 2 that specialized scholarly communities have more productive conversations if they share
a set of understandings. Likewise, members of a society can more easily interact
if they have a strong sense of how others will act and how others will expect
them to act in a variety of situations (cultures also are an important source of
meaning for at least some people). Cultural change is disorienting because we no

longer know how to behave or how others will behave (it also weakens the sense of meaning for many). Given this centrality of culture to human functioning, it is important that we understand both the internal and external causal links of cultural phenomena.

It may prove that some values are more important to the functioning of cultures than others. It may then be that societies should be more willing to alter some values than others – perhaps if a particular value is impeding the society's pursuit of valued economic or political outcomes. It may likewise be that a society can have a relaxed attitude toward diversity with respect to some values but really benefits from consensus on others (shared attitudes toward honesty might be invaluable, but shared expectations about how we greet strangers can also prevent a lot of misunderstanding).

Hellemans (2017, 74) notes that cultures determine what meaning is attached to a particular word. She follows immediately by asserting that learning another language introduces one to a different way of seeing the world. Yet this does not necessarily follow. Languages of course serve as a cultural barrier: the French are more likely to have cultural differences from Germans if French people mostly speak in French to other French people and Germans mostly speak German to German people. A French person learning German thus gains access to German conversations. Yet Hellemans and legions of other authors assert that languages also embody the essence of a culture (The Sapir Whorf hypothesis in anthropology asserts that languages shape how we think). But have the Irish ceased being Irish in some important way as they came to speak English rather than Gaelic – beyond the simple fact that they are then more likely to interact with the English next door? This link between language and other elements of culture deserves to be studied far more than it is. It has implications for public policy in many lands. The fact that nationalist politicians often assume a strong link between language and broader culture is no reason for academics to do so.

There is an important school of cultural studies that stresses that cultures can be an agent of political change. It was inspired by the observation that the working class often supported conservative (populist) politicians who pursued a political agenda aligned with property owners. It was then recognized that workers did not just vote for their economic interests but voted on the basis of a broader identity. It was hoped that if cultural identity could be better understood, it could be guided toward more progressive political outcomes (Chibber 2022) This school was largely founded by disenchanted socialists. It may be comforting, for those who no longer feel a clear ideological purpose, to imagine that they can instead work on the cultural front to achieve political change. It may be helpful to such people, given the lack of ideological clarity about what political changes they might want, to be somewhat vague about the precise mechanisms through which particular cultural phenomena might influence particular political phenomena. This is not, of course, a recipe for encouraging a cumulative or coherent academic conversation.[12]

We have, then, several recommendations for the study of culture. These can all be seen as reflecting a big if vague question of how cultures operate, change, and interact with other categories of phenomena. We need a shared understanding of culture as a particular set of values and practices. We need more focused research on particular links both within and beyond culture. We can note in closing that several disciplines at present study culture: anthropology, sociology, and across the humanities. It is perhaps not surprising that different fields pursue different definitions – though this does not explain the diversity of definitions within fields. Quite different conversations occur in these different disciplines with little effort at integration. Perhaps most seriously, much of the potential benefits of specialization are lost when scholars do not have shared understandings of either culture as a whole or its key components.

Art

While the public may often imagine that successful artists are geniuses pursuing their unique talents, scholars of art know that artists must balance a pursuit of novelty with a need to meet their audience's expectations. An artist who deviates too much from what other artists in their time and place are doing is more likely to be rejected than applauded. There is thus much value to studying a set of causal links within art that explore how one artwork influences others, and how different types of art – painting, theatre, literature – influence each other. Yet, as we shall see, the links from this art subsystem to other phenomena are also strong and worthy of study.

It seems that one of the glories of literature is that it helps us understand how human beings navigate lives of complexity. While we struggle in this book to figure out how human scientists as a community can comprehend how societies work, we each in our own lives must navigate complex human societies as best we can. We gain an intuitive feel for how humans cope with complexity by immersing ourselves in tales (novels or biographies) of how others do so.[13] The stories that grip us the most are likely those that capture elements of complexity that we readily comprehend. One of the beauties of reading about the lives of others is that we inevitably encounter both circumstances that are familiar and circumstances that are novel, and get a sense of how other humans cope in both cases. This gives us insight into both how we might behave and how others might behave. There is particular value in the fact that different authors – and different characters in the same novel – give us different perspectives on life. Steinberg (2014) draws an analogy to integrating the perspectives of different people in describing someone standing in the middle of a room, and argues that "all of us can use as many insights into being human as we can get."

It is clearly one purpose of the humanities to investigate how we learn about complexity from novels or biographies. Yet it is an enormous leap – and an incredible conceit – to imagine that we can learn about complexity by reading novels in the way that human scientists seek to understand complexity. Upton

Sinclair's *The Urban Jungle* can guide us to feel empathy with workers crushed by unfeeling capitalists. Nevertheless, it is no better guide to economic theory than Ayn Rand's *The Fountainhead, which* celebrates unfettered personal initiative. Scholars who draw conclusions about how the world works from works of fiction are making a hidden assumption that novelists have some intuitive understanding of human science theory. Yet surely, the appeal of a good novel reflects how its characters navigate their world rather than the author's deep understanding of why the world is the way it is. You need not be a good scientist to be a good novelist. If novelists have an intuitive feel for how the world works, how can Rand's and Sinclair's intuitions be so different? (We could, of course, try to investigate whether novelists do have some intuitive understanding of human science theory. The point here is that we should not simply assume this.)

The ubiquity of art across human societies cries out for explanation. What roles does art play in human societies that can explain why virtually every human society pursues art? Just as we would expect economists to study growth and political scientists to study the characteristics of successful democracies more than they do, we might imagine that humanists would devote most of their attention to grappling with this key question.[14] It is likely that art is more than a nice appendage to a healthy society – though many in the modern world view it in that way. Humanists have speculated on a variety of roles that art may play in human societies: it may be cathartic, educational, stabilizing, revolutionary, consciousness-raising, or empathy-inducing (and we have argued above that literature, at least, helps us grapple with complexity). If art does – or should – play critical roles in human societies we should seek to understand these better.[15] While some humans may engage little with some art forms (and perhaps suffer as a result), we all inevitably engage with architecture and industrial design, and should know how these shape our lives. In investigating how art affects us, the traditional humanistic approaches of examining "texts" can be combined with psychological methods of experiment and observation, and perhaps surveys to get at the question of how people respond to particular works.[16] There is also much scope for using scans of the human brain to establish how humans respond to works of art.

We have distinguished art from culture in recognition that art appeals to an aesthetic taste that transcends cultures. Yet we have appreciated that culture nevertheless influences art. One key task of the humanities is to attempt to disentangle the aesthetic and cultural appeal of art. In this endeavor, explicitly comparing works of art from different times and places may be critical. If we detect common elements across diverse times and places, these may reflect a shared aesthetic sensibility. When we detect clear differences these will most likely reflect cultural influences.[17] With respect to culture, we can then look at causation in the opposite direction: Does art reinforce certain values or encourage a sense of group identity?

As just one example of how art might affect the world, we can explore the emerging field of environmental humanities. Advocates of the environmental humanities may well be correct that one photograph or dystopian novel can do more to move people to care about the environment than a dry report on climate data. Yet most of the literature in the field seems to celebrate the work of particular artists rather than examine whether they have much effect. Merchant (2020, 9) lauds the field: "They are asking questions such as: what is nature, what does it mean to be human in the age of warming, and how can humans use technology to adapt to the new world?" Notably absent from this list is "How can we raise environmental consciousness?" Merchant then surveys several works in the field and wonders how we can choose between authors who blame capitalism and authors who blame globalization. It is too easy to suggest here that we move past analyses framed in terms of vague terminology in order to explore actual causal links. Merchant's third chapter supposedly addresses how art can change attitudes, and begins with "Artists and photographers who have engaged with global warming believe that the visual arts are an essential part of creating the largescale public awareness and understanding of climate change that can bring about substantive policy change" (46). Yet most of the chapter is about how artists in the nineteenth century celebrated railways and industrialization. At the end of the chapter, Merchant discusses some artists who glorify new environmentally friendly technologies or show what climate change is doing to various landscapes. Merchant asserts but does not show that such pictures can have more effect than prose. Chapter 4 turns to literature and notes that authors have often chronicled both our synergy with nature and the dislocating effects of rapid change[18]; Merchant asserts that literature can communicate such messages profoundly. Perhaps, but the fact that some authors have been doing so for centuries seems to have had limited impact.

Horn and Bergthaller (2019) talk about creating an "epochal consciousness" that the planet is in danger. They do not clarify whether this is a role for artists or for scholars. They later say that the environmental humanities take public outreach as critical. The authors make a puzzling argument (p. 5) that we have to change our very categories of analysis to recognize that a "politics" of nature is not just one issue among many but must take precedence, to appreciate that our culture threatens our environment, and that even humanity does so. They promise to map the key debates in the field but recognize that these are rapidly changing. We can worry, then, that the field is not carefully examining particular links, and is losing the advantages of academic specialization by switching topics of focus often. The authors recognize that environmental humanities must start with some understanding of natural science, but recognize that not all in the field share that view. How can one hope to raise epochal consciousness if one does not actually understand how the environment functions? They suggest that the rise of environmental concerns has forced humanists to recognize that culture both reflects and affects environment and social structure. We can celebrate this development while wishing that it had long been the case (and worrying that they are using "culture" when they mostly mean "art"). They say that the idea of the Anthropocene[19] radically alters our perspective, puts previous knowledge in a new constellation, and changes our epistemology (19). It should need to do none of these things. They cite Bruno Latour to the effect that it causes us to reject the distinction between nature and culture.[20] This would be unfortunate for we can hardly understand causal links to and from the environment if we lump everything together. (They also like the fact that the Anthropocene subsumes several distinct environmental challenges under one label).

Horn and Bergthaller (2019, 30) appreciate that many authors criticize the idea of the Anthropocene for being ideological, for still privileging the role of humans (if now in a bad way), for jumbling together diverse causal links, and for blaming humanity as a whole rather than particular classes or countries. They see all of these critiques as an invitation to debate the nature of the Anthropocene. I recognize that the Anthropocene (like globalization) may have a powerful rhetorical value, but think we will have a far more productive conversation if we avoid endless debates about what the Anthropocene means and instead focus scholarly research on particular causal links.

Alarm bells should ring in our heads any time an academic conversation engages questions of "What is X?" and "What causes X?" simultaneously. It is then far too easy for scholars to define X in a way that is congenial to their explanation of it.[21] Scholars will then have meaningless disagreements about causes simply because they are defining X differently. This is a recipe for unproductive science. In the case of the Anthropocene (and sometimes globalization or modernization), a similar concern arises with a "When is X?" question. If we think that the Anthropocene began with the Industrial Revolution we will seek different causes than if we think it began in the 1950s. Horn and Begthaller (Chapter 2) make it clear that there are indeed huge debates about when the Anthropocene began, and thus why. This is one further way in which organizing academic discourse around a complex term such as the Anthropocene can limit academic progress in understanding: We should have a clear place in our conversations for discussions of the causes of the Industrial Revolution and causes of the environmental policies of the 1950s. There should be no possibility of confusing those conversations.

The conversations that Horn and Bergthaller survey are intriguing, and they may throw up interesting insights. Yet it is hard to see how such conversations can be progressive in the sense of compiling evidence and argument that encourage consensus except by investigating in more detail the myriad causal links subsumed by these broad debates. If compelling evidence is found that a particular cultural attitude or institution plays a very big role in encouraging pollution or climate change, this might serve to decide broader debates. Without such information, these broader debates may be endless – or they will peter out to be replaced by the next big questions when authors find little new to say. As for whether art can move humanity to take environmental issues more seriously, this is an important hypothesis that deserves to be carefully investigated rather than assumed.

Technology and Science

As with the population/health subsystem there is no obvious disciplinary home for discussions of science and technology. A minority of universities have created interdisciplinary programs in Science and Technology Studies (STS) as a result. Yet there is no general appreciation that this is a missing discipline.[22] Even scholars of STS have long debated whether it should be a discipline or an interdisciplinary field (Jasanoff 2014). Scholars in many disciplines study science and technology. It is noteworthy that the main concentrations of such scholars are in Philosophy and History departments rather than in the departments that examine particular causal links.[23] We nevertheless have some appreciation that both technological and scientific innovation are evolutionary processes where new ideas necessarily build upon previous understandings – but an uneven process in which some new ideas open up novel and productive lines of inquiry. The selection environment for new ideas in science and especially technology is diverse, with economy, polity, culture, and social structure (at least) having large roles to play.

Some writers are technological or scientific enthusiasts, celebrating the many ways in which science and technology have improved our lives, and holding out hope that technology and science will solve human challenges such as climate change in future. Other writers are technological pessimists, highlighting the negative impacts of some innovations and fearing that science and technology will destroy human civilization in future. Optimists often celebrate the creativity of innovators, while pessimists often worry that technological and scientific innovation have a momentum of their own (or are guided in malign directions by capitalism or globalization) that may be hard to stop. Whether one tends to optimism or pessimism, it is clear that technology and science interact powerfully with economy, politics, culture, and more. A more robust and integrative conversation might guide us to a more nuanced understanding of how we might encourage beneficial technologies while limiting harmful technologies. Since evolutionary processes are unpredictable, we will need to be very conscious that causation in human science is probabilistic (see Chapter 3). The best we can do is hope to identify strategies that can increase the likelihood of good technologies and decrease the likelihood of harmful technologies. We can never erase technological pessimism but we can make pessimistic predictions less likely.

The study of technology and science lends itself to a variety of methods. Economists use quantitative methods to estimate the economic impact of particular innovations. Sociologists and anthropologists carefully observe research teams. Humanists wonder what science fiction tells us about humanity's hopes and fears for the future. Given that research is strewn across multiple disciplines, it is not surprising that efforts to integrate across the insights of diverse methods are limited.

Human Nature

There are two sets of individual-level phenomena in Table 2.1. One describes a set of common attributes of human beings. Though these various abilities, motivations, and emotions combine to make us human, we do not devote much effort to studying them. A minority of human scientists (mostly in anthropology departments) study how human characteristics evolved in human pre-history. These scholars tend to focus on the evolution of human abilities such as speech. A small interdisciplinary community speculates on how emotions and motivations might have evolved. The vast bulk of human scientists take our abilities and emotions and (most of our) motivations as given. We do not often ask how human societies reflect basic human abilities, motivations, or emotions. Perhaps if we encounter intelligent extra-terrestrial life-forms that differ from us in important ways, we will have cause to reflect more deeply on such matters. More ominously, the possibility of genetic engineering will force humanity to reflect on how human societies would change if humans became smarter, stronger, or less jealous.

The second set of phenomena are a set of differences in abilities, personality dimensions, schemas, and more that jointly define us as individuals. This subsystem of individual-level characteristics needs to cohere to a considerable degree if the individual is to be happy and successful. An individual that is clumsy but dreams of Olympic glory is destined for disappointment. Psychologists have studied this subsystem and especially the linkages among different personality dimensions.

Two key questions for the human science enterprise touch on both sets of phenomena. First, what is the human capacity for happiness, why are some humans happier than others, and how can we enhance human happiness? Arguably, this is among the most important questions in all of human science, for we pursue human science understanding in order to improve human wellbeing. Amazingly, psychologists devoted little attention to this key question until just a couple of decades ago, devoting the vast bulk of their effort to investigations of mental illness or other types of negative psychological outcomes. It is now a topic of much research both within and beyond psychology.[24] It would likely be an even bigger research field if not for a widespread suspicion of self-reports of happiness. The most common measure of human happiness comes from surveys in which people are asked how happy they are. Since there is no objective measure of happiness, people likely compare themselves to others when answering. A society might become happier but its individuals would look around at their happier neighbors and not report higher levels of happiness. Scholars of happiness naturally have sought to address this concern. Yet the best answer likely lies – as often in this book – in applying other methods to the question. One method with much promise is to scan human brains while exposing these to various stimuli.

A second big question involves how humans make decisions. An understanding of human decision-making could inform virtually every causal link from the individual to societal level. Here also there have been big advances in recent decades. Kahneman (2011) describes a set of experiments that have exposed a set of biases and errors that people commonly exhibit in making decisions. We are, for example, really bad at dealing with probabilities.[25] These psychological insights have encouraged some economists to alter economic theories that had assumed rational decision-making. Various human scientists and others have been guided to ask how we might nudge people toward making decisions that are better for society (The classic work is Thaler and Sunstein 2008) Yet some psychologists worry that experiments by their nature can only engage with relatively simple decisions. If we wish to understand how humans make complex career or voting or relationship decisions, we need to supplement our experimental insights with observations and interviews and surveys.

Environment

There is obviously a natural environment system out there. That system predates humanity by millions of years (though the realizations of various phenomena have changed a lot over the millennia). Humanity depends utterly on the natural environment for survival. Humanity has long exerted powerful influences on the environment: even hunter-gatherers set fires to shape landscapes to their purposes, and farmers turned forests and grasslands into planted fields on all but one continent. The effects of humans on the environment have expanded in recent centuries and decades. While we can leave to natural scientists the detailed study of natural systems, the important question of how humans are affecting the environment requires collaboration among natural and human scientists.

   We have already seen above some sign that some human scientists think that they can engage with environmental issues without having much understanding of natural processes. It is, though, hard to see how one can fully appreciate human impacts on the environment without having some appreciation of how environments work. For example, we cannot appreciate the impact of widespread agriculture on the environment without appreciating that each ecosystem tends toward some equilibrium in which diverse species of flora and fauna maintain a niche. When a farmer (or an industrial or mining operation, for that matter) displaces any species, we need to understand the role of that species in the local ecosystem, and how or if the ecosystem might function without it. We may at times be able to accept a particular piece of natural science knowledge – say, that carbon dioxide in the atmosphere increases global temperatures – and focus on how to address the human component: how to reduce carbon emissions. But if we wish to encourage humans to take the environment more seriously we really should understand how the environment functions. Human scientists will thus often need to collaborate with natural scientists in studying human-environment interactions, employing methods common in both areas.

   We discussed above some efforts to attribute the Anthropocene to globalization or capitalism. We are unlikely to progress rapidly in our understanding of how one vaguely defined complex thing affects another vaguely defined complex thing. We face enough difficulty establishing the precise causal relationship between carbon emissions and global temperatures. So we can as elsewhere encourage human scientists to focus on particular (sets of) causal links.

As with the study of culture or health, it might prove beneficial to have greater organizational unity among scholars of the environment. At the moment, these are dispersed across every discipline in human science.[26] Inevitably, scholars of different causal links have limited contact with those studying related links and are thus hampered in their ability to place their research in context.

History

Historians can play a role comparable to that of novelists in communicating the complexity of human lives, and showing how various humans have interacted within complex situations. There is thus an understandable emphasis in the field on telling a compelling narrative. There are concerns, first voiced persuasively by Hayden White decades ago (especially White 1975), that historians become biased in (usually subconsciously) pursuing a recognizable narrative form such as tragedy or comedy. History is a series of overlapping stories that only rarely have tidy and satisfying endings, and historians should be wary of making any historical episode appear self-contained. Yet there is nevertheless an important service performed by historians in detailing complexity. It should be unsurprising, given our discussion of literature above, that jargon-free historical narratives achieve a broad readership beyond the academy. In addition to informing readers about complexity, they tell us something about how our present circumstances have emerged from the past.

Yet this narrative complexity-oriented approach to history can and should be complemented by an approach that zeroes in on particular causal links or subsystems.[27] The vast bulk of research performed in human science examines only the last couple of decades of human existence. If historians will not explicitly study causal relationships that unfold over lengthy periods of time – like, say, how successful democracies become established (see above) – then our knowledge of such relationships will be extremely limited. Even for causal relationships that operate over shorter time frames, historians have much to contribute. We have emphasized in Chapter 2 that we should pursue contextualized generalizations, seeking to identify under what conditions a particular causal relationship holds. Human scientists focused on the last decades (and primarily in rich countries) have a limited evidence base from which to work.[28] Historians can usefully survey a much broader set of societal circumstances and give us a much more nuanced understanding of when certain relationships hold and when they do not. Historians can be an integral part of the human science enterprise if they are willing to study how particular causal links operated in different times and places; they can severely hobble the human science enterprise if they do not.[29] Historians often echo Santayana's famous observation that "those who do not understand the past are destined to repeat it," but only rarely put much effort into drawing lessons from the past. Identifying contextualized generalizations is a powerful way in which we could collectively learn from the past.

Historians shrink from this sort of activity because of a fear of bias. They worry that if they carry into the archives or archaeological dig some set of scholarly hypotheses, they will be biased in what they find there. They will see only what the hypotheses guide them to look for, and ignore salient material that the hypotheses ignore. This is an important concern. The solution (tell me if you have heard this before) may best lie in an appreciation of integrative historical research which tries to tease out causal relationships by comparing what many historians have reported finding in many different settings. In a discipline that understandably lauds detailed archival research (or occasionally archaeology or interviews), integrative research is not always applauded. The field of world history in which I have myself operated is an important exception, for it is appreciated that no one historian can master the archives of all lands encompassed in world historical enterprises. History, like all other fields, needs more integrative work to tie individual research into a broader whole. As in other disciplines, much of that integrative work can focus on particular causal links: how have states in different times and places attempted to instill supportive cultural attitudes, and how successful were they? Yet there is also scope for integrative works that focus on particular times and places, asking questions like how well our collective understanding of causal links allows us to understand, say, the French Revolution.

Though integrative works are important, even specialized research should be placed in context. History should be comparative in orientation, seeking generalization, recognizing that we can best appreciate uniqueness and the role of individuals in comparisons.[30] We may think that a particular king is bloodthirsty or cowardly. We can only really evaluate such a conjecture by comparing this king to other kings in (hopefully) similar situations. Maybe kings with dominant forces generally attack and kings with weaker forces lay low. We can only understand so much about a particular historical episode without comparing it to other episodes. There may, then, be no alternative than for the historian to head into the archives with some understanding of other historical cases that might be comparable. Only if they know how other kings acted will they be able to recognize when the particular king they are studying does something unusual. The historian's natural desire to comprehend the uniqueness of events is not in conflict with the need of human science for generalization. The two activities complement each other. Though we can reasonably worry about bias, even specialized historians should have some idea of context before initiating their research.[31]

Note that humans may have a tendency to exaggerate the human role. It is often observed that if students are given a narrative that emphasizes society-level forces, and then asked questions about it, they will re-produce a narrative that stresses the behaviors of individual human actors. Individual humans do have a role to play in history, of course, but we should be careful not to exaggerate this and thus under-appreciate the role of societal-level forces.

The key method employed by historians involves interpreting written sources, though there is an important role for archaeology and interviews. These need to be integrated. As someone trained in economic history, I can note that there is much scope for quantitative analysis in history. Economic historians have not only attempted to estimate many economic variables (and then run regressions on this data) but also some non-economic variables. Most notably, perhaps, economic historians have used both army (and other) records and skeletal remains to estimate average heights in diverse human populations, a variable that potentially tells us much about the health of those populations. The results of different kinds of research are not integrated as well as they could be: economic historians privilege quantitative analysis while other historians shun it.[32]

Philosophy

One of the key challenges in defining the humanities lies in the fact that philosophy serves an entirely different purpose(s) from other human science disciplines. For the most part, it does not study individual causal links, nor particular times and places. Rather, philosophy's purpose is to provide general guidance: on how to do science of any sort, how to live our lives, and how to attach meaning to those lives. It thus operates on a plane above the pedestrian pursuits of other human or natural scientists. It does not properly belong to human science for it devotes even more effort to worrying about how natural science should proceed than about how human science should proceed. Yet since philosophers play with words more than numbers they are generally housed administratively with other humanists. We shall find that we can apply much of our advice for human scientists also to philosophers

We have repeatedly emphasized the value of integration above. This may be even more important in philosophy than in science. Philosophers have long focused on an impossible search for the perfect argument. The result of thousands of years of philosophical speculation is that we have inherited a set of strong but necessarily imperfect lines of argument. In epistemology – the study of what and how we can know – philosophers sketch a variety of arguments: some applaud experiments as "the" way to do science while others argue that there is no real distinction between science and non-science. Others fall at various places along a spectrum between decreeing scientific uniformity to proclaiming that anything goes. In ethics, philosophers have tended to advocate three distinct ways that we might judge an act to be good: examine its consequences, ask whether it accords with certain values we hold dear, or inquire whether it accords with certain rules (such as the Golden Rule) that we have previously adopted. There is, to be sure, a recognition among philosophers that each of these three approaches have merit, but in their research philosophers argue fervently for their favorite one. Without a concerted effort at integration, philosophy cannot provide clear guidance on either how to live or how to do science properly.

In recent decades, the pursuit of one perfect argument has often given way to a recognition of the value of different perspectives. Different genders, ethnicities, nations, or classes are expected to view the world differently. Yet the desire to pursue one line of argument exclusively is generally maintained within this recognition of diversity. Each perspective is to be valued on its own with little or no attempt to integrate across different perspectives. In place of a misguided search for perfection, we thus have a search for independent and incompatible views of the world. We have applauded a respect for diverse perspectives but urged integration across perspectives in Chapters 2 and 3. We can do so again here.

We have urged methodological flexibility above. Philosophers do not employ methods in the way that human or natural scientists do. Philosophy is a reflective exercise, and philosophical arguments are judged by coherence rather than direct observations of reality (with obvious exceptions: philosophers of science try to explain science as it exists, and consequential ethicists examine the consequences of particular acts). Yet we have often seen value in combining qualitative and quantitative analyses above, and can make a similar recommendation to philosophers. Philosophers tend to shun numbers (except perhaps in the area of logic). They do not engage questions of "How much?" or "How often?" We saw in Chapter 2 that language is inherently ambiguous, but argued that we could transcend this ambiguity in the pursuit of enhanced understanding. Philosophers have been satisfied to show that language is ambiguous and have not much cared how ambiguous it is. Yet the "how much?" question is critical to scientists. And not just with respect to ambiguity: Philosophers might address each of the postmodern concerns of Chapter 2, identifying to what degree these can be overcome. More generally, philosophers rarely evaluate the strength of their arguments. They are either perfect or they do not care. Such an attitude supports the general antipathy to integration. Philosophers could usefully reflect on how strong they judge particular arguments to be.

The result is that scientists have less clear advice from philosophers than they might have on how best to perform science. And people have less guidance on how to live and how to find meaning than they could have. We noted in Chapter 3 that we would in this book follow Williams (2020) in drawing on philosophy but stopping far short of developing a detailed philosophical justification for the arguments made in this book. We would, like Williams, instead focus on the level of practical methodology, and show how this book was consonant with many practical suggestions on how to reform human science. We noted that we could surely find philosophical justification for any reasonable argument among the array of philosophies of science on offer. We could benefit, then, from integrative works that weighed the strengths and weaknesses of different philosophies, and identified arguments that received support from different philosophical theories.[33] Such integrative works would close the gap between philosophy of science and practical methodology as pursued within human science disciplines. Integrative works might also feed back into specialized philosophical research: Critics of a particular point of view might stop pretending that attacking its weakest points means destroying the entire edifice, and advocates (this is more of a stretch) might stop pretending that there are no caveats to which they have no response.

My sense is that most philosophers would agree with the following statements:

- There is a real world.
- We are limited in our understanding of it.
- We can develop guidelines to address a range of challenges to understanding.
- Different methods have different strengths and weaknesses.
- Proof and disproof are impossible in practice.
- Thus, the best evidence for any hypothesis is that it receives support from multiple methods.

I suspect that a robust integrative exercise in philosophy would support – albeit imperfectly and with caveats – this set of guidelines.[34] At the moment, though, there is no body of integrative philosophy of science that can provide assurance (even textbooks tend to provide a survey without integrating).

Ethical philosophy is important in our study of societal values. And ethics plays a role (often implicit) anytime that a human scientist moves from examining how the world is to investigating whether it might be improved in some way. In the area of ethics, we very much need integration beyond philosophy itself. In addition to the three ethical approaches studied by philosophers, humans commonly make ethical decisions in two complementary ways. First, we are guided by the traditions of the communities in which we operate and peer pressure from those we interact with. We are thus guided to act in ways that those we interact with will understand and respect. Anthropologists rather than philosophers examine this approach to ethical decision-making. Second, we are guided intuitively to do things that make us feel good and avoid things that make us feel guilty. (Some) Psychologists study intuitive processes. One important lesson from an integrative ethics is that the five types of ethical analysis often point in the same direction. Honesty and responsibility and compassion generally have good consequences, accord with values and rules, are respected and encouraged by most human societies, and make us feel good. Another important lesson is that the five approaches are potentially complementary: Societies will hopefully develop guidelines with good consequences (but societies may need to change as circumstances change, and some guidelines may reflect the interests of the powerful more than the average person). Most importantly, philosophers have no powerful answer to the question of why a person should behave ethically when nobody is looking. Only our sense of guilt guides most of us to do so.

Note that integrative efforts in ethics combat two common errors. First they address a feeling that "anything goes" in ethics (grounded in the fact that we are mostly exposed to ethical examination of issues like abortion where consensus seems elusive). Second, they address a sense that we cannot have a respect for diversity and a sense of common ethics simultaneously (which ignores the fact that the vast majority of human societies have valued honesty and responsibility and compassion). To be sure, we can never detail perfect arguments in favor of any ethical position. Yet we can achieve a degree of consensus that would allow us to collectively expect that deviations from honesty or compassion or responsibility require an explanation.

Maxwell (2020) makes similar arguments with respect to metaphysics – the study of meaning – that we have just made with respect to ethics and epistemology. He urges integration across both science and philosophy in the pursuit of a new metaphysics (p. 38). He notes that modern natural science understandings of the nature of reality need to be incorporated into our metaphysics. Yet he – like us – appreciates that human beings are more than just physical objects – and thus that human science is distinct from though connected to natural science. "We are, in other words, doubly comprehensible. We are comprehensible physically (as physical systems); and, simultaneously, we are comprehensible humanly (as conscious persons, as persons acting in the world). The miracle of miracles is that we are comprehensible in both ways, simultaneously, the two kinds of comprehensibility intermeshing subtly and intricately, so that both can be valid at one and the same time." He identifies evolutionary advantages for human abilities to imagine different behaviors and outcomes and thus not just follow instinctive patterns. Yet though those capabilities may have evolved to support hunting and gathering activities, they allow humans to grapple with mortality and contemplate human purposes beyond survival and reproduction. He urges us to each love ourselves and to love others. And he thus urges an integrated philosophical and human science project devoted to enhancing human flourishing in a complex age.[35]

We have argued many times above that we can have the greatest confidence in any scientific hypothesis when it is supported by evidence from multiple methods. We can make a similar argument for philosophy. We can have the greatest confidence in any philosophical hypothesis when it is supported by multiple philosophical theories or approaches. In the area of epistemology, we can seek consistency between philosophy and practical methodology as pursued in other disciplines. In ethics, we can seek consistency with guidance from tradition and intuition. And in metaphysics we can seek meaning that is consistent with scientific understandings.

Concluding Remarks

By looking in turn at each subsystem or set of causal links within human science from the perspective of the system as a whole, it was straightforward to identify questions that are receiving far less attention than they deserve regarding the causes of growth, characteristics of successful democracy, nature of art's effect on humanity, and more. These questions each call for both interdisciplinarity and methodological plurality. We did not have to delve deeply into the literatures of each discipline in order to identify these questions: the logic of the larger system drove our analysis. It also in each case proved straightforward to identify methods that are receiving less attention than they deserve. I am not aware of this exercise – of examining all human science subsystems from the perspective of the system as a whole – being performed elsewhere, and would submit that these observations are worthy of deep reflection throughout human science. Yet the disciplinary character of human science militates against scholars placing their research within a broader context.

We were also able to make important suggestions regarding philosophy and history. These disciplines do not focus on particular causal links. Rather, each in their own way has something potentially to say about all links. Philosophy could be giving us clearer advice on how to study any link, and history could be allowing us to examine each causal link across a far wider range of contexts. Again, a systemic perspective allows us to identify important tasks that could be performed better.

Our systemic perspective also raises some intriguing questions about the way the human sciences are organized into disciplines. The economic and political subsystems have clear disciplinary homes. So also does the study of individual-level phenomena. The study of the cultural and social subsystems is strewn across multiple departments or programs. The study of art is also pursued in many different disciplines. The technology/science and population/health subsystems have no clear disciplinary home (sociologists study population but study health less than economists do). The study of the environment requires collaboration with natural science; the human science component of that collaboration is widely dispersed. The disciplinary structure of human science does not represent some logical division of human science subject matter. It is rather the result of a complex historical evolution. This evolutionary process has jumbled the study of culture, social structure, and population (and criminology!) together in sociology departments, despite the fact that these categories of phenomena are as closely linked to economy and politics and other categories of phenomena as they are to each other. More seriously, the disciplinary structure that we have inherited from the past does not give us clearly defined disciplinary homes for most of the subsystems that constitute human science. If we value the interplay between specialized and integrative work that this book has advocated, then we should tidy up the organizational structure of human science. This is not something that can be accomplished overnight but perhaps an evolution toward a more logical division of specialized research among disciplines can be encouraged.[36]

Summary

- We should want specialized research communities to specialize by subject matter: on subsystems or sets of causal links.
- Some subsystems are less open than others.
- Economy is more closed than most subsystems, but there are still important links to other phenomena. Economists should devote more attention to economic growth; this will require both interdisciplinarity and methodological

flexibility. Economists should also pay more heed to the links between economy and social structure.

- Politics is a very open system. Political scientists should devote more attention to studying the causes and characteristics of stable democracy; this will require both interdisciplinarity and methodological flexibility.
- Social structure is also a very open system. Social structure is studied in many fields that are not well integrated. One obvious question is how discrimination is encouraged or discouraged. In this as in other matters, scholars must strike a careful balance between studying internal and external causal links.
- It is important to appreciate that cultures are both internally diverse and changing. It is then important to carefully investigate the links within the cultural subsystem. Values likely need to be broadly consistent, but links from values to some cultural expressions and to languages may be far weaker. Cultures seem to play a critical role in human functioning and thus we need to understand the roles that particular cultural phenomena play in human societies. We are hampered by vague definitions of culture. Research should focus on particular causal links rather than attempting to grapple with culture as a whole.
- Art is also a very open subsystem. We should pay more attention to how and why art moves us. There is scope for application of diverse methods. Scholars of art should focus on particular causal links involving artistic phenomena rather than theorizing about all of human science. Scholars should be more comparative in orientation so that we can better distinguish the aesthetic from cultural effects (and causes) of art.
- The field of environmental humanities should show, rather than assume, that art can encourage environmental sensitivity. It should examine particular causal links, rather than embracing an ever-changing series of broad topics. The Anthropocene is a useful term, perhaps, but research is better focused on particular phenomena and causal links rather than seeking to define the elusive essence of the Anthropocene.
- A more robust and integrated study of (the missing discipline of) science and technology might generate a more nuanced understanding of how to encourage beneficial innovation while discouraging harmful innovation. We should integrate across applications of diverse methods.
- Psychologists in recent decades have added much to our understanding of two key questions for human science: the sources of human happiness and the nature of human decision-making. In both cases, there is scope for integrating across a wider range of methods.
- The efforts of scholars in many human science disciplines to study the natural environment could be better integrated; these efforts should also be integrated with natural science understandings.
- Historians (in addition to detailing how humans cope with complexity) can clarify the nature of contextual generalizations by comparing causal links

across a diverse range of contexts. They can allow us to comprehend causal links that unfold over long time frames.

- We need far greater efforts at integration in philosophy. In epistemology, we could better know which practices are justified by a range of epistemologies and more practical methodologies. In ethics, we could better know which practices receive strong justification from each of the five types of ethical analysis. In metaphysics, we could integrate scientific and philosophical understandings in a manner that encourages enhanced human science understanding. Human science would benefit if philosophers appreciated that no argument is perfect and thus we should identify hypotheses (both philosophical and scientific) that can be justified in multiple ways.
- Our system-wide perspective allowed us to identify for every subsystem (and for philosophy and history) important questions that deserve more attention, and methods that deserve wider application.
- Our system-wide perspective also exposes the fact that the disciplinary structure of human science is illogical, and does not provide a clear disciplinary home for specialized research into most human science subsystems.

Notes

1 These are not, of course, the only questions that scholars should ask. Szostak (2022) suggested a wide range of policy-oriented questions such as "what are the likely effects of a basic income?" and "how can we encourage beneficial cultural attitudes?" We focus in this book on questions suggested by our systemic approach to human science.
2 I had made similar arguments in Szostak (1999). At the time, such critiques were not widely accepted.
3 Non-political scientists may be less curious about democracy than economic growth simply because most live in and study democracies that have been stable for decades or centuries – but recent events in several countries should remind us not to take this stability for granted. Surely, political instability and the rise of authoritarianism would interact powerfully with culture, social structure, economy, and more.
4 When Morlino (2018) provides examples of five big questions that are under-studied in political science but could benefit from comparative research, all have something to do with the conditions that support democracy.
5 They worry that advocates of experiments often disdain all other methods. This is especially worrying because experiments can easily explore the effects of information on human decisions but less easily the effects of other factors such as ideology.
6 "Most scholars in this school thus would emphatically agree with Andrew Abbott (1997) when he points out that abstracting a case from its context in the interest of parsimony can lead to deeply misleading results. As he puts it, if such "decontextualization is merely the removal of excess detail, then it's a fine thing, scientifically." But if it eliminates crucial variables and interactions, "it is a scientific disaster" (Mahoney and Thelen 2015).
7 Collins and Bilge (2016) recognize that "intersectionality" has been defined in many ways but suggest that it generally recognizes the complexity of the world, that a person's experience is shaped by membership in a variety of groups, and that social divisions build on one another and work together. There is a stress on inequity and power relations. The authors approve of a strong link between scholarship and activists, while noting some dangers.

8　Vertovec (2021) urges a systems approach to social structure, where we recognize interactions among different kinds of difference (race, gender, etc.) but also the uniqueness of each, and how these are configured (a term he prefers to stratification). We should then study how these differences interact with both societal beliefs and what he calls "encounters." He recognizes "encounters" as a vague term (he talks about how people interact in markets and on trains) and we might substitute for it with reference to institutions and a variety of other phenomena, and perhaps especially elements of the built environment. He notes that different authors have stressed different links.

9　I have had the great pleasure of interacting with scholars in Physical Education who combine human and natural science understandings of the causes and effects of exercise (especially for people with impairments; see Szostak 2018). In Szostak (2018), I drew on conversations with that group to recommend the principle of "No intervention based on just one type of research."

10　Daniels et al. (2017) concur, and stress the importance of qualitative analysis.

11　Hellemans devotes much of her book to arguing that culture shapes human lives. She begins her chapter on Classics with an absurd question about whether it makes sense to still speak of Western culture – a question that makes little sense once we appreciate that cultures are always diverse and changing (and have subcultures). Yet she does recognize that culture is not passively received but rather actively interpreted by individuals (2017, 136).

12　Hellemans (2017, 74) worries that students sometimes do not see a difference between a cultural framework and an ideology. Vagueness in definition will further limit our ability to understand how culture influences politics. Chibber (2022) notes that many authors worried that scholars in focusing on culture ignored earlier emphases on social structure. As in many places in this book, we see the advantages of integrating understandings of diverse causal relationships. Chibber argues that the working class has become resigned to their fate (he also occasionally recognizes the economic benefits that capitalism has at times generated) but does not make the seemingly obvious point that they need to recognize viable policies for, say, reducing income inequality without reducing average incomes in order to transcend a feeling of resignation. A "progressive" research agenda that eschews the hard task of identifying the sort of policies that workers could be guided to identify seems unlikely to succeed.

13　"literature forces readers to confront the complexities of the world, to confront what it means to be a human being in this difficult and uncertain world, to confront other people who may be unlike them, and ultimately to confront themselves." (Steinberg 2014, 15). In addition to the joy of grappling with complexity, there is the joy of language well employed.

14　Much of the effort of literary scholars in recent decades has been to establish that texts are ambiguous. Authors convey messages that are contradictory without being aware of this. This is an important point, to be sure, but there may be limited value in showing ambiguity in yet another text. This extensive literature has tended to focus on finding ambiguities rather than attempting to measure how big or important these are. In earlier decades, literary scholars often focused on criteria by which one work might be judged superior to another. This type of endeavor is less popular as literary scholars have broadened the "canon" of works deemed worthy of scholarly appreciation. Yet we can see that efforts to identify the strengths of individual works might contribute to a more general understanding of why art moves us – if we recognized the latter as our goal and integrated across understandings of particular works.

15　Rust (2007) outlines ways in which artists might contribute to research in human science. He suggests that artists may make tacit contributions that (subconsciously) encourage novel approaches in others.

16　Klein (2005, 127) notes that we need a critical mass of researchers for the potential of an interdisciplinary understanding of art to be achieved.

17 Horn and Bergthaller (2019, 170) appreciate that it is a challenge for humanists to pursue comparison: "Their bailiwick are traditions that are specific to particular languages and cultures, and historical epochs which rarely span more than a century. The Anthropocene challenges the humanities to place their knowledge and their methods in relation to the supersized image of the planet that Earth system science and other scientific disciplines have drawn. They are thus compelled to think of the whole, but they must not lose sight of the parts." Happily, the emerging field of World Art pursues comparisons across time and place. See the journal *World Art.*

18 Horn and Bergthaller (2019, ch 3) describe a debate about whether we should appreciate that some have pursued environmental objectives for centuries. Surely, we are best guided by accuracy and honesty?

19 They note that artists often use the word because it is trendy. It then means nothing more than "contemporary."

20 They pursue this idea further in their fourth chapter before finally concluding that we need to understand a system in which humans and nature interact. Yet they still assert that the need to bridge the nature/culture divide lies at the heart of the environmental humanities. This could, of course, merely mean an assumption that some causal links between culture and environment are strong, but unless carefully considered could be an invitation to vague theorizing.

21 Epstein (2015) remarks that we would not wish to reduce the murder rate by simply redefining murder.

22 Klein (2021, 72) quotes Sheila Jasanoff, a leading scholar of Science and Technology Studies: "The future of STS, and once again other fields, by extension, depends on redrawing the map of the disciplines to demonstrate they are all islands of happenstance, with unmapped waters between them. Then they can claim a space for themselves as another fertile territory in these wide waters, offering resources for understanding some of humanity's most impressive accomplishments, but without threatening anything achieved, or yet to be achieved, in other quarters of the disciplinary archipelago." The quote is interesting in many ways: for referring to a map, implying that interdisciplinary fields investigate unique sets of causal links, and recognizing that disciplines evolve through time without reflecting much on how or why they do so. Klein likes the archipelago metaphor; I would stress the importance of recognizing the links among phenomena studied on different islands.

23 I should perhaps confess that as an Associate Dean I helped launch an STS program at my university over a decade ago. I thereafter occasionally taught in the program. And I have co-authored three editions of a history of technology textbook (Cross and Szostak 2018).

24 The annual World Happiness Report provides a good summary of research in the field. See https://worldhappiness.report/ed/2021/ (Helliwell et al 2021).

25 Notably, even trained mathematicians are not immune to certain common errors in grappling with probabilities. These basic human biases should be kept in mind by human scientists as we struggle to engage probabilistic causation.

26 Geography departments, where these exist, might seem like a place that could emphasize natural processes. Physical geography does stress human relations with our natural environment, but human geography casts its gaze far more widely. Geography, as a whole, then, is associated with a method of mapmaking more than any particular set of phenomena. Geography is then similar to history (discussed below) and for a similar reason: Just as all human activity takes place in time, it also takes place in space.

27 Historians often distinguish these two approaches as "humanities-ish" and "social science-ish." We have in this book blurred the distinction between the two and urged the methods of both to be applied across human science.

28 Area studies programs could, but generally do not, play a similar role in examining how particular causal links operate in the quite different circumstances of non-Western societies. As a result, human science theory often casually assumes that the Western societies that receive most scholarly attention are the whole universe.

29 Wallerstein (1996) famously urged the reduction of barriers among human science disciplines. One proposal was for historians to be attached to other human science disciplines.

30 Recall our discussion of comparative historical analysis above under Politics. Streek (2015) argues that comparative historical analysis became popular because of a desire to understand fascism and communism, and later to comprehend political realities in Asia. Streek (2015) compares comparative analysis to several different kinds of historical exploration. Most obviously, Streek contrasts it with a more traditional focus on unique events with an emphasis on the role of individuals. We address these concerns below. Streek also surveys Machiavelli's search for general rules that apply everywhere, Ibn Khaldun's general theory of history, and 19th century scholarship (including some versions of Marx) that sought to identify inevitable historical processes. We can agree with Streek that a search for what we have called contextualized generalizations – seeking to identify when certain causal relationships hold without assuming any are universal – provides for a more progressive historical enterprise.

31 In this chapter, we have urged comparison in the study of politics, art, and history. In each case, we have noted that academic specialization hinders comparison. We can note here that comparison is invaluable across human science. Morlino (2018) discusses how comparison allows us to identify important differences, test hypotheses (he speaks of "conditional generalizations"), and suggest policy interventions. He also identifies how best to perform comparisons.

32 I have reviewed the approach of economic history in Szostak (2006) and (2015).

33 Perhaps in some future philosophers (and scientists) will even attach confidence intervals to their conjecture: "I am 80 percent confident of this conjecture," or maybe "I think this conjecture holds 80 percent of the time." At present this is such apostasy that I bury it in a footnote.

34 Merchant (2020) urges philosophers of science to pay greater attention to the complexity and uncertainty of the world we study. I naturally concur. A philosophical recognition that contextualized generalizations should be the goal of human science research would be invaluable. 6 and Bellamy (2013, 57) dispose of several arguments for skepticism regarding the possibilities of a progressive social science, observing that "philosophers of science moved on long ago, and today interest in relativism among philosophers has waned considerably."

35 "The human is made up of all those features that are distinctive of our human world: the look, sound, feel, smell, and taste of things; the mental aspects of our inner experiences, our feelings, desires, and thoughts; what it is to be a certain kind of physical system (a conscious person); the human character of human actions and lives; the meaning and value of things; our friendships, quarrels, and loves; our dreams, our plans, decisions, deeds; our works of art, our literature, music, and science; our technology and architecture; our laws, traditions, and institutions" (p. 38). In addressing a metaphysical problem he neatly distinguishes natural from human science, and lists most of the phenomena in Table 2.1.

36 Darbellay (2019) develops four scenarios for the future of interdisciplinarity, one of which involves the complete eclipse of disciplines by interdisciplinarity. Darbellay sees this as an unlikely outcome. I would think that we will always need communities of specialized researchers but we might imagine a quite different configuration of such communities than our existing disciplinary structure.

5

TEACHING IN HUMAN SCIENCE

The American Association of Colleges and Universities (AAC&U) regularly surveys employers regarding what they think about a Liberal Arts (effectively, a human science) education (AAC&U, 2021). The latest AAC&U survey of business leaders finds appreciation of a broad liberal arts education, but room for improvement. Notably, employers value both depth and breadth in education. As elsewhere in this book, we can approach our discussion of teaching with a sense that we are already doing good things but can do even better. We can ask how we might better blend depth and breadth of understanding. We can note that employers care about attitudes as well as understandings. We can suggest that an integrative approach to education will encourage students to see value in multiple perspectives and work better in teams, two attitudes that potential employers care much about. These skills, we might stress, will serve them well in their communities as well as in their careers.

Hanstedt (2012) reports a steady movement away from distributional models of General Education (in which students are required to take courses in a variety of fields) in the United States toward what he terms a more integrative approach. He identifies four key drivers of this transition: the recognition that student lives are complex; a desire to help students draw connections across courses and cope with information overload; the recognition that workplaces require diverse knowledge and skills; and the challenges of citizenship, which requires familiarity with many fields.[1] The proposals we outline below are consistent with the trend identified by Hanstedt, and would serve to better prepare students for coursework, employment, citizenship, and the complexity of life in general.[2]

The modern research university is predicated on a belief that research and teaching are mutually supportive enterprises: that our research informs our teaching and our teaching informs our research. It is noteworthy, then, that it is distinctly unusual for authors to address questions of research and teaching

DOI: 10.4324/9781003275237-5

practice in the same work. Yet there is good reason to suspect that integrative teaching practices and integrative research practices will be mutually support-ive. Researchers called upon to teach integrative material will be more likely to perform integrative research and to do this well. In turn, efforts at integrative research will enhance our ability to give students a coherent education (yet one that respects diverse perspectives). I would note in this respect that multiple authors in Barry and Born (2014) discuss how teaching programs – in diverse interdisciplinary fields such as science and technology studies and medical humanities – encouraged the consolidation of theoretical understandings in these fields. There is undoubtedly a symbiotic relationship between the research strate-gies outlined in the preceding two chapters and the teaching practices advocated in this chapter. (We will in Chapter 8 note a further synergy: that integrative teaching provides job opportunities for integrative researchers.)

What Every Student Can and Should Know

The typical Liberal Arts degree, especially in North America, requires students to Major in some field but take courses in many fields. With only a few excep-tions, little effort is expended to help students tie their diverse coursework into some coherent whole.[3] Even the move toward an "integrated approach" chroni-cled by Hanstedt (2012) only rarely involves explicitly teaching students how to integrate. It is hoped (generally implicitly) that students will somehow figure out how to integrate all on their own. This regrettable situation reflects not a lack of will[4] – though it is encouraged by the disciplinary hegemony that we have discussed in previous chapters – but a failure to appreciate that we can easily give students a far greater capacity to tie the little bits of understanding we throw at them into a greater whole. This educational coherence is invaluable in its own right but also dramatically increases the chances that they will remember some of what we teach them. Our understanding of human memory indicates that we are more likely to remember X if X is nested within a structure of related memories. Students who can connect one bit of understanding to other bits of understanding are more likely to remember all of these things. They are then better prepared for lifelong learning, for they can readily connect what they learn after graduation to what they learned in university.

The Structure of Human Science Knowledge

We have spent much of this book outlining a map of human science and explor-ing how we can best explore this map. We should then expose our students to this map. They should appreciate that human science as a whole studies relationships among dozens of key phenomena. They should not have to memorize Table 2.1 but should be able to recognize where their Major and any course they might take – or indeed any issue they encounter on social media – fits within that table. They should appreciate that human science disciplines are not a logical division of the subject matter of human science. They should nevertheless appreciate how disciplines in practice do carve up the subject matter. Among other things, this will make it far easier for students to both find and evaluate relevant information about any topic – a skill widely recognized as one of the key purposes of general education programs (Wells 2016, 34).

How can we justify not teaching this material? Why would we not try to give students an organizing structure on which they can hang every bit of understanding they achieve in their studies? It is surely easy enough for an instructor to master the map of human science well enough to communicate it. This will perhaps be easiest for an interdisciplinary researcher but should be entirely feasible for a specialized scholar. Students who are cognizant of how one course they are taking relates to other courses they have taken may then ask challenging questions in class, but this should be seen as a positive development.

Key Strengths and Weaknesses of Methods and Theory Types

Likewise, we should not ask students to memorize Table 2.2. Yet they should learn that no method is perfect, that each method has strengths and weaknesses, and that we can be most confident of a hypothesis that is supported by multiple methods. When confronted with evidence generated by a particular method, they should know where to look to identify the method's strengths and weaknesses. They should be curious about what other methods might suggest. This skill will make them both better employees and better citizens, for they will know how to evaluate evidence generated by any scholarly method.[5]

There will likely be pushback from scholars who still think that *their* method is *perfect*. Few scholars may say this explicitly, even to themselves, but such a belief runs deep in many disciplines. Certainly, scholars in some disciplines view the methods employed in other disciplines (or even alternative methods in their own) with deep suspicion.[6] I hope that the arguments that generated Table 2.2 – and in particular employment of the innocuous 5W questions – can allow these suspicions to be transcended. The simple fact is that our students will confront evidence from all our methods in their lives and we have a duty to prepare them to grapple with all of this information. We can and should prepare them to make the best possible decisions.

Strategies for Integration

What should students do when they encounter disagreements? These may occur within a course, across courses, or in life more generally. We should equip students with skills at both evaluation and integration so that they can transcend such disagreements and develop a more comprehensive understanding of the issue at hand. As with the map of human science above, the main reason we only rarely do so is that universities are largely comprised of specialized scholars who do not appreciate that it is entirely feasible to do so. Yet there is now a well-articulated interdisciplinary research process that outlines successful strategies for evaluation and integration (Wernli and Darbellay 2016).[7]

It is important that we expose students to scholarly disagreements. Science develops through a process of disagreeing, marshalling evidence and argument, and working toward consensus. The public often seizes upon examples of scientific disagreement as an excuse to disdain scholarly insights in their entirety. We do students a disservice if we do not expose them to disagreements and explain that these are a good thing.[8] Yet if we expose students to disagreements without also exposing them to strategies for addressing these, we can leave them disillusioned, frustrated, and even angry.[9]

Luo (2021) finds that students who engage in conversations across ideological boundaries during university are more likely to do so in later life and also report superior skills and greater career success. Yet faculty members must guide students to have constructive conversations, for students are naturally tempted to adhere closely to their ideological preferences. Here again, it is important that we not just expose ideological disagreements but provide students with strategies for evaluating opposing arguments and seeking to integrate when possible. The advantages for democratic citizenship should be obvious.[10] Yet as Luo notes, the skills of respecting opposing points of view, engaging in constructive discourse, evaluating diverse arguments, and pursuing integration, are also useful in careers and life more generally.

Though it has not been our purpose in this book to describe the interdisciplinary research process, we have already touched on a couple of important strategies. One challenge in integrating is that different authors employ terminology differently (Chapter 2). We will often find that apparent disagreements disappear when we clarify the meanings that different authors are attaching to key terminology. Another challenge in integrating is that scholars tend to assume that the things they study are the most important. A diagram such as in Figure 2.2 can serve to show students how they might tie the researches of different scholars regarding different causal links into a coherent whole. Many other strategies have been found useful for each step in the interdisciplinary research process. Students learn these best when they apply them in their own integrative research projects.

The world is complex. Our students will in their careers and lives inevitably encounter a series of challenges that do not fall into a neat disciplinary silo. They will necessarily need to know how to find information from different disciplines, evaluate this, and integrate across it. Integrative research on the issues they investigate can aid them in these tasks, but they will still need to comprehend the nature of integrative research and tailor its findings to their particular circumstances. An understanding of how to perform interdisciplinary research empowers our students to grapple with any problem they face.[11]

We should also wish to enhance our students' creative potential. There are strong similarities between the interdisciplinary research process and the creative process as outlined by scholars of creativity. Both processes involve starting with a good question or problem, gathering relevant information from diverse sources (connecting previously unconnected information is the source of much creativity), an act(s) of inspiration, critical revision of that inspiration, and communication to diverse audiences (with persuasion being appreciated as a creative act in its own right) (Szostak 2017a). The creativity literature recognizes that we all have creative potential and can learn strategies for becoming more creative. Familiarity with the interdisciplinary research process will itself encourage creativity. It is particularly useful for students to appreciate the creative potential of integrating previously unconnected understandings. The skill of seeing issues from multiple perspectives is critical to both interdisciplinarity and creativity. Finally yet importantly, both processes recognize the importance of (creatively) communicating one's discoveries to others. Indeed, the creativity literature appreciates that persuasion may be as or more important than developing creative insights in the first place. The history of both art and science is littered with people who made creative advances but failed to convince others of their value.

In sum, an understanding of the interdisciplinary research process is important to students both in their studies and in their lives. It is entirely feasible to teach the interdisciplinary research process to all students. Therefore, we should do so.

Some Epistemology

We have urged in this book a sensible methodological approach in which we seek to achieve consensus around hypotheses by compiling argument and evidence from diverse methods. In Chapter 4, we urged an integrative approach to epistemology, and suggested that this would likely support our methodological approach. We should expose students to modern debates in epistemology. Indeed, how can we justify teaching them heaps of stuff without ever acquainting them with philosophical speculation regarding how and how much humans can know? Yet as with any academic conflict that we might teach them, we should explore with them how we can integrate across different epistemological arguments.

Some Ethics

We should likewise expose students to the five types of ethical analysis (Chapter 4) *and* show them that these often point in the same direction. Skeptics often wonder if we can teach ethics to people. Yet in fact, most western societies have done a great job of teaching young people to respect diversity in recent decades. However, this success has come at a cost: Young people, when surveyed on other ethical issues tend to respond that it is up to any social group to decide what is right and wrong.[12] It is thus critically important at this point in human history for us to appreciate that there are a set of values – honesty and both personal and social responsibility among them – that are supported by all five types of ethical evaluation, including the traditions of the vast bulk of human societies. We can respect diversity while still also having a reasonable expectation that *all* people need to justify acts that seem dishonest or irresponsible.[13]

Rhetoric and Critical Thinking

The skills and understandings outlined above are complemented by a further set of skills that we have not had much cause to speak about previously. First, we should teach all students some of the key elements of "rhetoric" and "critical thinking." Students can only integrate across the insights of different authors if they can first distinguish the author's conclusions from the supporting arguments and evidence, recognizing when an assertion is provided with no justification. The student should be able to distinguish appeals to evidence from appeals to authority and appeals to emotion. They should distinguish attacks on people from critiques of arguments. They should recognize generalizations and analogies, and how these can be abused. They should understand the criteria for judging a causal argument (see Chapter 4). If we teach our students how to dissect works, and recognize manipulative strategies, we prepare them for the deluge of misinformation that they will inevitably encounter in life.[14]

Students also need to write and make presentations. Most of our students will need to write reports of one sort or another in life (including PowerPoint presentations). Yet university writing courses often stress creative writing more than practical writing. They often also stress literary appreciation rather than writing skills for the simple reason that they are generally taught by experts in literary analysis rather than writing. Universities need to think hard about what they wish to accomplish in a required writing course, and ensure that instructors and course syllabi reflect this. Universities need also to think about where in the curriculum students develop presentation skills.

World History and Future Studies

I recommend here two courses that can reinforce an understanding of the complexity of the world, and of how scholars can grapple with it, while at the same time pursuing other valuable goals. I am so devoted to these courses and goals that I have written textbooks for each (Szostak 2021, 2022). The first course engages world history. As noted in Chapter 4, history can serve two purposes. First, like a good novel, a good history can show us how humans grapple with complexity. Second, history can show us how particular causal links operate in quite different times and places. World history can excel at the second task, for it engages the broad sweep of human history. In Szostak (2021), for example, I outline a set of challenges facing rulers, farmers, merchants, parents and dozens of other agents, and then compare how these agents addressed each challenge in different times and places. I also compare how empires rise and fall, how trade expands, and myriad other historical processes. In addition to its lessons regarding complexity, world history communicates to students how the world they inhabit came to be. It thus allows them to place their life within human history. World history teaches that all regions of the world have contributed to a shared human story, an invaluable lesson in today's world.[15] It also can teach about our common humanity: merchants and rulers and parents in quite different times and places often make similar decisions when faced with similar circumstances. One of the challenges faced in teaching world history in the past has been incoherence: Instructors and students may enjoy tales of pharaohs and Aztecs and Polynesian seafarers, but cannot comprehend why they are all in the same course. Yet a course that is deliberately comparative, that integrates understandings across disciplines and regions and time periods, and that shows how key phenomena in Table 2.1 (reprised in Szostak 2021) interact throughout human history, is coherent. Further coherence can be achieved by carefully explicating how the events and processes of one time and place built on the events and processes of earlier times and places.[16]

The second course is in future studies. The field of future studies has been transformed in recent decades. Scholars in the field now appreciate that we cannot predict the future very well. Nevertheless, we can identify a set of plausible futures and a set of desirable futures and ask how to transform the former into the latter. Future studies grapples explicitly with complexity, and seeks to understand how various trends will interact into the future. Systems analysis – and a recognition that systems are open – dominates the field. Whereas world history shows us how to grapple with complexity in understanding our past, future studies shows us how to grapple with complexity in engaging our future. Futurists recommend certain methods that instructors can employ as class exercises. The Futures Wheel exercise starts with a particular trend and asks us to identify effects of that trend. We then identify effects of the effects, and how these might interact. The Backcasting Wheel operates in reverse, starting with some desirable future outcome and looking at influences on this, and then influences on influences. Both of these are obviously exercises in identifying a related set of causal linkages and understanding how these interact. Futurists decades ago developed the Delphi method of engaging experts around an issue (usually around predicting plausible futures), sharing the initial responses of each expert, and engaging them again. The general finding is that experts developed more nuanced analyses through interaction and moved toward consensus. Student exercises employing the Delphi method can potentially show them the value of respecting multiple perspectives and the possibility of integrating across these. As with world history, future studies serves important goals beyond reinforcing our understanding of how to grapple with complexity. It guides students to think about what kind of future they want and how to work toward achieving that. Importantly, it can guide them to identify societal goals that are widely shared. On a personal level, it should help them to both cope with change and plot a future-oriented career path.[17]

I am a big believer in capstone courses that gather students from different majors. These should discuss their research projects with each other, and perhaps work in groups on such projects. Future studies is an obvious theme around which to structure a capstone. Students can learn from each other as they discuss how the future might and should unfold. They can gain a sense of self-efficacy from contributing to class discussions and exercises. They can come to appreciate how their education has shaped their worldview, and how they can learn from others with a different worldview.

Structuring Interdisciplinary and Thematic Majors

We noted in Chapter 4 that disciplines do not divide the subject matter of human science in a logical manner. A student with an interest in a particular subsystem may wish, then, to structure a set of courses from multiple disciplines that address that subsystem. In particular, we identified a set of "big questions" that should be pursued with respect to each subsystem. Students with an interest in any of these questions should be able to pursue this interest across multiple courses.[18] We have noted in multiple earlier chapters that the world faces a set of challenges – climate change, urban poverty, racism, among many others – that usefully can be informed by several disciplines. Here too, students may want a major that combines courses from different disciplines.

Put differently, students might reasonably wish to focus on a wide variety of sets of causal links in our map of human science (and sometimes some links to natural science phenomena also). If they can identify a good reason for wanting to study this particular set of links then our universities should facilitate this educational strategy. Our map, that is, highlights the fact that there are myriad useful educational pathways, far more than the handful of Majors that most students are allowed to choose from.

A university can pursue two complementary strategies here. The most obvious is to structure a set of thematic interdisciplinary Majors around subsystems and/or themes that span multiple disciplines. Most universities in North America already have a couple programs like this, though these are less common elsewhere.[19] Groups of faculty members with a shared interest have generally developed these programs. Very few universities have thought hard about what sorts of programs their students might want. A glance at our map of human science might be helpful here, as would looking at lists of the sorts of Majors that other universities offer. Yet such a strategy will surely not satisfy the interests of every student. The second strategy involves creating "self-designed Majors" where students with an unusual but sensible interest can themselves suggest a program of study around a theme that they describe. This sort of program exists at a minority of universities (enough that there is an association of directors of such programs), but involves some significant administrative costs: Some administrator(s) must approve each student program and advise the student along the way.

There is a hybrid option whereby a university offers a degree in interdisciplinary studies (sometimes called liberal studies). Such programs usually require students to take a variety of core interdisciplinary courses – which usually but not always include courses about how to integrate. Yet these programs are often structured so that students then specialize in one or two interdisciplinary areas or themes. These specializations require fewer courses than a free-standing Major and are thus easier to put together for both university and student.

It should be obvious that in any of these three approaches students will need advice on how to integrate information from different courses in or spanning different disciplines. We have argued above that we should teach integrative skills to *all* students. Yet these skills become even more important to students pursuing interdisciplinary Majors. Some interdisciplinary programs have a set of required courses that both teach and practice integrative strategies. Yet others leave it to students to figure out how to integrate material from different disciplines. This last strategy is academically irresponsible, especially given how easy it is to teach students integrative strategies.[20]

One challenge in structuring an interdisciplinary Major is how to deal with methods. Disciplinary Majors naturally acquaint students with the one or two methods (sometimes more) most common in that discipline. Some students may be tempted to pursue an interdisciplinary Major just to avoid challenging courses in methods. This should not be countenanced. We have argued above that all students should have some appreciation of the strengths and weaknesses of each of the dozen methods pursued across human science. Students should also have a deeper familiarity with one or two methods. Students might be allowed to choose courses in any method that is commonly applied to the theme of their Major or specialization.

This book is unusual in treating the humanities and social sciences together (and in treating research and teaching together). Yet the sorts of interdisciplinary programming advocated above will often link courses in social science with courses in the humanities.[21] This may attract new audiences to coursework in the humanities. Hayot (2021) notes that there are many reasons why enrolment in the humanities has declined in recent years. One of these may be that the traditional disciplinary Majors in the humanities do not resonate with students as they once did, in part because career opportunities are unclear.[22] Hayot doubts that many want to be historians or experts in literature. Hayot suggests that students may be much more attracted to Majors organized topically around "social justice, migration studies, the problem of God, translation, journalism, wealth and inequality, conflict, ideas of beauty, television, society and technology, and the like." I could quibble a bit with the list of topics – some appear a bit vague and would certainly need clarification – but can support the thrust of the argument. Most of these topics would require that humanities scholarship be connected to social science scholarship.[23] As argued in Chapter 4, humanist scholars should be careful of drawing lessons about economic or social subsystems from the artworks they study. Hayot also recommends sets of courses focused on "practices," by which he means something a little broader than the methods we have discussed in this book.[24] I again can quibble on details but appreciate the need to teach students about methods.

The preceding paragraphs have focused on undergraduate education. Similar arguments can be made at the graduate level: graduate students also should be enabled to pursue interdisciplinary degrees. This too can be facilitated by a combination of thematic degree options, interdisciplinary studies programs, and individualized study options. Note that there is an important synergy between disciplinary graduate and undergraduate programs in that graduate students are often funded to teach (or assist in teaching) undergraduates (and later may be hired as professors in interdisciplinary teaching programs). Interdisciplinary programs can benefit from the same synergy. Since graduate students must perform independent research, it is critically important that interdisciplinary graduate students be acquainted with strategies for performing interdisciplinary research (Rashid 2021). Given that interdisciplinary researchers face a set of common challenges, research seminars in which graduate students can discuss their work with each other can be invaluable (Lyall et al. 2011).[25]

Teaching in an Integrative and Comparative Manner

We have urged a symbiotic relationship between specialized and integrative (both within and across fields) research in preceding chapters. We can urge a similar symbiosis in our teaching. Students need to see numerous examples of specialized research in order to understand how this proceeds. Yet within a field, students need to be exposed to integrative work that ties the pieces together into some coherent whole. And students need also to appreciate how any subject they study fits within human science as a whole and thus also need exposure to interdisciplinary analyses.

Universities have long focused on teaching specialized research. We can thus focus here on how to teach in an integrative manner. We have already highlighted one key message above: instructors need to guide students through the process of integration. It is not fair to simply expose them to scholarly differences and leave them to deal with these. Instructors in any integrative course can usefully remind students of integrative strategies and guide them in the application of these. Nevertheless, integrative instructors should see themselves as coaches rather than sages. The process of integration lends itself to collaborative pedagogies such as team teaching, class discussions, group projects, and problem-based learning (where we start from a problem and explore how to address it). Integrative courses and programs are also well suited to experiential learning opportunities such as community-service learning or internships (Dezure 2017).[26]

Integrative instructors should be self-aware regarding a set of skills that are associated with integrative teaching. We want students to learn how to analyze complex problems or questions, to appreciate multiple perspectives, to appreciate the strengths and weaknesses of the different theories and methods relevant to a particular inquiry, to evaluate diverse sorts of evidence, and to integrate insights into a more comprehensive understanding. We want them to embrace complexity, accept nuance, and communicate respectfully and constructively with those from different perspectives. We should never lose sight of the goal of preparing students for a lifetime of integration and collaboration.[27]

We should also never lose sight of the fact that our goal is to identify contextualized generalizations. We will want always to expose students to different cases so that they can evaluate under what circumstances a particular causal link holds. We want to encourage students in their own research projects to pursue comparison and contextualized generalization whenever possible. In the social sciences, both instructors and students should be open to looking beyond western societies of the last two decades. In our study of art, we should deliberately compare artworks from quite different times and places: As noted elsewhere only then can we distinguish the aesthetic from the cultural. In our study of history, we should also compare across both time and space.[28] The value of comparison is obvious but it is challenging in practice for the simple reason that most human science research focuses on one time and place. In the absence of lots of integrative/comparative research, comparative teaching requires lots of extra work. Moreover, specialized researchers unsurprisingly find it easier to teach their specialization.[29] Yet this is also an opportunity to empower students: teach them the guidelines of good comparison (such as making sure you are comparing the same phenomena or causal links across cases) and ask them to compare different cases.

Some Thoughts on High School Social Studies and English

Like many parents, I found my children's social studies courses unfathomable. They seemed to be a random congeries of topics. Each of these might be valuable in its own way. Yet without any obvious organizing structure, students could easily wonder what the point was (no matter how great the teachers were). Students need to be motivated to learn, after all, and will inevitably have a hard time motivating themselves to master a disparate bunch of isolated treatments of history and geography and little dribbles of social science.[30]

I am far from alone in querying the way that social studies is taught. "Educators have never fully agreed on a common definition of social studies. We have not yet decided whether the subject is singular or plural, a unity or a collection. We have experienced considerable conflict over goals, and this is ongoing. As a result, all social studies teachers confront certain dilemmas at the outset: what to teach, how to teach, and why to teach it. A major question is what lies at the heart of the subject." (Zevin 2015, 3–4). Zevin (5) then highlights a big debate in the field: "Is the social studies a single, integrated field, or are the social studies a series of related disciplines?" He notes that the National Council for Social Studies in the United States has recommended an interdisciplinary approach, but provides no curricular advice on how to do so. He disdains the idea of teaching each discipline separately (26–30).[31] Importantly, he recognizes that previous attempts to introduce interdisciplinarity into high school curricula were challenging because teachers lack interdisciplinary training, and had no access to an integrated curriculum (274).

I would naturally propose that one of our goals should be to provide students with a sense of how the pieces fit together.[32] We should give them a map that guides them through the social studies curriculum and shows how each topic addressed connects to others. Even more than university students, they need a structure on which to hang little bits of information, and will be more likely to remember structured information. We can then articulate a set of important sub-goals: to understand how the world came to be as it is, to have some sense of how the future might unfold, to appreciate democracy and understand the characteristics of successful democracy, and to appreciate social diversity but also our common humanity (and ethics).[33] It may be that the pieces we already have just need to be better motivated. Alternatively, it may be that once we have artic- ulated clearer goals we will tinker with these. Either way, we can do far better than a seemingly random set of topics.[34]

Ross et al. (2014) identify five main purposes advocated in the literature on social studies. The first is to communicate democratic values. I would argue that we should communicate to students what we know about the conditions that support stable democracy (They do not seem to be getting the message that respect for those we disagree with may be essential to stable democracy.) It might also be useful for them to hear more about what life under non- democratic regimes is like.[35] The second is to acquaint students with the social science disciplines. I suggest that this proves problematic in large part because these divide the human science terrain so illogically. It would be useful to show students how the pieces fit together. The third is to teach students the decision-making skills they will need in life. Since life is interdisciplinary, we should expose students to the true complexity of the world, guide them on how to look for information on any topic, and teach them how to integrate.[36] The fourth is to teach them to question the status quo. Here again an ability to grapple with diversity and integrate across divergent points of view will be critical. The fifth is to develop a sense of efficacy among students. I would argue that teaching them that they have the ability to evaluate and integrate the arguments of others is critical here.[37]

Most high school students are asked only to do creative writing and five paragraph essays. They are thus poorly prepared for university term papers. Universities have thus created mandatory writing classes. (As noted above, these often also teach the wrong stuff.) Students are also poorly prepared for the writ- ing tasks associated with employment. American businesses spend billions of dollars annually on remedial writing programs for employees. We could do a far better job in our high schools of teaching students to write the sorts of things they will have to write later. Motivation is again important: We need to show them how important writing is before teaching them how. Then we can expose them to examples of good writing while they practice the craft: They will appreciate good writing more after struggling to produce it themselves.

One of my joys in writing this book has been to discover that some of my adolescent objections to high school literature classes are borne out by modern scholarship. Why do teachers force students to identify one theme in a work when we now appreciate that one of the main purposes of literature is to show us how to grapple with complexity? Why do we study a series of works in isolation rather than comparing these? What is the point of it all? I think I would have found high school literature courses more interesting if I had been told that I was supposed to be learning about coping with complexity, and if class discussions had focused on what we might learn from a particular work. I would have been intrigued if connections had been drawn between literature and social studies.

Summary

- The reforms to teaching practices suggested in this chapter will benefit from and reinforce the reforms to research practices urged in preceding chapters.
- We can and thus should provide all students with a map of human science, a sense of the strengths and weaknesses of different methods, skills at integration, an integrated understanding of epistemology and ethics, skills in rhetoric and critical thinking, appropriate writing skills, and some world history and future studies.
- We should enable students to pursue the interdisciplinary study of themes or subsystems. We can create a set of thematic Majors, create a self-designed Major, and/or create an Interdisciplinary Studies program with a variety of specializations. In any of these options, we need to actively teach integration skills, and ensure that students gain expertise in some method.
- Interdisciplinary thematic Majors may prove particularly valuable to instructors in the humanities. These have much to contribute but this contribution needs to be carefully understood.
- Integrative teaching lends itself to interactive pedagogies. Instructors should be conscious of a set of skills they are trying to communicate, and especially integration itself.
- Comparison is invaluable for teaching about contextualized generalizations, among other things.
- High school social studies curricula should be more coherent.
- High school English courses should teach students to write the sorts of things they will need to write later in life. They should focus literary appreciation on learning how to grapple with complexity.

Notes

1 General Education programs in the United States have great potential to institutionalize an integrative approach to education (Holley and Szostak 2022). The drivers identified by Hanstedt can be observed in other countries (e.g. Litre et al. 2022 and other chapters in that book).

2 There are numerous recent works that worry about the state of a "Liberal Arts" education. Some suggest curricular reforms while others doubt that these will stem the decline in enrolments in Liberal Arts colleges (e.g. Ferrall 2015). Yet if the curriculum is uninspiring then public relations efforts and testimonials from alumni may have a limited impact.

3 There is little consensus on why we require students to take General Education or core requirements. "Whereas some consider general education to mean skills and abilities, others endow general education with specific content. Still others equate general education with particular academic disciplines. Recent articulations have framed general education to be a set of learning outcomes" (Wells 2016, 6).

4 Many scholars regret the decline of "Western Civilization" as an organizing theme for Liberal Arts education precisely because it lent some coherence to a Liberal Arts degree. Yet we can have coherence without privileging one region of the world in our understanding of how the world works. Other scholars are wary of coherence as a goal because they value multiple perspectives. We have shown in earlier chapters that we can and should integrate across diverse perspectives.

5 The distribution model of a general education program in which students are required to take courses in quite different disciplines is generally justified with a desire for students to be acquainted with different types of scholarship. Yet distribution models are widely seen as problematic, and it is not clear that students gain a deep appreciation of scholarly differences (Wells 2016, 42–44). It is likely far better to compare different approaches in the same course.

6 "[S]ocial scientists do not typically accept the idea that all approaches might comfortably coexist, side by side and tolerated, as just so many alternative ways of pursuing knowledge. Far from it. Instead, they tend to *identify* themselves with their favored paradigms and to *denigrate* the approaches they regard as *inferior* (the "cult of arrogance"). … Sectarianism in the social sciences involves the drift of theoretical and methodological preferences toward the sacred, which believers embrace with fervor (the "cult of defensiveness"). Simultaneously they lash out at other approaches—as critics and opponents of their own—with equal, negative fervor" (Smelser and Reed 2012, 331).

7 Wernli and Darbellay cite Repko and Szostak (now 2020) as a resource. That book also describes strategies for asking good questions, searching the literature, communicating, and reflecting. Another good resource (that I also co-authored) is the Interdisciplinary General Education set of webpages under Resources on the website of the Association for Interdisciplinary Studies at https://interdisciplinarystudies.org/. Wells (2016, 38) identifies integration as a goal of general education but says nothing about how this might be achieved: "Making sense of the varied and fragmented experiences associated with a college education demands an intentional context for integrative learning that general education uniquely provides."

8 A classic work is Graff (1992). Notably, he urges teaching the conflicts as the best way to address the culture wars.

9 Hanstedt (2012, 25) argues that we should not expect students to integrate anything that instructors cannot. This is invaluable advice. We should not expose students to diverse material and leave it up to them to integrate. Yet while Hanstedt provides numerous examples of integrative courses he does not suggest actually teaching strategies for integration.

10 I focus in this chapter on curricular suggestions that flow naturally from the analysis in this book. Yet I would follow Daniels (2021) in urging a much greater effort to educate university students about democracy. This important matter is touched upon below in our discussion of high school, for it has long been argued that high schools should teach students about how democracy functions.

11 Ari (2020) reports the experience of undergraduate students taught interdisciplinary research strategies while performing an interdisciplinary group project. Careful assessment indicated that students learned both important strategies and much about

the topic they investigated. "The competencies, on which students showed some of the largest gains, were some of the most highly desired by today's employers including communicative competence and critical thinking."

12 I have in several publications, including Szostak (2022) spoken of the "ethical challenge of our times": learning how to respect diversity while also recognizing a set of universal ethical principles. If we do not do so, there will surely be a backlash against diversity. If we need to choose between diversity and honesty, which do you pick? It is far better to appreciate that we can have both.

13 Wells (2016, 36) reports that general education is widely expected to provide ethical guidance, but she provides no advice on how this might be done.

14 I found Groarke and Tindale (2012) very useful. Hanscomb (2016) urges us to not just teach students how to distinguish different types and elements of argument, but to give them lots of critical thinking practice (both to learn and to gain confidence), and to guide them toward self-reflection. Moll (2019) stresses the importance of "citizen epistemology" in which students learn to evaluate arguments and evidence in public discourse, and argues that an interdisciplinary education is essential to this task.

15 World history also teaches that circumstances change, and that circumstances shape human behavior. It is a healthy thing to be shocked at the casual racism and sexism and homophobia of many past societies. This did not stop agents from engaging in acts of kindness or creativity or courage. History can serve to remind us that humans are multifaceted. We should not be surprised that Churchill and Jefferson did both things that we celebrate and things that we find deeply offensive. Future generations may well scorn people of our time for our sluggish reaction to climate change, callous disregard of the plight of refugees, or willingness to wink at injustices both locally and globally. All of us might reflect on how easily we assume that "what is" is "what should be" and simply behave as our friends behave without thinking.

16 In Szostak (2021), I employ dozens of flowcharts to capture the main causes and effects of important historical transformations. Often, the results in one flowchart become influences in a later flowchart. I also carefully apply (social) evolutionary analysis to show how particular developments built on what went before. And I have in-text boxes that discuss certain complex developments across a longer timeframe than any chapter, such as the history of rubber or timekeeping. These boxes provide a microcosm of world history showing how diverse phenomena, agents, and regions interact. Other in-text boxes explore a particular causal link across time, such as how epidemics spread.

17 Burke (2021) notes that many defenders of the Liberal Arts have argued that it prepares students to deal with uncertainty. Yet Burke doubts that the Liberal Arts generally do this very well. A required course about the future could change this.

18 This may at times be possible within disciplines. Economics departments might expand their course offerings in economic growth and development, and enhance the interdisciplinary content of these. Literature departments might focus on the central question of how and why literature moves us (comparing this to how and why other art forms move us). For most of our big questions, though, interdisciplinary coursework will be essential.

19 On the North American situation, see Holley and Szostak (2022). Other chapters in that book discuss the growth of interdisciplinary teaching programs in recent decades in Mexico (Villa-Soto et al. 2022), Brazil (Litre et al. 2022), and Australia (Sebastian, Fam, and Prior 2022). Lyall (2022) discusses exciting experiments but limited institutionalization in the United Kingdom. Other chapters look at the potential for the expansion of interdisciplinary teaching programs in Ghana, China, Russia, Armenia, and Georgia. Adomßent (2022) describes a unique German program. Litre et al. (2022, 66) voice a common complaint that interdisciplinary programs often suffer from being evaluated by disciplinary standards: "Hence, programs end up being evaluated and rated not according to what they offer but what they do not offer or intend to."

20 I am biased, of course, being the co-author of two texts on how to perform interdisciplinary analysis (Repko and Szostak 2020, Repko, Szostak, and Buchberger 2020). Yet I think the case I make here is straightforward. I am also conscious that I have advocated multiple courses in this chapter for which I have written textbooks. I have written all of these books due to a strong feeling that students needed access to a certain kind of material.

21 Martinelli (2017) bemoans the malign impacts of combining his school of humanities with his university's school of social sciences. Yet he appreciates some synergies.

22 There are other reasons. Both Hellemans (2017) and Steinberg (2014) worry that we may take much of the joy out of art (especially literature) with excessive jargon and forcing students to dissect rather than appreciate works. Yet a greater problem may be that the humanities are not clear about what they are trying to achieve in their teaching. Clune (2021) begins his article with "The most basic questions for any educator are: Why should students listen to me? What claim do I have on the public? When these questions can no longer be answered clearly and convincingly, a discipline risks extinction. This fate looms for literary studies." Clune doubts that humanists can reasonably claim to provide an ethical education, and thus should stress teaching a kind of artistic appreciation (which requires us to judge some works as better than others). Hayot says "I'm trying to teach my students, in no matter what class I teach, how to understand a problem, a process, or an event — a document, a social form, an inflection point — and to use that understanding to increase their more general capacity to reason humanistically. I hope that doing this kind of thinking increases their capacity to relate to, appreciate, understand, and engage themselves in their own lives and in the lives of others." I doubt that such a vague statement will inspire many students. My advice, of course, is to focus on how and why art moves us toward a variety of individual and societal goals.

23 I could make the same observations with respect to Rosenberg (2021): "Should we take it as a given that building your education around ten literature courses is preferable to building it around a global challenge like food insecurity or climate change or around the development of an ability like creativity or clarity of expression? This is not about the value of studying literature, but about how that study should be organized in relation to other areas of study in order to prepare students for work they will do and the problems they will need to solve." Dorot and Davidovitch (2020) argue that the humanities are essential but need to change, and urge connecting humanities coursework to courses in the social and natural sciences. Campion (2018) makes a similar argument for graduate programs (he mentions medical humanities and environmental humanities).

24 He speaks of "language learning, writing and speaking, historical, cultural, and social analysis."

25 Rashid (2021) describes how he teaches interactively using Repko and Szostak (2020) in an integrative science and engineering PhD program at the National University of Singapore. Rashid notes that instructors trained in disciplines often do not adequately acquaint interdisciplinary students with either an understanding of the nature of interdisciplinarity or of strategies for performing interdisciplinary research. His techniques can also be applied in human science. Another useful resource is Menken and Keestra (2016), a short textbook designed for an interdisciplinary graduate program at the University of Amsterdam.

26 The Association for Interdisciplinary Studies website at https://interdisciplinarystud ies.org/ provides a host of resources for the integrative teacher. There is lots of advice in both the *About Interdisciplinarity* and *Scholarship of Interdisciplinary Teaching and Learning* webpages. There is also a collection of peer-reviewed course syllabi, and a couple of rubrics that can be used in evaluating integrative work. I am a big believer in community-service learning, and helped launch such a program at my university. I join with Mintz (2021) in thinking that working on a local project as students may be the best way to instill citizenship.

27 The British Academy (2016) urges scholars to teach both interdisciplinary and disciplinary courses. This may be great career advice, especially in the contemporary European environment in which there are limited interdisciplinary course offerings at many institutions. But we should not lose sight of the fact that the goals of integrative teaching, and thus the skills required for it, are different.

28 Doing so allows us to appreciate our common humanity while also appreciating cross-societal differences.

29 In literature especially, there is also some feeling that only people from a certain ethnic group or region should teach the literature of that ethnic group or region. Such a point of view could only emerge within an academic community that does not appreciate the value of comparison.

30 "Social studies are the most inclusive of all school subjects ... Given this, it is not surprising that social studies has been racked by intellectual battles over its purpose, content, and pedagogy since its very inception as a school subject in the early part of the 20th century" (Ross et al. 2014, 20).

31 Niemelä (2020) instead urges that we both teach students about disciplines and about how to integrate across disciplines. That is similar to the approach taken in this book. He argues that only in this way can we achieve curricular coherence, and that coherence enhances student learning.

32 "In the current model, subjects, even when linked, tend to be presented without their relation to the general framework. This leads to shards of understanding. It also supports the belief that knowledge consists of fragments alone, that viewpoints cannot be reconciled, and that specializations are their own goal" (Ramadanovic 2021, 212). He urges, though, a shared narrative rather than a shared map.

33 There are, of course, already goals articulated in most high school curricula. Some of these are quite vague. I am urging here that we identify a manageable set of well-defined goals, and tie these into a coherent bundle. Each of these goals have been discussed earlier in this book.

34 Adams and Kerr (2021) describe a topic-oriented approach where topics or activities (such as visiting a museum or walking through a neighborhood) are approached from multiple disciplines simultaneously.

35 Daniels (2021,88) urges a democracy requirement at the college level because students are not adequately educated in high school: "The fact is that our students, who show such remarkable sophistication and mastery across so many different fields upon entering university, are woefully undereducated in democracy's core precepts." He appreciates that there is considerable debate about how best to teach about democracy. He recommends teaching the institutions, values, and history of democracy, but most importantly having students constructively debate policy issues to experience tradeoffs and hopefully learn to respect those they disagree with. Kahne and Westheimer (2006) also encourage such debates. Yet Zevin (2015, 360) understandably worries about the challenges of addressing controversial issues in a high school classroom. It can be useful here to show how scholars from different disciplines approach an issue, and seek to integrate.

36 Zevin (2015) laudably urges us to teach students to recognize and respect differences of opinion. Yet students can easily become frustrated if we do not also teach them how to integrate across differences of opinion.

37 Most of the Ross et al. volume addresses the vexed question of standardized testing. I fully appreciate their concern that some of what we want to teach is hard to test, and that an emphasis on testing squeezes such topics out of the curriculum. We can, though, test students about their understanding of how the pieces fit together, and how to integrate or compare.

6

REORGANIZING OUR LIBRARIES

Phenomenon-Based Classification

We have urged in preceding chapters a more integrative approach to both research and teaching. In pursuing this, researchers and students will often need to search for relevant works from different disciplines. They can be greatly aided by the sorts of integrative works that we have advocated in Chapter 3. However, where will they find these? If some scholar performs an integrative analysis of the effect of a particular cultural attitude on economic output, where will such an analysis appear in a library? It might be in Economics or in any of the disciplines that study culture. Where and how should the scholar or student look for it?[1]

Libraries have in recent decades moved away from encouraging searches using the subject headings that are assigned to each book and journal. They instead mimic online search engines: A library user inputs some search terms and the library search interface identifies books or journals in which the search terms appear in title or abstract. As in online searches, this is a very imprecise approach. The user will miss any works that employ even slightly different terminology. Yet the user may nevertheless receive hundreds or thousands of "hits" and have to skim many of these in order to identify relevant works.

I have long been active in the field of Knowledge Organization. This interdisciplinary field asks how information of any sort, but especially scholarly output, is best organized so that users can find the information they seek. The field recognizes that the sorts of searches increasingly employed in libraries are both imprecise and time-consuming. Yet there is a general appreciation that there are/were problems in the alternative approach of searching by subject. The main classification systems employed by libraries (such as the Library of Congress Classification or the Dewey Decimal Classification commonly employed in North America) were first developed in the 19th century long before the advent of computers. They

DOI: 10.4324/9781003275237-6

are "enumerated": Long schedules of subjects were developed for each discipline. These have necessarily been much revised over the centuries to reflect both new topics and changes in societal attitudes (toward gender identity, homosexuality, and a host of other issues). Yet most scholars in the Knowledge Organization field have come to accept the value of what is called "facet analysis": Subject headings are not enumerated but rather formed synthetically by combining terms that capture key facets of the document (or idea or object) in question. The Library of Congress and Dewey Decimal Classifications have adopted some elements of facet analysis over the years: most obviously, they have schedules of geographical locations and time periods that might be combined with other subject headings (Poetry – France – 18th century). Yet they remain primarily enumerative in approach. Some other classification systems, such as the Colon Classification in India (which pioneered a faceted approach decades ago) and the Universal Decimal Classification in Europe, have pursued a faceted approach to a much greater degree (Szostak, Gnoli, and Lopez-Huertas 2016).

A faceted approach has the potential to greatly facilitate searches across multiple disciplines (and to facilitate searches across libraries, museums, archives, and other information repositories). A user interested in the effects of a particular cultural value on economic growth should ideally be able to search for precisely that relationship and readily find all works that study that relationship. Note that this will be a boon for integrative researchers themselves: They can identify with one quick search all works that have examined the particular causal relationship they hope to survey. Unfortunately, even faceted classifications have tended to be organized by disciplines and this has limited their effectiveness in facilitating interdisciplinary searches.

There is a better way. We could appreciate that the vast bulk of scholarly works examine one or more causal relationships among the phenomena identified in Table 2.1 (or more precise phenomena that can be identified by further subdivision of some of the phenomena in that table). [A minority instead analyze processes internal to a single phenomenon.] We could then seek to classify works in terms of the links that are studied: (Phenomenon X) (Exerts effect N on) (Phenomenon Y). This will be virtually impossible within an enumerated classification, but straightforward in an approach that synthesizes subject headings by combining terms from schedules of phenomena with schedules describing causal processes.

I have developed to this end the Basic Concepts Classification (Szostak n.d.). That classification adds considerable detail to Table 2.1 in identifying schedules of human science phenomena. (It also has schedules of natural science phenomena.) It then adds schedules of "relators": These are mostly verbs and describe the many ways that one phenomenon might influence another. Over time, I added a schedule of "Properties": These adverbs or adjectives help to clarify the nature of a phenomenon or relator. The classification has been applied to random sets of both books in libraries and artifacts in museums. The general finding is that it is able to give far more precise indicators of the contents of a document than the classification systems in widespread use while not requiring lengthier notations (if it were to be used for shelving purposes) (e.g. Smiraglia and Szostak 2018).

The Basic Concepts Classification is also potentially very easy to use. Libraries have moved away from searches by subject heading because existing systems of subject headings are hard to navigate. With the right search interface and the BCC, though, a user merely types in a question about a particular causal relationship, and is shown all relevant works. I have (well, actually, a great research assistant has) developed a thesaurus that can translate search terms into the vocabulary used in the Basic Concepts Classification. The user need not, then, identify the terminology employed in BCC in order to prosecute a successful search. I have identified a simple set of grammatical rules for the search interface to employ in turning a search query into an appropriate synthetic subject heading (Szostak 2017c).[2] If, for some reason, the user does not get the results they desire, the schedules in the BCC, grounded as they are in Table 2.1, are easy to navigate so that the user can develop the precise complex subject heading they wish to search for.

Once a user gets started, they can easily tweak their query. They originally wondered about phenomenon X having effect N on phenomenon Y. They might then get curious about the influences on X or the effects of Y. They might also wonder where else effect N is observed (since existing classification systems focus on nouns rather than verbs this is virtually impossible at present). It is thus quite easy to navigate a related set of causal relationships.

So far, we have spoken only of causal links. Scholars and students will also be curious about what methods and theory types have been applied to a particular causal link. Yet we rarely classify scholarly works in terms of the theories and methods they employ (only works about theories or methods are classified that way, not works applying particular theories or methods). The Basic Concepts Classification includes detailed schedules of methods and theory types to facilitate the classification of all works in these ways. Recall that we can be most confident in any hypothesis if it is supported by evidence from multiple theories and methods. Scholars and students should be able to identify easily whether this is the case or not. They might then be inspired to apply theories or methods to a particular causal link that had not (often) been applied before.

A library can be a forbidding place for even seasoned researchers, much less students. Most specialized researchers may become comfortable with a very limited stretch of the library's shelves, and view the rest as alien territory. It need not be that way. We have seen in chapter 3 that we can imagine a coherent research enterprise. We have seen in chapter 5 that we can imagine a coherent teaching enterprise. Our libraries should reflect and reinforce this coherence. At present, our libraries institutionalize a mistaken impression that scholarship consists of hundreds of distinct topics. Libraries should instead institutionalize an accurate sense of a unified human (and natural) science comprising a set of interrelated causal influences and the application of a finite set of methods and theory types.

Ambiguity Again

Though the approach to library classification advocated above fits very well within the tradition of facet analysis, it appears to conflict with the other key analytic tradition in Knowledge Organization. "Domain analysis" suggests that terminology will only be well understood within a domain. The term "domain" is generally understood to refer to any group with shared understandings of terminology. It is often assumed, though, that disciplines are domains. If so, then domain analysis implies an approach to classification that entrenches the difficulties in interdisciplinary searches noted above. We would have to abandon all hope of a classification that extended beyond single disciplines and resign ourselves to a set of discipline-specific classifications employing terminology generated by the discipline itself. The best we might manage is a set of translation devices across disciplines.

The motivation for domain analysis is the recognition that language is ambiguous. Domain analysts draw upon philosophers such as Wittgenstein to argue that different people will have different understandings of terms. A classification system is of little use if different users interpret the terms used in the classification differently. We must then only classify within communities that will share understandings of key terminology.

A lot of great research has been performed within the domain analytic tradition. Researchers examine particular fields of inquiry seeking to identify the meanings attached to key terminology. Domain analysis can thus be harnessed to the approach recommended above: We can seek to identify key phenomena, relators, and theoretical or methodological terminology in each field.

It is then an empirical question as to whether we can render the terminology of each discipline in a manner such that scholars from both within and beyond the discipline can understand it similarly. Note that we do not need different users to have identical understandings of terminology. If we needed that, we would be doomed for philosophers have long since established that absolute precision in definition is impossible. Indeed, absolute precision is not achievable even within domains. We just need enough shared understanding that diverse users will be able to find what they are looking for. Philosophers have agonized for thousands of years over the fact that we cannot define a word such as "freedom" precisely; this has not at all prevented diverse users from finding books about freedom in our libraries.

The Basic Concepts in the Basic Concepts Classification are defined as concepts for which there is a broadly shared understanding across both disciplines and cultural groups. Economic output, population, and occupation are terms for which we can reasonably anticipate that diverse users will have similar understandings. Other terms such as class or ideology are trickier (and thus we may want to clarify these terms by providing both brief definitions and examples of their use). Even there, we can imagine that most people will have some shared sense of what "working class" or "socialist" mean – though definitions of "conservative" and "liberal" may be harder to pin down. Note, though, that ideologies are likely the vaguest terms in the Basic Concepts Classification. Arguably, diverse users will understand the vast majority of the terms in the classification in quite similar ways.[3]

We should not leap from a recognition of ambiguity to a costly conclusion that there is too much ambiguity for us to even attempt a cross-disciplinary classification. I have had no difficulty in classifying works from all disciplines. I am confident that users from diverse disciplines and cultural backgrounds could readily find works using that classification. Indeed, I am confident that scholars can find works in their own discipline more readily using the Basic Concepts Classification than within existing classification systems.

Summary

- We could classify the resources in our library in terms of causal links and theories and methods applied. This would greatly facilitate integrative research by both scholars and students. It might also facilitate specialized research.
- It is an empirical question as to whether users from different disciplines or cultures can understand terms in a similar enough fashion for the purposes of finding relevant documents. There is good reason to think that a classification that spans disciplines is entirely feasible.

Notes

1 Buvke (2019) devotes several pages in his concluding chapter to advice on how to perform a literature review. This is a common practice in works on research methodology. It need not be so challenging or time-consuming.

2 I also in that chapter and elsewhere have argued that the approach I pursue makes the application of facet analysis easy. Other attempts at facet analysis generally employ "facet indicators" in their notation. In my approach, subject headings are structured as sentence fragments, and the grammatical place of a term indicates its facet: verbs are relators, adjectives are properties, and the place of a noun indicates whether it is subject or object or intermediate. A huge further advantage of a grammatical approach is that humans find it far easier to understand and remember information formulated in the format of a sentence.

3 This is most obviously the case in human science. In natural science, there are a host of terms for species or organs or subatomic particles that may only make sense to experts in a particular field. But even these can be appreciated by outsiders with a bit of effort.

7

INFORMING PUBLIC POLICY

We turn our attention in Chapter 7 to public policy.[1] One obvious point here is that an integrated human science can provide much better policy advice: We will reduce scholarly bias in advice and do a much better job of identifying possible negative side effects of proposed policies. Yet I will also urge a further type of integration: between academics and policy-makers. It is naïve to think that policy-makers will take academic research off the shelf and act upon it. It is much better for academics to engage with policy-makers about the precise problems these face and then collaborate with them in addressing these.

The Advantages of an Integrative Approach to Research

Reduced Bias

We should want the human science enterprise to provide the best possible advice to policy-makers.[2] We have recognized both the strengths and weaknesses of specialized research in earlier chapters. By its very nature, specialized research ignores the insights that might be gained by engaging alternative theories or methods, or by engaging with a broader set of phenomena and causal links. It follows necessarily that integrative research will provide a less biased, more comprehensive understanding. Whereas specialized researchers will tend to provide policy-makers with one perspective on an issue, integrative researchers will report on multiple perspectives and how these can be integrated. This point was recognized by the British Academy (2016, 81): "even if the research findings originate in distinct disciplines, their full value to policymakers will be revealed only after they have been combined into a coherent, IDR package." Notably, this finding reflected extensive surveys with both researchers and policy-makers.

DOI: 10.4324/9781003275237-7

We inhabit a complex world that faces many complex challenges such as climate change and urban poverty. We can best face these if we integrate understandings.[3] Specialized researchers will focus on only a subset of the phenomena and causal links involved. An expert on how X influences Y is too easily tempted to give advice on how W might lead to Z without bothering to consult experts on how W affects X or Y might lead to Z. Only integrative research will try to fit the pieces together. Complex problems will almost inevitably benefit also from the application of different theories and methods.[4]

Smelser and Reed (2012) worry that social science research is not as "usable" for decision-making in the real world as it might be. Their view of the models developed by specialized researchers is worth quoting at length:

> We return to these kinds of models periodically in this book, approaching them from different angles. Our general orientation toward them is mixed. On the one hand, they define decision problems precisely and help enormously in developing scenarios for decision and action—for example, applying economic reasoning to issues such as the impacts of minimum wage, tax levels, and fringe benefits on hiring and spending behavior. At the same time, we regard all such formulas as "unreal" in the sense that in the empirical world, all decisions involve taking many uncertainties and contingencies into account. Almost never are all other things "given" or "equal" or even known. Making those decisions, moreover, often involves uninformed simplifications and mental shortcuts. Only in rare circumstances can a fully rational model be the sole basis for decision-making and assessing consequences. As a result, all such models are best regarded as idealized or normative statements, to be consulted as sensitizers for decision-makers, but not as full scenarios or directives for action.
>
> *(2012, 5)*

We see here much of what we have argued in this book: that specialized research is valuable, that it nevertheless needs to be placed in the context of related causal links, and that we need to exercise collective judgment. These arguments become particularly important for policy-making where the general insights of human scientists need to be tailored to particular situations.

Policy-makers – especially politicians but also some bureaucrats – may have strong preferences of their own with respect to policy. They may thus prefer some of the perspectives summarized by integrative researchers to others. We will still benefit as citizens if they are aware of the full set of options, and guided to choose among perspectives they find appealing, rather than seek out some specialized researcher whose ideas they find congenial. We can hope that in the search for compromise that often guides political decisions, the integrative efforts of integrative researchers, which combine the best elements from the insights of specialized researchers, will gain favor. If not guided by integrative research, it is all too easy for political compromise to enact the worst elements of competing proposals.[5]

Another tangential comment about the culture wars is appropriate here. Since conservative politicians will seek conservative policies, we should want them to have access to academic research that reflects conservative values. If not, they will be forced to conjure policies that may have little grounding in our collective understanding of how the world works. We should want them to advocate for the best policies that are consistent with their perspective. Moreover, we would want them to see, through integrative research, how they might compromise and gain even greater public support for policies that appeal to voters with different guiding principles.[6]

This book has set out to grapple with complexity. We should note that one reasonable response to complexity is to argue that humans will likely never understand the world very well. We should thus be very hesitant to try to change the world for we are quite likely to do more harm than good. This was the position taken by the economist and political philosopher Friedrich Hayek, and many others (Epstein 2015). We can perhaps see the task of human science as advancing our level of understanding to a point where we can have some confidence in our capacity to act in the world. Yet the very act of integrative research should guide us to humility.[7] In attempting to integrate different insights, we should be aware that reasonable people can disagree about how the world works. We can integrate across these differences but should still appreciate that we cannot prove that our integrated understanding is a close approximation of reality. Our integrative efforts are thus ideologically neutral: They can help us to grapple with complexity while warning us that this is no easy thing.

Matthews (2016) argues that we should state public policy analysis in probabilistic terms. Complexity and uncertainty combine to mean that we cannot be sure of the effects of any policy. We should be wary of experts who pretend to certainty. We should strive to increase the probability of good outcomes while minimizing the probability of bad outcomes. This we can only do by exploring all of the potential risks and side effects associated with a particular policy. We should not be frightened into inaction by small risks but nor should we ignore these. Involving academics and the public in policy development is necessary to ensure that all potential effects of a policy are taken into account (Matthews 203). I would add to Matthews' analysis that we need to involve diverse academics (and members of the public) and then integrate their understandings.

Martini and Boumans (2014) explore how social science expertise should influence public policy. While science is spurred forward by disagreement, public policy benefits from consensus.[8] They wonder how we can achieve an unbiased consensus among experts. They also wonder which experts we should trust. Our answer to both questions would be to turn primarily to the community of integrative scholars. Martini and Boumans recognize both the need to appreciate different types of evidence and the role of judgment in interpreting this. These are both points we have made above and in earlier chapters, and can appreciate that they are critical again in the realm of policy analysis. We can likewise concur with them on the danger of achieving consensus among a group of experts that excludes certain perspectives: The only solution is to integrate across all perspectives. One debate is whether voting or deliberation among experts is best. We have urged in this book an ongoing conversation among integrative scholars (and with specialized scholars).[9] Yet we can see where votes among relevant groups of scholars can be very informative. The twin facts that 95 percent of climate scientists believe in human-caused climate change and 95 percent of economists think placing a price on carbon emissions is the best way to arrest this deserve to inform public policy. It is possible that one or both groups is wrong but highly unlikely.

Martini and Boumans (2014) wonder about the nature of expertise itself. Experts are those who can draw on previous experience in suggesting solutions to present challenges. A dentist can draw upon years of training in deciding how best to treat a particular tooth. The dentist's level of confidence will depend on how much this tooth resembles others they have treated. For the human scientist, the danger is that present circumstances may differ from past circumstances in unappreciated ways. An appreciation of contextualized generalizations is thus critical to the exercise of expertise. We need to know as precisely as possible under what conditions a particular causal relationship will hold. Otherwise, we can easily recommend a policy that is not well suited to present realizations of phenomena. There are few things in the world more dangerous than an expert who does not know the limits of their expertise.[10]

Specialized researchers may well protest our suggestion that integrative researchers are better placed to give policy advice. Yet there are several reasons to think so. Integrative researchers communicate multiple perspectives and insights rather than just one. They integrate the best elements of diverse insights. They incorporate evidence from diverse theories and methods. They examine all relevant causal links. They seek to identify contextualized generalizations. They, quite simply, have a much firmer base from which to provide advice. Yet they are guided to be humble and careful in their advice.

Mayer, van Daalen, and Bots (2013) usefully identify six steps in policy analysis: researching the situation, outlining policies to address it, identifying the values and assumptions behind alternative viewpoints, giving strategic advice on how to achieve policy goals, encouraging public understanding and participation, and mediating between competing interests. We have focused so far on the first two of these. We can note here that the other steps depend heavily on understanding why people disagree about both goals and means. We will be better able to inform, persuade, and mediate if we first appreciate where people are coming from. Integrative researchers are experienced in identifying the sources of disagreement and strategies for transcending these.

We could add to Mayer, van Daalen, and Bots' list the important task of evaluating policies after they have been instituted. Here an ability to perform unbiased research becomes particularly important. Bureaucrats that manage a new program, and policy-makers that advocated for it, will have a natural tendency to recognize the good effects of a policy while downplaying its costs and negative side effects (Shapiro 2016). We want an evaluation that dispassionately evaluates *all* of the costs and benefits associated with a particular policy.[11] We also want one that is clear: governments often produce reports that are incomprehensible, and academics can usefully provide analysis that is comprehensive but still comprehensible. The evaluations should also make clear recommendations regarding not just whether the program should continue but if so how it might be improved (Matthews 2016 notes that most program evaluations in OECD countries do not make constructive suggestions for program improvement).

We have talked in earlier chapters of a synergy between specialized and integrative research. We should recognize here a synergy between research and policy. If human science can provide better advice, this will not just benefit public policy but human science itself. Human scientists should still follow their curiosity but will be encouraged to grapple with complex public policy challenges. They will be encouraged to be practical and to engage in conversations that result in sound policy advice. Just as natural science and technology exist in a symbiotic relationship, human science and public policy can do the same.[12]

One challenge in the contemporary world is that many people are suspicious of both governments and academics. One partial solution is transdisciplinarity. "Transdisciplinarity" is a word that has meant many things but today most often signals integration not only within the academy but beyond. A transdisciplinary project investigating a local environment would involve local residents. These would play an active role in the research project, from research design through to final results. One challenge in transdisciplinary research is that community partners are most interested in identifying practical policies while the academic partners are looking for academic publications. Yet the two goals are hardly incompatible, and there have been numerous successful transdisciplinary projects.[13]

Recognition of Side Effects

Bastow et al. (2014) note that a key problem in public policy advice from social sciences is that they "over-claim authoritativeness" and fail to appreciate that their area of expertise is nested within a broader network of causation. They pursue law-like relations that can never be found. By promising more than they can deliver, they have inevitably disappointed. This connected set of problems in policy advice has been touched on in the foregoing but deserves special emphasis. Specialized researchers inevitably know one piece of a larger puzzle – especially when engaging complex policy challenges. They inevitably give advice that reflects their narrow expertise. And this advice is necessarily incomplete. If we want to decrease the popularity of gangs among young men, we likely need to stitch together the insights of psychologists, sociologists, economists, and others. Any one of these will provide policy advice that is unlikely on its own to do much to address the problem. A concerted effort that examines a set of related causal links and identifies a complementary set of interventions is far more likely to achieve results.

Integration is important not just for success in achieving a particular public policy goal. It is critical to avoiding the greatest challenge in modern public policy: avoiding negative side effects. We do not want anti-poverty policies to discourage work or for infrastructure projects to destroy communities. It is all too easy for an expert that is focused on a small set of causal links to be completely oblivious to negative side effects. We should instead be seeking policies that minimize these, or ideally pursue multiple public policy goals simultaneously.[14] This we can only do by integrating across our understandings of a variety of causal links.

Integrating Academics and Policy-Makers

We advocated above an integration of human science research and human science policy-making. We advocate here an integration of human scientists and policy-makers. It is simply naïve for academics to imagine that policy-makers will just take academic research "off the shelf" and apply it. Policy-makers have very particular interests and needs and these are unlikely to be met by academic research unless academics are interacting with policy-makers. (Some) Academic research can then be guided by the specific challenges faced by policy-makers, policy-makers can give advice on research, and as a result policy-makers will feel invested in the academic research that results.[15] It is worth stressing that there should be a two-way conversation: academics influence policy while policy-makers influence what academics research and teach (British Academy 2021, 7).[16] Those academics that have the greatest influence on public policy do so by regularly interacting with policy-makers (Barstow et al. 2014).[17]

Gabriele Bammer of Australian National University has been advocating linkages between integrative research and policy-making for decades. She (and Peter Deane) founded Integration and Implementation Sciences, a network and website that advocates for and provides advice on the interconnected acts of integration and policy implementation.[18] Bammer urges a separate discipline of integration and implementation scientists whereas I imagine such people strewn across the academy (but hopefully interacting as a community). As noted in the next chapter, the best way to organize integration in the academy is unclear. It would be no bad thing if some universities developed a unit whose twin goals were integration and interaction with policy-makers.

As noted in the previous section, it is valuable for academics and policy-makers to draw the wider public into their conversations. Transdisciplinary research is one important way of doing so. Yet academics can also do much good through maintaining relationships with community groups, advocacy groups, and media, among others.[19] Muhonen, Benneworth, and Olos-Peñuela (2020) identify sixteen types of policy collaboration including media dissemination of research, publications intended for the wider public, educating policy-makers, performing research in response to social needs, and several types of interactions with policy-makers.[20]

Barstow et al. (2014) interviewed large numbers of academics. They found that some think that there is a division of academic labor where some do research and others are great communicators to the public and policy-makers; while others think that the same people often do both. They compiled measures of both publications and policy impact for large numbers of scholars in many fields, and found some truth in both hypotheses. Some academics do specialize in providing policy advice while others do both research and policy advice. We can easily imagine a future, then, where many scholars pursue both integration and implementation, but others specialize in one or the other. In the latter case, those giving policy advice will need to be closely associated with those doing integrative research.

Barstow et al. (2014) also appreciate that some scholars focus on giving advice aimed at political parties or advocacy groups rather than bureaucrats. They applaud these efforts for "speaking truth to power," while remaining aware of the inherent limits of social inquiry. They note that academics may have an important indirect impact on policy by interacting with advocacy groups – and media – that may in turn influence government policy. We also can applaud efforts to give sound advice to all who are active in policy creation. We can see the advantages of working in collaboration with parties or advocacy groups. The obvious danger to avoid is twisting the facts to serve partisan interests. Interactions with media may be safer – and blog posts safer still – but the impacts on public policy are hard to measure.[21]

Barstow et al. (2014) also look at academic relationships with business. They find that the hard part is firms and academics finding each other and establishing a relationship; once they do so they have little difficulty sustaining this. They calculate that one in 200 employees in government, business, and civil society organizations have a job of digesting social science research for their organizations. This is a vast number of people who would benefit from integrative research. In the absence of this, they are each forced to perform their own surveys of the literature. This repetition of activity is incredibly wasteful. Moreover, many of these employees may lack integrative skills and thus can at best provide their organizations with a bewildering array of insights from different authors.

Educating Future Policy-Makers

Where do policy-makers come from? What about the one in 200 employees identified just above by Barstow et al. (2014)? Most of these will have university degrees. Vanishingly few will have been taught how to integrate during their education. Almost none will have been invited to grapple with the complexity of the human science enterprise. Few will have deep familiarity with more than one or two of the methods employed in human science. Their educations, that is, will not have equipped them as well as they could to appreciate diverse kinds of research and then identify the best policies. The sorts of educational reforms that we have advocated in Chapter 5 would, among other things, better prepare the next generations of policy-makers.

Our public policy programs in particular should stress integrative skills. Yet those programs tend to focus on political science, usually with a strong dose of economics. They focus on how policy processes work more than on how to iden-tify the best policy. In Szostak (2005b), I responded to three criticisms of public policy programs by DeLeon and Steelman (2001). They had worried that policy programs do not educate students on how to first identify policy goals. I pointed out that the sort of integrated understanding of ethics advocated in Chapter 5 could guide students in setting policy goals that would be widely appreciated. They worried that students were taught a limited set of theories and methods as if these were the only possible theories and methods. I urged a more nuanced appre-ciation of the strengths and weaknesses of different methods and types of theories. They worried that teaching in public policy programs abstracts away from the complexity of the world. Students are taught a set of cases in such a way that only certain key elements of those cases are highlighted. I advocated a broader approach where students would be acquainted with the entire map of human science, and encouraged to identify potential side effects of policies. Sadly, those recommenda-tions remain as important today as they were 15 years ago.

Summary

- Integrative research will better inform public policy. It will be less biased and more comprehensive.
- In particular, it will identify how combined interventions can best achieve policy goals, and will limit negative side effects on other policy goals.
- (Some) Human scientists should interact regularly with policy-makers. There is a symbiosis here that will lead to both better policy and better human science.
- The educational reforms advocated in Chapter 5 will better prepare the policy-makers of the future. They should infuse public policy programs in particular.

Notes

1 We may under-appreciate the myriad ways in which human science research influences policy. Chambers (2017, Preface) cites a British report that identified some 450 policy impacts of psychological research alone, including "the design and uptake of electric cars, strategies for minimizing exam anxiety, the development of improved police interviewing techniques that account for the limits of human memory, setting of urban speed limits based on discoveries in vision science, human factors that are important for effective space exploration, government strategies for dealing with climate change that take into account public perception of risk, and plain packaging of tobacco products."

2 Greenwood and Levin (2008) worry that much social science research has no policy relevance. They attribute this mostly to strong disciplinary structures in which each discipline has developed internal criteria for success and backed away from complex real-world concerns. They also worry that there is not enough sustained contact between academics and policy-makers, a matter we return to below. Maxwell (2020, 159) criticizes the academy for not addressing the key questions about how to improve society, and for focusing on small questions without tying these together. Maxwell concludes (p. 174) that the basic academic task should be to identify social problems and solutions, and then educate the world on how to implement these.

3 The same conclusion is reached (for all of science) by Renn (2020, 415) from a history of science perspective: "To conclude, the very possibility of addressing our current global challenges continues to depend on processes of knowledge integration based on globally shared experiences and mediated by critical reflection that includes the societal conditions for the evolution of knowledge as well as its eschatological dimension." Renn recognizes, as we have, that we need to respect the value of curiosity-driven science, reform our teaching, and communicate better with the wider public.

4 Martini and Boumans (2014) urge theory and method plurality in search of consensus, which can then guide policy. Smelser and Reed (2012, 289) conclude a chapter exploring various methods employed in human science with the observation that "each method carries both strengths and weaknesses with respect to its transferability to practical settings—that is, its usability." Mobley (2021) also urges the integration of theories, methods, and concepts from different disciplines.

5 Indeed, politicians might be tempted to bargain for the least appealing elements of their desired policies, hoping that they can achieve the more appealing elements later. This strategy might gain them more favor with lobbyists than urging elements that seems like common sense.

6 Daniels (2021, ch. 4) urges universities to hire conservative faculty to mentor conservative students and to encourage constructive conversations. He cites John Stuart Mill to the effect that democracy depends on interacting with those who differ from us, and notes that universities are one of the few places where diverse people are thrown together. Universities can thus do much to model constructive respectful discourse for students. He worries that universities are becoming less open to engaging opposing points of view. See also Marks (2021) on the importance of reasonable discourse among scholars with different perspectives.

7 Shapiro (2016) urges another sort of humility. Policy-makers are likely to ignore proposals for dramatic changes. Analysts may accomplish more by suggesting smaller changes that are easier to achieve. Though Shapiro is guided by dozens of interviews with key policy-makers and analysts, I think there is still value in placing more radical suggestions before policy-makers and the public.

8 "Most people seeking knowledge useful for making decisions do not understand what the wars between disciplines, within disciplines, and among paradigms are all about, and if they did, they would likely conclude that academics are wasting their time, and certainly not producing anything like knowledge that might be usable" (Smelser and Reed 2012, 331–332).

9 Bastow et al. (2014) urge a more coherent social science effort. They think that if disciplinary organizations worked together as STEM fields do, they could encourage greater institutional support for academic research influencing policy. Gorard (2017) worries that social science does not influence policy as much as it could because much research is poorly designed. Integrative research can build on the best elements of research programs and suggest improvements.

10 Economists, I might note, have been guilty of lots of simplistic advice in recent decades. This has at times been because of simplistic views of human behavior (not appreciating that bankers will do foolhardy things if facing losses and not prevented by regulations), or neglect of the importance of institutions (rapid privatization in the Soviet Union of course led to massive corruption because institutions to patrol insider trading and other abuses were not in place).

11 Shapiro worries that critical evaluations will often be ignored. Yet his analysis suggests that this will not be the case if the costs greatly exceed the benefits.

12 I noted in chapter 1 that this book is associated with but distinct from Szostak (2022) in which I develop a set of strategies for public policy. A more integrated human science can very much help guide us toward desirable futures.

13 The Network for Transdisciplinary Research, sponsored by the Swiss Academies, operates a very useful website at https://transdisciplinarity.ch/en and hosts regular conferences. Hirsch Hadorn et al. (2008) provide an overview as well as 21 case studies. We have not often used the word "transdisciplinarity" in this book because of our focus on the internal workings of the academy, but transdisciplinarity builds upon the integrative approach that we have advocated throughout. The British Academy (2021, 32) concurs that public and community engagement can reduce the distrust of experts. The Organization for Economic Cooperation and Development (2020) urged governments and universities to collaborate in transdisciplinary research, and further urged universities to adjust hiring and career progress decisions, teach about transdisciplinarity, develop links to the community, and share best practices in pursuit of this goal.

14 If you doubt that this is possible, I invite you to peruse Szostak (2022).

15 "The analysis of successful projects shows that the involvement of these stakeholders is necessary to realise impact. It means going beyond a mere dissemination of results, allowing the creation of real collaborations that include discussions to agree on the very content of the project and the co-creation of knowledge in the framework of the project; this can have social, political and scientific impacts" (Aiello et al. 2021, 138).

16 The British Academy worried that it is hard to measure – and thus encourage – this sort of ongoing collaboration. So do Muhonen, Benneworth, and Olos-Peñuela (2020). Reale et al. (2018) appreciate that it is hard to measure the social or policy impact of research, though considerable effort is now devoted to doing so.

17 Barstow et al. find that a key challenge is maintaining relationships since bureaucrats (in the United Kingdom) move between departments a lot and are often required to make open tenders for policy work. Policy-makers often complain that academics are too slow and impractical, while academics complain that it is hard to keep track of changing personnel and priorities and to react quickly to windows of opportunity.

18 See https://i2s.anu.edu.au/ I have had the pleasure of publishing a couple of blogs on the I2S website and have been impressed by the quality of responses these have received.

19 Lyall (2021) provides a very useful set of tips on policy advice. She encourages interactions with policy intermediaries and communication via social media.

20 As noted elsewhere, academic communication to the public will be distrusted if academics are perceived to be either biased or arrogant (see Daniels 2021).

21 Aiello et al. (2021) recommend a type of public dissemination that encourages feedback.

8

ADMINISTERING TRANSFORMATION; TRANSFORMING ADMINISTRATION

This book has started from a simple observation that all human science phenomena interact. From that simple but under-appreciated fact, we have derived a set of recommendations for a coherent, integrated human science that appreciates the strengths and weaknesses of different methods and theories, and pursues terminological clarity. The simplicity of our argument deserves emphasis: Our recommendations flow readily from this one observation. Yet the recommendations are at odds with the vast bulk of human science practice. Most human science researchers (implicitly or explicitly) ignore the relationships between the phenomena they study and any other phenomena. Most human science researchers reify one or two methods. Most human science researchers are entirely comfortable with an unnecessarily wasteful enterprise that does not make a concerted effort to tie the insights of specialized researchers into a coherent whole. Most human scientists are far more interested in disciplinary Majors than reflecting on either interdisciplinary practices or what all students need to know (see Chapter 5).

Specialized researchers may wish simply to ignore our analysis. They have succeeded within the existing system, and identified research agendas and teaching practices that they find congenial. They will find change – even a set of changes that promise to make their efforts more productive and meaningful – threatening. They have been trained for many years to believe that their subsystems are effectively closed and their methods superior, and will not let go lightly of such core beliefs. We can calm but not erase these fears by stressing the symbiosis between specialized and integrative research, and by sharing a vision of a more productive human science enterprise that facilitates better teaching and policy advice.

The intellectual case for our recommendations is strong. We might quibble a bit about how strong the causal interactions are across subsystems, but there can be little doubt that they are potentially strong enough to merit greater investigation.

DOI: 10.4324/9781003275237-8

There can be little doubt that the existing human science enterprise is forgetful. We can show so easily that all methods (and theories) have both strengths and weaknesses. The disadvantages of terminological confusion and unnecessarily ambiguous styles of presentation are painfully obvious (even to those who might argue that I have under-appreciated alleged advantages). Our recommendations mesh nicely with those of other scholars worried about inadequate progress in humanities or social science.

I am skeptical, though, that this battle will be won on the plane of ideas alone. As with any social change, we can expect that the greatest resistance will come from those who have succeeded the most within the existing disjointed approach to human science. Those who garner the most citations may worry about how integrative research will treat them. Those who have instigated academic fads will mourn the decline of faddishness. Those who are famous for one idea may have much to lose from stitching ideas into a coherent whole. Those who provide narrow policy advice will not welcome the arrival of more integrated advice. Finally yet importantly, those who administer universities will have a natural urge to protect the system that nurtured them.

Thoughts on Administrative Structures

Though the ideal administrative structure for a university may not be obvious, we can at least identify what we want that structure to achieve:

- More and better integrative research, both within and across fields
- More and better integrative teaching, both within and across fields
- Increased respect for methodological diversity in both research and teaching
- Enhanced pursuit of the questions identified in Chapter 4 in both research and teaching
- Teaching of the core material identified in Chapter 5
- Fair systems of evaluation that do not punish integrative researchers or teachers

Having spent the last few years of my career as a department chair fighting turf battles over financial resources, I think there is a lot to be said for transparency in resource allocation. I think that my time is far better allocated to human science research than to battling with other chairs and a dean over funding. *Much better allocated.* I have thus become a big advocate for funding to largely follow students. We should strive for a broad coverage of human science. We should give students a good idea of the career prospects associated with various degree programs, and then let students choose. The vast bulk of student tuition (and any government grants for teaching those students) should follow them into their programs of study and any General Education courses that they take (with, of course, some slice taken off the top for university administration: it is no bad thing if students know how big this slice is).[1] Practices whereby some students subsidize others should be viewed with suspicion. Students in all human science courses should do lots of written (or video) work, engage in class discussions, and make presentations. There may of course be cases where a university decides that a certain program is important to its mission even if student numbers do not justify it.[2] However, such exceptions should be rare and well justified – and regularly reviewed. There should also be a funding envelope for experiments with new course offerings – but these should be expected to fund themselves after a couple of years. Such a funding model can be invaluable for interdisciplinary programs. These are often the first to be cut in budget crises even if student numbers are buoyant, due to the simple fact that disciplines tend to wield more power in most universities (Augsburg and Henry 2009 speak of "disciplinary hegemony").[3]

Courses within disciplines are often integrative, trying to give students an overview of a particular field of inquiry. We can hope that disciplinary departments going forward will find it useful to hire some integrative researchers. We will discuss below some reasons why this might prove advantageous. Since research universities are predicated on the synergy between research and teaching, we can imagine that integrative researchers will be well suited to teaching integrative material.

That still leaves a question of how best to institutionalize interdisciplinary programs.[4] One option is to create interdisciplinary departments. Another is to cross-appoint professors between disciplinary departments and interdisciplinary teaching programs. The latter practice may dis-serve scholars with no clear disciplinary home. Yet it might give interdisciplinary programs some support in disciplinary departments. Neither strategy has proven perfect.[5] But the sort of funding model advocated above could strengthen both options. Interdisciplinary departments would be funded just like disciplinary departments. In the case of cross-appointed faculty, student numbers would still translate into a certain number of (partial) faculty positions. The alternative to a funding formula is somehow to ensure administrative support for interdisciplinarity. Wernli and Darbellay (2016) urge research universities to institutionalize interdisciplinary research and teaching from the top. Some senior administrator needs to take responsibility, ensure adequate budget allocation, ensure space allocation that puts interdisciplinary research teams together, provide training in interdisciplinary strategies, and ensure sensitivity in tenure and promotion practices to the fact that interdisciplinary research often takes longer and is published in outlets that disciplinary scholars may be unfamiliar with. Such practices are valuable even if a transparent funding formula is in place.

Our analysis in Chapter 4 raised some important questions about how to structure human science disciplines. If we had a magic wand and could re-engineer human science from scratch, we would wish to have human science disciplines organized around the ten subsystems or sets of causal links addressed in Chapter 4. We might lump the two individual-level subsystems together into a department of Psychology. We might leave Economics and Political Science in place, but urge them to both change their priorities and embrace a wider range of methods. But no other extant discipline serves to anchor the specialized study of only one subsystem or set of causal links.[6] Can we group together the various scholars who study culture (excluding those who study art but call it culture) into one discipline? Can we provide some sort of disciplinary umbrella in which those who study visual art, music, or literature can recognize their common concerns? Can we break sociology and anthropology into disciplines that make logical sense?[7] Should we fashion new disciplines to address technology/science, population/health, or the human science component of environmental studies? I hesitate to encourage enlightened administrators to force a logical division of labor from above, but fear that scholarly inertia will limit innovation from below. The sociologists that exist today managed to be hired into sociology departments as they exist, and have fashioned careers within such departments, and may be fearful of change. The ideal division of labor in human science is obvious but the path to get there from where we are is unclear. Yet I would note that disciplines inevitably evolve through time, taking on new topics while paying less attention to others, and thus a widespread appreciation of the nature of human science as a whole might encourage evolution toward a more logical set of specialized research and teaching communities.

Universities may also wish to award scholars and perhaps departments for research excellence. If they do so, they need to reward all types of research excellence. We will get virtually no integrative research if universities only reward specialized research. And we will have gaps in understanding if universities only fund certain fields.[8] This is not to say that universities should not pursue research clusters of scholars with related expertise. However, universities – and especially government funding agencies – should be careful not to privilege some research questions at the expense of others.

One insidious practice in the modern university is to award scholars and departments for the amount and size of research grants they receive. There is a certain logic to this practice: universities cream off some research grant funds to cover administrative costs, research grants often employ (especially graduate) students, and (perhaps most importantly) universities brag to local governments about the amount of money they bring in to the community. Yet as taxpayers, we should all be horrified. Universities and scholars regularly complain that governments do not put enough money into funding research. Yet those same universities encourage those same scholars to apply for grants *that they do not need.* I remember a glorious time mere decades ago when we valued research grants for the research they made possible. Historians need to visit archives and psychologists need labs in which to run experiments. Without research grants, valuable research in these fields could not be done. Some other fields require far less funding: a scholar of literature or philosophy may just need access to a good library, and many economists just need a good computer and access to publicly available data.[9] It is often harder for researchers in these fields to train students than to do the work themselves. Integrative work by its nature tends to be less expensive than specialized research: the integrative scholar needs a good library (that subscribes to most journals and can get its hand on most books) and needs probably to attend multiple conferences annually.[10] For the project of this book, then, this now-common practice of rewarding departments and scholars for getting big grants will mean that some causal links are studied more than others are and integrative work will be less valued than it should be.

Government granting agencies could stop this stupidity. They could refuse to provide grants to those universities that provide financial incentives for scholars to obtain grants. Note that I have no objection to universities having research offices that help scholars write grant proposals. These serve a valuable function in allowing scholars to spend more time doing research and less time applying for funding. My objection is to funding formulas that reward departments for the number and size of grants received, and to evaluations of scholars that treat getting a grant as being valuable in its own right rather than as a necessary input into the publications that the scholar should be judged on.[11]

If we could wean universities from glorifying big grants, they might then recognize that some scholars just need some thousands of dollars annually for attending conferences, buying computers, and buying books. It is rather silly to pay decent salaries but force such scholars to waste time and effort groveling for smallish funds to be able to do their jobs. We should be happy that some scholars have limited needs, help them meet those needs, and not force them to get in the way of others in competitions for large grants.

We can also celebrate the successes of interdisciplinary research centers both within and across universities. These tend to be focused on particular topics and serve a critical function in drawing together academics from diverse backgrounds with shared interests.[12] These scholars are then better able to identify innovative interdisciplinary research questions and mixed methods approaches. Such centers are often then able to advocate for further policies to support interdisciplinarity. Universities often establish such centers in the hopes of applying for large external grants, but they can nevertheless serve as incubators (and seed funders) for exciting interdisciplinary research.[13] There is now a ton of advice on how best to manage interdisciplinary team research,[14] and institutes can strive to ensure that researchers associated with the institute are aware of best practices. Note, though, that there is a "critical mass" problem here: integrative research centers or teaching programs are best evaluated by peers who will not judge these by the standards of specialized research and teaching, but this is only possible when there is a large number of such programs or centers in a country, and especially interdisciplinary graduate training of researchers and teachers (Litre, Lindoso, and Bursztyn 2022 make this point in the Brazilian context but it has wide applicability).

We should pay special attention to issues of career progress. If we want to have integrative research and teaching, we need to ensure that there are career opportunities for scholars interested in integrative research and teaching. We noted at the start of Chapter 5 that there are important synergies between integrative research and integrative teaching. We can stress another synergy here: The combination of integrative research and integrative teaching should generate many jobs for integrative scholars. At present, such scholars may struggle to find stable employment. This challenge is felt especially strongly in Europe, where there are still very few interdisciplinary teaching programs.[15] This is a theme that runs through many of the documents generated by the European Union's Shape-ID project. The British Academy (2016, 8) while finding "a broad and deep support for IDR" from those it surveyed due primarily to "its essential role in addressing complex problems and research questions posed by global social challenges," nevertheless recommended against pursuing interdisciplinarity early in a career. They instead recommend establishing a disciplinary home first, and maintaining disciplinary expertise. They did so despite appreciating that interdisciplinarity requires unique skills. Lyall (2019) found that many British scholars who had been supported to pursue interdisciplinary PhDs thereafter struggled to find permanent posts but rather cobbled together temporary jobs on interdisciplinary research projects.[16] The situation is better in North America where there are a much larger number of interdisciplinary teaching programs. Yet even there interdisciplinary scholars are often urged to have a disciplinary home for career safety (Holley and Szostak 2022).[17]

Once hired, the integrative scholar faces the challenge in many institutions that specialized scholars will evaluate them. They often suffer in tenure, promotion, and salary decisions by being judged by disciplinary/specialized standards. We have in Chapter 4 identified a set of rigorous standards by which integrative research might be evaluated. Pohl and Fletcher (2021) provide a useful set of tips on evaluating interdisciplinary research. One that deserves emphasis is to appreciate that it takes time to forge interdisciplinary research teams. The Association for Interdisciplinary Studies has a set of guidelines for tenure and promotion decisions on its website at https://interdisciplinarystudies.org/ (under Resources). It is thus entirely feasible for universities to evaluate integrative scholarship fairly. Appropriate guidelines need to be followed by those making decisions.[18]

Barry and Born (2014) stress the importance of contingency: No administrative structure can guarantee the success of interdisciplinary endeavors.[19] The personal characteristics of administrators may be of crucial importance.[20] We may, then, need to change institutional cultures as much or more than institutional structures. Indeed, it is widely understood in the general literature on institutions that these will only function well if supported by cultural values. Think of the challenges that governments face in enforcing laws against drugs or littering if (large swathes of) the public are not supportive of such laws. We have identified several ideas for an improved institutional structure but should stress in closing that these can only operate well if the academy comes to appreciate the value of integration.[21]

Overcoming Academic Inertia

We need first to realize that institutional inertia is powerful in academia (Daniels, Shreve, and Spector 2021). There are, first of all, powerful financial barriers to change. Some readers may be surprised that I start with financial issues rather than with intellectual barriers to change. Yet universities like any big organization have procedures that allocate funds to various activities. Any change – such as encouraging a greater amount of integrative research or teaching – must mean moving money from one place to another. I can assure the reader that department chairs will not let a single penny slip away without a fight – regardless of how worthy the transfer may be. It might be hoped that a group of academics could have a sensible conversation about the university's priorities, recognize that these need to be changed, and agree to a reallocation of resources. I have seen no sign that this is possible. The potential losers will marshal arguments in their defense to be sure, but these may be very thinly disguised expressions of self-interest.

As in any organization, those with the most decision-making power are those who have succeeded under existing rules. In most universities, this means that specialized researchers rather than integrative researchers occupy senior positions. This is why Augsburg and Henry (2009) speak of disciplinary hegemony. This is why Wernli and Darbellay (2016) stress the importance of a senior administrator with power to support interdisciplinarity. This is (in large part) why I encourage transparent budgetary mechanisms.

Intellectual barriers reinforce the financial barriers to change. Recall again that humans substitute questions they know how to answer for questions that are hard to answer. Scholars know how to do specialized research. Communities of specialized scholars have developed standards for judging specialized research. Their self-image is tied up with their participation in a community with clear standards. It takes an act of will, and threatens positions of power and influence, to recognize that we need to do something more to answer the questions that humanity cares about.[22]

Academic reputations and expertise – and thus the sense of self-worth of many academics – at present depend on knowing a lot about one little thing. There will be inevitable resistance to the idea of tying these little bits into a bigger whole. It is natural to think that the thing you know is the most important thing in the world. In time, experts may come to recognize the value of placing one's expertise in context, but the transition will be difficult. Doctors, we might note, are often hesitant to participate in medical teams precisely because these dilute their authority, despite compelling evidence that patient care can be enhanced.

How, then, might those in positions of power come to accept that change is desirable? It is important to appreciate here that universities compete with each other. They compete for students and they compete for faculty members, and they compete for reputations in order to attract both. University presidents have been giving lip service to interdisciplinarity for decades now, though their actions have rarely matched their words. If they become convinced that integration both within and across fields is of critical importance moving forward, they will hire integrative researchers, and make sure that these are not penalized by tenure and promotion standards. They will create integrative courses for these faculty members to teach, and to attract students by offering a more coherent curriculum. There can be a huge first-mover advantage here, in that institutions that develop a reputation for integrative research and teaching will find it easier to attract both faculty members and students well into the future.

The diversity of universities in the world increases the likelihood that some will be enticed by a change in vision. A bold new strategy may be most attractive to universities keen to move up the rankings.[23] It may be particularly attractive to universities fearful of declining enrolments or facing financial pressures. It may be easier for smaller universities to agree on a new vision. Universities dedicated to serving their communities or preparing their students for lifelong learning may find that integration and coherence resonate with their mission.[24] Once a few universities pursue a more coherent and integrative vision, and find success in doing so, others will follow.

There are important financial advantages of doing so. Most kinds of integrative research are less expensive than specialized research. The integrative researcher often needs only a good library and the ability to attend conferences. Integrative research should then be attractive to universities that struggle to finance the research initiatives of their faculty members. Such universities could provide successful integrative researchers (that is, those who publish regularly in good outlets) with a few thousand dollars annually to attend conferences. This would make it easier to find the much larger sums that (some) specialized researchers need for data, laboratories, or trips to the archives. It would also allow the funding of the more expensive sort of interdisciplinary research in which teams apply multiple methods in pursuit of answers to complex questions. Unfortunately, as noted above, universities these days often value researchers for their ability to obtain grants from outside agencies. They are thus blind to the potential advantage of having a group of researchers that may never require huge grants. If granting agencies would change the rules of the game, as recommended above, then universities would be far more interested in hiring integrative researchers.

The present scholarly enterprise is incredibly wasteful. Some waste is inevitable: the scholarly community will find some ideas better than other ideas over time and cast away the ideas that seem misguided (but note here that a good integrative effort will tend to find some value in research programs even if the core hypotheses may seem misguided). Yet two kinds of waste are avoidable. One is the regrettable tendency for scholars to "reinvent the wheel" by duplicating research of which they were not aware. This might count as replication – but, crucially, not if they do not know about the work they are replicating. The second is that not all scholars are successful at specialized research. We reviewed in Chapter 2 the standards that should guide both specialized and integrative research. These are similar in some ways but different in others. Some scholars may thus be good at both while others may excel at only one. It is likely, then, that some of those that add little to the body of specialized research will find that they have a capacity for integrative research. These underemployed resources can be put to work at little net cost.[25] University administrators may not be too worried about the first kind of waste – unless it affects publications or citation counts – but may be keenly interested in reducing the second kind of waste.

There may also be savings on the teaching side. Integrative researchers, and especially interdisciplinary researchers, will generally be able to teach a wider range of courses than their specialized counterparts will. Smaller universities may especially find it congenial to hire integrative scholars who can teach in multiple areas. Yet all universities should have an interest in hiring integrative scholars to teach the core materials outlined in Chapter 5.[26] It may prove easier to change the way we teach than the way we do research. Yet the former will encourage the latter: The people we hire or encourage to do integrative teaching will be more likely to do interdisciplinary research, and their students will grow accustomed to integrative thinking. The next generation will be even more integrative.

At this moment in history, some universities and some regions of the world have proceeded farther in institutionalizing interdisciplinary teaching and research. Those universities and regions have an obvious advantage in further changing institutions and culture going forward. For institutions that are dominated by specialized research and teaching, there must first be an acceptance (not necessarily unanimous but extensive) of the synergies that we have outlined between specialized and integrative scholarship.[27] Yet such universities have a potential advantage in that they can learn from others what administrative strategies have worked best in encouraging a productive balance between specialized and integrative research and teaching.

Though I started this section with financial arguments, I would appreciate in closing that we need to make a powerful intellectual argument in favor of integration, methodological plurality, care in defining terminology and expressing argument, and pursuing epistemological integration. We need, that is, what Frickel and Gross (2005) call a Scientific/Intellectual Movement. This involves a group of scholars who are self-conscious about their shared goals, and cognizant of the need to challenge existing power structures within academia. Scholars within such a movement may disagree on many points but work together on a shared agenda.[28] In the case of the agenda outlined in this book, this means both fleshing out the academic case for an integrated human science and figuring out how best to instantiate this administratively. Frickel and Gross suggest that such movements are more likely to succeed when high-status individuals are unhappy with the status quo; when members of the movement can gain resources (and especially jobs, but also intellectual prestige); when conferences and graduate training come to support the movement: and when movement members are able to articulate core ideas in a manner that resonates with others. We have suggested above how resources might be available. We can hope that academic competition, and concerns that human science is not as successful in advancing our understanding as it could be, will attract influential people who will make compelling arguments. The fact that the various proposals made in this book flow from the simple observation that the phenomena studied in different disciplines interact should facilitate the articulation of a shared vision – but one that clearly will offend the sensibilities of scholars who define themselves in terms of their discipline.

Changes beyond the University

Changes within the university may be encouraged by changes outside it. We spoke of granting agencies above. These could wean universities from wasteful practices with respect to research grants. They could also encourage the pursuit of the big questions we identified in Chapter 4. Moreover, they could encourage the application of a wider range of theories and methods to these and other questions. They could exhibit a far greater understanding of the characteristics of quality interdisciplinary team research. If granting agencies could force universities to see research grants as the means to an end of quality research, and simultaneously move to better fund the sorts of research that we need more of, universities will in turn be encouraged to hire and nurture researchers interested in those types of research.

Governments could act to create closer contacts between academics and policy-makers. As we argued in Chapter 7, this should encourage both better policy and better research and teaching. Universities do generally see giving policy advice as one of their roles. It is, though, not particularly easy to measure the impact of academic research on public policy.

Governments and granting agencies might encourage an even more profound change in the way scholarship operates. Many granting agencies have already started to insist that the research they finance be made readily available. That is, it should not be published in journals that are expensive to subscribe to. Many journals now publish in an Open Access format. This move on its own can facilitate integrative research. As noted above, the integrative researcher today needs access to a good library: a library that subscribes to most/all journals and buys (access to) lots of books (see Gamsby 2020). Scholars at universities with limited library budgets may struggle to do integrative research.

I wonder if the Open Science movement will create an opening for the publication of something other than the standard research article. We have recognized throughout this book that scholarship is a conversation. It is thus worthwhile for us to reflect on how we might address shortcomings in that conversation. We have discussed above possibilities such as brief reports of stylized facts, the recognition of gaps in the literature, or the posing of questions.[29] Perhaps we can develop some standards for each of the above type of contributions. And of course we need much greater scope for the publication of integrative research. We have suggested the standards by which this could be judged in Chapter 2. Our map of human science may be helpful here in providing a clear structure in which to place new ideas: for example, we do not know much about the link from X to Y but it may be important (especially to scholars that study X or Y). Some journals already focus on short papers, and so it should not be inconceivable that these various types of publication could be encouraged. Should existing journals take on new tasks or should new journals emerge to cater to new needs? Perhaps a bit of both. Who will pay for this? There are several models of Open Access being tested in the world and each might be expanded to embrace a wider range of types of publication.

Chambers (2017) in his concluding chapter champions a system suggested by others of an online platform that referees papers for quality (perhaps in stages) but also allows post-publication ratings and comments that can raise the paper's profile on the platform. Note that novelty becomes important after publication rather than before.[30] Chambers hopes that such a system would facilitate replication and reduce the bias toward only publishing positive results (see Chapter 3). Yet such a platform could easily be tweaked to facilitate the broader range of publications that we have advocated.[31]

We can think even more boldly. Imagine a website that regularly published jargon-free surveys of the literatures on each causal link or subsystem in human science – or on complex questions that involve interactions across multiple links. This could be a wonderful resource for people everywhere, and particularly for those engaged in policy-making or policy advocacy. It could guide them to further reading if they wanted to pursue particular ideas further. (They could easily follow their own curiosity if our libraries were organized around phenomena and causal links; see chapter 6). Such a website might allow journalists to more readily analyze policy proposals. Rather than finding random sources to laud or pillory it, they could see what the scholarly literature says about the issue in question, and maybe follow up with those often cited in integrative works, or the authors of the integrative works themselves.[32]

The public pays for most of the research performed in the world. It should not be so hard for the public to access that information. The sort of website mentioned above would not be costless, but its cost would be a miniscule proportion of the funds at present devoted to research. Such a website would be valuable to scholars too: it will give them a more complete view of their own fields and make it much easier for them to draw upon related fields. It will likewise be useful to students for precisely the same reasons. Finally, it will encourage scholars and students to recognize and seek to fill gaps in the literature identified by integrative works – while in no way limiting them from following their own curiosity.

Summary

- We want universities to support more integrative research, both within and across fields; more integrative teaching, both within and across fields; increased respect for methodological diversity in both research and teaching; enhanced pursuit of the questions identified in Chapter 4 in both research and teaching; teaching of the core material identified in Chapter 5; and fair systems of evaluation that do not punish integrative researchers or teachers.

- Transparent systems of resource allocation save time, reduce the intensity of turf wars, and provide safety for interdisciplinary programming.
- Human science disciplines are not structured logically around human science subsystems.
- Granting agencies should discourage universities from encouraging scholars to apply for grants they do not need. This would in turn cause universities to better appreciate research that is inexpensive.
- There is powerful inertia within universities but the diversity of universities creates possibilities of innovation toward more integrative structures. These should prove both intellectually and financially beneficial, and thus encourage imitation.
- A Scientific/intellectual movement is needed to change institutional cultures.
- Governments and granting agencies can push universities in beneficial directions.
- Open Access publishing may generate opportunities for a wider variety of publication, which would in turn support a more coherent and cumulative research enterprise.

Notes

1 Smith (2021) worries that our funding of academic research is thus determined by student's choices about courses to take. He worries in particular that this may delay the funding of research as new fields open. Such a delay will be shorter if new courses are created in new fields, and funding follows students. Universities might nevertheless devote some funding to interdisciplinary research institutes.
2 What to do with programs that are expensive to offer (say, because of labs). When possible, student tuition should be adjusted to reflect the cost of programming. If this is not possible, the university should be transparent that it is transferring funds from one group of students to another.
3 Lyall (2019, 111) discusses how battles over resources distract from sensible discussions of the best curriculum for students. Departments instead focus on what is best for them.
4 Lyall (2022, 15) observes that virtually every university in the United Kingdom lauds interdisciplinarity in their strategic plans. "Nevertheless, UK higher education largely remains structured on a conventional, disciplinary basis and is still grappling with the complexity of how to manage institutional structures unsuited for interdisciplinary teaching."
5 Holley (2017) concurs that there is no recognized administrative structure best suited to interdisciplinarity.
6 Smelser and Reed (2012, 322–323) look at the fields within social science disciplines, and find that these also represent a complex historical development rather than a rational plan. They note that the emergence of diverse fields, plus the increased importance of interdisciplinarity, have decreased the importance of disciplines – but that these maintain institutional importance.
7 This judgment may seem harsh. But we can ask an empirical question (hinted at in Chapter 4): Are the causal links between population, social structure, and culture (three categories of phenomena studied by sociologists) stronger than the links between any of these and economy or polity? We could add criminology to the

mix, another topic primarily addressed by sociologists, despite the fact it is at least as strongly linked to politics as to the other topics addressed by sociologists. Nor is there any obvious reason to think that the theory types or methods that are applied in studying these four classes of phenomena should be more similar to each other than to those applied elsewhere in human science.

8 Lyall (2022) reports that university administrators in the UK often speak of wishing to support interdisciplinarity but in practice their pursuit of government funding for research excellence is focused almost entirely on disciplinary measures of research excellence. Interdisciplinary research and researchers inevitably suffer. Litre et al. (2022) report on a dramatic increase in both interdisciplinary teaching programs and research centers in recent decades in Brazil (driven partly by government support but also demand from below that itself reflected Brazilian democratization), but note that in Brazil as in many other countries such programs and centers tend to be evaluated by non-peers that employ disciplinary standards.

9 Barrow (2019) notes that philosophers rarely need large grants and suffer when universities expect large grants from faculty members.

10 I have only rarely needed big research grants in my career. Early in my career, I received some much-appreciated grants to do archival research in four countries. More recently, I had a fairly large grant that supported computer science and information science graduate students who did invaluable work on my classification system. In between, I annoyed the administrators of my university's internal granting competitions by regularly applying for small sums to attend conferences. They wanted me to use these funds as a springboard to applying for bigger grants that I did not need. I could not ethically justify applying for funds that I could do without when I knew that other scholars had research plans that were completely dependent on funding. I have served on grant adjudication committees many times and know that it is heart-breaking when there isn't enough money for everyone who needs it and has a good proposal.

11 Chambers (2017) is also highly critical of the way universities encourage scholars to apply for large grants.

12 Many scholars stress the importance of physical spaces (and events) in which scholars from different disciplines can interact (e.g. Vicente and Lucas 2022). One huge barrier to interdisciplinarity is simply that scholars do not often meet scholars from other departments in an environment where they can explore shared interests.

13 Bardosh et al. (2020, 13) interviewed 75 leaders in academic research and policy related to health issues. "Our analysis found that the growth of agile social science research units and centers that actively engage in preparedness and response was seen among many respondents to be fundamental for knowledge generation and capacity strengthening."

14 See the Science of Team Science website at https://www.inscits.org/. One key insight is that it is not enough to just throw researchers with overlapping interests together. Bloom, Curran, and Brint (2020) investigate the increasingly popular practice of "cluster hiring" in which universities hire a handful of people with shared interests into different departments. They find that cluster members often interact little with each other except when affiliated with a research center.

15 Adomßent (2022) describes a unique German program at Leuphana College near Hamburg where interdisciplinary education is institutionalized across the college. He notes that this is much harder to accomplish in institutions originally structured around disciplines. The universities of Amsterdam and Utrecht in the Netherlands are other important sites of interdisciplinary education. Lyall (2022) reports on many experiments in the UK but still limited institutionalization.

16 "Universities still give greater credence to the disciplinary specialist and do not yet fully appreciate the broader skill sets that individual interdisciplinarians, trained through these and similar studentships, have to offer" (Lyall 2019, 111).

17 Villa-Soto et al. (2022) describe promising new initiatives in both interdisciplinary research and teaching in Mexico, but note that these have suffered from being evaluated according to disciplinary criteria.

18 Klein (2021, 126) identifies 6 criteria for successful interdisciplinary administration. Two of these address issues of evaluation. She urges transparency and fairness in allocation of resources and expertise across different types of activity. She also urges informed use of best practices. And she urges a systematic approach rather than a bunch of fragmented efforts.

19 O'Rourke and Fam (2021) identify several ways in which interdisciplinary research and teaching projects can fail. Often, but not always, failure is a precursor to later success.

20 Shape-ID (2021b) provides a set of reflexive questions that administrators committed to interdisciplinarity should ask themselves.

21 Klein, Baptista, and Streck (2022, 2) appreciate that interdisciplinarity is "confronted by a gap between widespread endorsements and continuing impediments. Nothing less than a culture change is needed to elevate both inter- and transdisciplinarity to a norm within the academic system."

22 White and Deevy (2020) apply design methods in generating an interdisciplinary research culture.

23 Citations are highly skewed so that in most fields a small minority of scholars garner most of the citations. Yet integrative works, both within and across fields, tend to be more highly cited than specialized research. Citations are one key way that universities are ranked (though more so in the natural and social sciences than the humanities at present, for citation indices have tended to capture journal publications better than books; this may change; see Sooryamoorthy 2021). A university that hires integrative researchers could see much higher citation totals. There are, I should stress, problems in relying on any metric. Some professors and journals game the system by citing each other (see Chambers 2017, Biagioli and Lippman 2020). And some citations are criticisms of the work in question. As in anything, judgment needs to be exercised in looking at citation data. But integrative research is likely much-cited for very good reasons: it sets the stage for future specialized and integrative research.

24 Elman et al. (2020) in their conclusion concur with us that there is much inertia in universities but also potential for change. They stress that reforms must be feasible and accord with academic incentives. They suggest that private universities with small endowments may be the most open to change.

25 Wernli and Darbellay (2016) suggest that research universities need to expand the number of interdisciplinary researchers.

26 The American Association of Colleges & Universities in April 2021 championed a consortium of small colleges that have been able to create new Majors by sharing some online courses that supplement local courses. There may be potential for some shared offering of core content.

27 "First, we must stop seeing interdisciplinarity as an epiphenomenon: the prevailing ethos within research-intensive universities is discipline excellence first, then interdisciplinary collaboration. If we are to nurture and indeed benefit from the expertise of true interdisciplinarians, interdisciplinarity has to be entrenched and embedded rather than epiphenomenal" (Lyall 2019, 118).

28 Bammer (2021) provides a set of suggestions on how to institutionalize transdisciplinarity.

29 Gerring, Mahoney, and Elman (2020) urge top journals to find a place for new ideas. These cannot be judged by the same standards as the usual article. They worry that we lack space for exploratory research. They build upon Swedberg (2020). In the same volume, Lieberman (61) describes what an exploratory study might look like in political science: "A descriptive study in political science ought to use the best available conceptual, measurement, and sampling tools to depict a phenomenon of

interest. What are citizens' political attitudes? How have certain institutions evolved over time? In order to be considered important, such studies generally need to focus on a subject that is truly novel or that disrupts conventional wisdom about a particular state of affairs; for example, documenting either a new type of institution or set of political attitudes or behaviors, describing some aspect of political life in the wake of an important historical moment, or showing that a particular way of understanding some existing phenomenon is no longer correct, given superior data or measurement techniques, which in turn might cast some existing causal theories in doubt."

30 Gerring, Mahoney, and Elman (2020) also urge that a work's significance should be judged separately from its quality.

31 We can note here that journals in many fields increasingly require authors to publish their data. Open data is an important component of open science, and makes replication much easier.

32 Renn (2020, 400–407) notes that the World Wide Web has an unachieved potential to integrate knowledge. He urges us to somehow make integrated knowledge available to the wider population. Different users will have different entry points but can each readily find relevant information.

9

CONCLUDING REMARKS

It is quite simple really. The human world comprises dozens of key phenomena that interact. Our research, teaching, and policy advice should reflect that complex reality, but do not. Our libraries should be organized to capture and facilitate the exploration of that complex reality, but are not. Our universities should be structured in a way that encourages us to embrace that complexity in our research and teaching, but are not.

This book has sought to identify the implications for academic practice of this complex reality. Each chapter has closed with a summary of the main arguments in that chapter. We can briefly reprise here the point of each chapter:

- Chapter 1 motivated our inquiry, outlined the book, and identified key characteristics of its approach.
- Chapter 2 outlined a set of key implications for human science research: that we need to map human science inquiry, seek a symbiosis between specialized and integrative (both within and across fields) research, clarify terminology, recognize the strengths and weaknesses of the dozen methods pursued in human science, and pursue clarity.
- Chapter 3 surveyed a number of recent works on methodology in the social sciences and humanities. The approach recognized in this book was found to complement these diverse works. They suggested some important clarifications to our arguments in Chapter 2. Yet we in turn provided answers to questions or problems they had identified.
- Chapter 4 then looked at particular subsystems or sets of causal links within human science. In each case, our big-picture perspective guided us to identify important research questions. We also pointed to methods that should receive greater attention. We performed a similar exercise for history and philosophy, two disciplines with broader remits.

DOI: 10.4324/9781003275237-9

- Chapter 5 turned to teaching. We identified a handful of things that all students should know (including our map, and some understanding of the strengths and weaknesses of methods). We explored how to better offer interdisciplinary programming and courses. We discussed how to teach integration skills.
- Chapter 6 showed how we could and should organize our libraries to reflect complexity and thus encourage integrative research and teaching.
- Chapter 7 argued that integrative research and teaching would facilitate superior policy advice. We then advocated a close connection between (some) academic researchers and policy-makers.
- Chapter 8 explored how universities might be structured to encourage integrative research and teaching. We then asked how we can achieve reforms (within and beyond universities) to move us from where we are to where we should be.

REFERENCES

6, Perri, and Christine Bellamy (2013) *Principles of Methodology: Research Design in Social Science*. London: SAGE.

Abbott, Andrew. (1997) "Of Time and Space." *Social Forces* 75(4): 1149–182.

Adams, Erin C., and Stacey L. Kerr (2021) "Always Already There: Theorizing an Intra-Disciplinary Social Studies." *Pedagogies: An International Journal*, January. https://www.tandfonline.com/doi/full/10.1080/1554480X.2020.1870470

Adomßent, Maik (2022) "Taking Inter- and Transdisciplinarity to Eye Level with Scientific Disciplines: Teaching and Learning in Complementary Studies at Leuphana College, Lüneburg, Germany." In Bianca Vienni Baptista and Julie Thompson Klein, eds., *Interdisciplinarity and Transdisciplinarity: Institutionalizing Collaboration Across Cultures and Communities*. London: Routledge, 27–42.

Aiello, Emilia (2021) "Effective Strategies That Enhance the Social Impact of Social Sciences and Humanities Research." *Evidence & Policy: A Journal of Research, Debate and Practice* 17(1), 131–146.

American Association of Colleges and Universities (AAC&U) (2021) *How College Contributes to Workforce Success*. https://www.aacu.org/new-report-employer-views-higher-education

Ari, Omar (2020) "Undergraduates as Interdisciplinary Researchers: Gains in Competencies and Conceptual Knowledge." *College Teaching*, December.

Ásta (2018) *Categories We Live by: The Construction of Sex, Gender, Race, and Other Social Categories*. New York: Oxford University Press.

Augsburg, Tanya, and Stuart Henry, eds. (2009) *The Politics of Interdisciplinary Studies: Essays on Transformations in American Undergraduate Programs*. Jefferson NC: McFarland and Company.

Bammer, Gabriele (2021) "What Is Needed to Institutionalise Transdisciplinarity?" *Integration and Implementation Insights Blog*, August 3. https://i2insights.org/2021/08/03/institutionalising-transdisciplinarity/

Bardosh, Kevin Louis, Daniel H. de Vries, Sharon Abramowitz, Adama Thorlie, Lianne Cremers, John Kinsman, and Darryl Stellmach (2020) "Integrating the Social Sciences in Epidemic Preparedness and Response: A Strategic Framework to Strengthen Capacities and Improve Global Health Security." *Globalization and Health* 16, 120.

Barrow, Robin (2019) "Social Science, Philosophy and Education." *Philosophical Inquiry in Education* 26(2), 146–155.

Barry, Andrew, and Georgina Born, eds. (2014) *Interdisciplinarity: Reconfigurations of the Social and Natural Sciences.* London: Routledge.

Bastow, Simon, Patrick Dunleavy, and Jane Tinkler (2014) *The Impact of the Social Sciences: How Academics and Their Research Make a Difference.* Thousand Oaks CA: SAGE.

Bate, Jonathan, ed. (2011) *The Public Value of the Humanities.* London: Bloomsbury Academic.

Bertolaso, Marta (2011) "Epistemology in Life Sciences. An Integrative Approach to a Complex System Like Cancer." *Journal of Philosophy of Life Sciences* 19(36), 245–249.

Biagioli, Mario, and Alexandra Lippman, eds. (2020) *Gaming the Metrics: Misconduct and Manipulation in Academic Research.* Cambridge: MIT Press.

Bloom, Quinn, Michaela Curran, and Steven Brint (2020) "Interdisciplinary Cluster Hiring Initiatives in U.S. Research Universities: More Straw than Bricks?." *The Journal of Higher Education* 91(5), 755–780.

Boero, Riccardo (2015) *Behavioral Computational Social Science.* Hoboken NJ: John Wiley & Sons.

Bowen, John R., Nicolas Dodier, Jan Willem Duyvendak, and Anita Hardon (2021) "Introduction." In John R. Bowen, Nicolas Dodier, Jan Willem Duyvendak, and Anita Hardon, eds., *Pragmatic Inquiry: Critical Concepts for Social Sciences.* London: Routledge.

Boyer, Ernest L. (1990) *Scholarship Reconsidered: Priorities of the Professoriate.* New York: Carnegie Foundation for the Advancement of Teaching.

Bracken, L.J., and E.A. Oughton (2006) "'What Do You Mean?': The Importance of Language in Developing Interdisciplinary Research." *Transactions of the Institute of British Geographers* 31, 371–382.

Brigandt, Ingo (2020) "How Are Biology Concepts Used and Transformed?." In Kostas Kampourakis, and Tobias Uller, eds., *Philosophy of Science for Biologists.* Cambridge: Cambridge University Press.

Brint, Steven (2017) "New Concepts, Expanding Audiences: What Highly Cited Texts Tell Us About Scholarly Knowledge in the Social Sciences." *Social Research* 84(3), 637–668.

British Academy (2016) *Crossing Paths: Interdisciplinary Institutions, Careers, Education, and Applications.* https://www.thebritishacademy.ac.uk/publications/crossing-paths/

British Academy (2021) *Knowledge Exchange in the Shape Disciplines.* https://www.thebritishacademy.ac.uk/publications/knowledge-exchange-in-the-shape-disciplines/

Burke, Timothy (2021) "An Unconvincing Argument for the Liberal Arts." *Chronicle of Higher Education,* July 13. https://www.chronicle.com/article/an-unconvincing-argument-for-the-liberal-arts

Buvke, Oddbjørn (2019) *Designing Social Science Research.* Berlin: Springer.

Campion, Corey (2018) "Whither the Humanities? – Reinterpreting the Relevance of an Essential and Embattled Field." *Arts and Humanities in Higher Education* 17, 4.

Carnap, Rudolph (1934) *The Unity of Science.* Republished, 2011. London: Routledge.

Chambers, Chris (2017) *The Seven Deadly Sins of Psychology: A Manifesto for Reforming the Culture of Scientific Practice.* Princeton NJ: Princeton University Press.

Chapman, Karen (2021) "Characteristics of Systematic Reviews in the Social Sciences." *Journal of Academic Librarianship* 47, 5.

Chibber, Vivek (2022) *The Class Matrix: Social Theory after the Cultural Turn.* Cambridge MA: Harvard University Press.

Clune, Michael (2021) "Are Humanities Professors Moral Experts?" *Chronicle of Higher Education,* May 3. Based on his *A Defence of Judgment.* Chicago: University of Chicago Press.

Collins, Patricia Hill, and Sirma Bilge (2016) *Intersectionality*. London: Polity Press.

Collins, Randall (1998) *The Sociology of Philosophies*. Cambridge MA: Harvard University Press.

Cross, Gary, and Rick Szostak (2018) *Technology and American Society: A History*, 3rd Ed. New York: Routledge.

Daniels, Karen, Johanna Hanefeld, and Bruno Marchal (2017) "Social Sciences: Vital to Improving Our Understanding of Health Equity, Policy and Systems." *International Journal for Equity in Health* 16, 1–3.

Daniels, Ronald J., Grant Shreve, and Phillip Spector (2021) *What Universities Owe Democracy*. Baltimore: Johns Hopkins University Press.

Darbellay, Frédéric (2019) "From Interdisciplinarity to Postdisciplinarity: Extending Klein's Thinking into the Future of the University." *Issues in Interdisciplinary Studies* 37(2), 90–109.

DeLeon, P., and T.E. Steelman (2001) "Making Public Policy Programs Effective and Relevant: The Role of the Policy Sciences." *Journal of Policy Analysis and Management* 20(1), 163–172.

Denscombe, Martyn (2010) *Ground Rules for Social Research*. New York: McGraw-Hill Education.

Dezure, Deborah (2017) "Interdisciplinary Pedagogies in Higher Education." In *Oxford Handbook of Interdisciplinarity*. Oxford UK: Oxford University Press.

Dorot, Ruth, and Nitza Davidovitch (2020) "The Status of the Humanities in the 21st Century: A Case Study." *European Journal of Educational Sciences* 7(3), 141–159.

Elman, Colin, John Gerring, and James Mahoney, eds. (2020) *The Production of Knowledge: Enhancing Progress in Social Science*. Cambridge UK: Cambridge University Press.

Emmeche, Claus, David Budtz Pedersen, and Frederik Stjernfelt, eds. (2017) *Mapping Frontier Research in the Humanities*. London: Bloomsbury Publishing.

Epstein, Brian (2015) *The Ant Trap: Rebuilding the Foundations of the Social Sciences*. Oxford UK: Oxford Online.

Ferrall, Victor E. (2015) *Liberal Arts at the Brink*. Cambridge MA: Harvard University Press.

Frickel, Scott, and Neil Gross (2005) "A General Theory of Scientific/Intellectual Movements." *American Sociological Review* 70(2), 204–232.

Fusari, Angelo (2014) *Methodological Misconceptions in the Social Sciences: Rethinking Social Thought and Social Processes*. Berlin: Springer.

Gamsby, Patrick (2020) "The Common Ground of Open Access and Interdisciplinarity." *Publications* 8(1), 1.

Gavens, L., J. Holmes, J. McLeod, E.S. Hock, P.S. Meier, G. Bühringer, M. Neumann, and A. Lingford-Hughes (2018) "Interdisciplinary Working in Public Health Research: A Proposed Good Practice Checklist." *Journal of Public Health* 40(1), 175–182.

Gorard, Stephen (2017) *Research Design: Creating Robust Approaches for the Social Sciences*. London: SAGE.

Greener, Ian (2013) *Designing Social Research: A Guide for the Bewildered*. London: SAGE.

Graff, Gerald (1992) *Beyond the Culture Wars: How Teaching the Conflicts Can Revitalize American Education*. New York: Norton.

Gerring, John (2020) "Comprehensive Appraisal." In Colin Elman, John Gerring, and James Mahoney, eds., *The Production of Knowledge: Enhancing Progress in Social Science*. Cambridge UK: Cambridge University Press.

Gerring, John, James Mahoney, and Colin Elman (2020) "Proposals." In Colin Elman, John Gerring, and James Mahoney, eds., *The Production of Knowledge: Enhancing Progress in Social Science*. Cambridge UK: Cambridge University Press.

Greenwood, Davydd J., and Morton Levin (2008) "The Reformed Social Sciences to Reform the University: Mission Impossible?" *Teaching and Learning* 1(1), 89–121.

Griffiths, Paul E., and Karola Stotz (2014) "Conceptual Barriers to Interdisciplinary Communication: When Does Ambiguity Matter?" In Michael O'Rourke, Stephen Crowley, Sanford D. Eigenbrode, and J. D. Wulfhorst, eds., *Enhancing Communication & Collaboration in Interdisciplinary Research*. Thousand Oaks: SAGE.

Groarke, Leo A., and Christopher W. Tindale (2012) *Good Reasoning Matters! A Constructive Approach to Critical Thinking*. 5th Ed. Oxford UK: Oxford University Press.

Gross, Neil, and Christopher Robertson (2020) "Ideological Diversity." In Colin Elman, John Gerring, and James Mahoney, eds., *The Production of Knowledge: Enhancing Progress in Social Science*. Cambridge UK: Cambridge University Press.

Guerin, Bernard (2020) *Turning Psychology into a Social Science*. London: Routledge.

Hanscomb, Stuart (2016) *Critical Thinking: The Basics*. London: Routledge.

Hanstedt, Paul (2012) *General Education Essentials: A Guide for College Faculty*. San Francisco: Jossey-Bass.

Hayot, Eric (2021) "The Humanities Have a Marketing Problem." *Chronicle of Higher Education Review*, April 2. https://www.chronicle.com/article/the-humanities-have-a-marketing-problem

Hayot, Eric (2014) *The Elements of Academic Style: Writing for the Humanities*. New York: Columbia University Press.

Hellemans, B. (2017) *Understanding Culture: A Handbook for Students in the Humanities*. Amsterdam: Amsterdam University Press.

Helliwell, John F., Richard Layard, Jeffrey Sachs, and Jan-Emmanuel De Neve, eds. (2021) *World Happiness Report 2021*. New York: Sustainable Development Solutions Network.

Henry, Stuart, and Lindsay M. Howard (2019) *Social Deviance*. 2nd Ed. London: Polity Press.

Hesse-Biber, Sharlene Nagy, and R. Burke Johnson, eds. (2015) *The Oxford Handbook of Multimethod and Mixed Methods Research Inquiry*. Oxford UK: Oxford University Press.

Heyck, Hunter (2015) *Age of System: Understanding the Development of Modern Social Science*. Baltimore: Johns Hopkins University Press.

Hirsch Hadorn Gertrude, Hoffmann-Riem Holger, Biber-Klemm Susette, Grossenbacher-Mansuy Walter, Joye Dominique, Pohl Christian, Wiesmann Urs, and Zemp Elisabeth, eds. (2008) *Handbook of Transdisciplinary Research*. Berlin: Springer.

Holley, Karri (2017) "Administering Interdisciplinary Programs." *Oxford Handbook of Interdisciplinarity*. Oxford UK: Oxford University Press.

Holley, Karri, and Rick Szostak (2022) "Interdisciplinary Education and Research in North America." In Bianca Vienni Baptista and Julie Thompson Klein, eds., *Interdisciplinarity and Transdisciplinarity: Institutionalizing Collaboration Across Cultures and Communities*. London: Routledge, 72–86.

Holosko, Michael J., and Bruce A. Thyer (2011) *Pocket Glossary for Commonly Used Research Terms*. Thousand Oaks: SAGE Publications.

Horn, Eva, and Hannes Bergthaller (2019) *The Anthropocene: Key Issues for the Humanities*. London: Routledge.

Jasanoff, Sheila (2014) "Fields and Fallows: A Political History of STS." In Andrew Barry, and Georgina Born, eds., *Interdisciplinarity: Reconfigurations of the Social and Natural Sciences*. London: Routledge.

Jungmeister, Alexander (2016) *Innovation and Reflexivity in the Research Process*. Newcastle UK: Cambridge Scholars Publishing.

Kahne, Joseph, and Joel Westheimer (2006) "Teaching Democracy: What Schools Need to Do." In E. Wayne Ross, ed. *Social Studies Curriculum: The Purposes, Problems, and Possibilities*, 3rd Ed. Albany: SUNY Press.

Kahneman, Daniel (2011) *Thinking Fast and Slow*. New York: Farrar, Strauss, and Giroux.

Klein, Julie Thompson (2021) *Beyond Interdisciplinarity: Boundary Work, Communication, and Collaboration*. Oxford UK: Oxford University Press.

Klein, Julie Thompson (2005) *Humanities, Culture, and Interdisciplinarity: The Changing American Academy*. Albany: SUNY Press.

Klein, Julie Thompson, Bianca Vienni Baptista, and Danilo Streck (2022) "Introduction: Institutionalizing Interdisciplinarity and Transdisciplinarity: Cultures and Communities, Timeframes and Spaces." In Bianca Vienni Baptista and Julie Thompson Klein, eds., *Interdisciplinarity and Transdisciplinarity: Institutionalizing Collaboration Across Cultures and Communities*. London: Routledge, 1–10.

Lebow, Richard N. (2020) *Reason and Cause: Social Science and the Social World*. Cambridge: Cambridge University Press.

Leezenberg, Michiel, and Gerard de Vries (2019) *History and Philosophy of the Humanities: An Introduction*. Amsterdam University Press.

Levenson, Michael (2018) *The Humanities and Everyday Life: The Literary Agenda*. New York: Oxford University Press.

Liao, Tim F. (2020) "Peer Review." In Colin Elman, John Gerring, and James Mahoney, eds., *The Production of Knowledge: Enhancing Progress in Social Science*. Cambridge UK: Cambridge University Press.

Lieberman, Evan (2020) "Research Cycles." In Colin Elman, John Gerring, and James Mahoney, eds., *The Production of Knowledge: Enhancing Progress in Social Science*. Cambridge UK: Cambridge University Press.

Litre, Gabriela, Diego Pereira Lindoso, and Marcel Bursztyn (2022) "A Long and Winding Road Toward Institutionalizing Interdisciplinarity: Lessons from Environmental and Sustainability Science Programs in Brazil." In Bianca Vienni Baptista and Julie Thompson Klein, eds., *Interdisciplinarity and Transdisciplinarity: Institutionalizing Collaboration Across Cultures and Communities*. London: Routledge, 57–71.

Lumsden, Karen (2019) "Introduction: The Reflexive Turn and the Social Sciences." In Karen Lumsden, Jan Bradford, and Jackie Goode, eds., *Reflexivity: Theory, Method, and Practice*. Routledge.

Luo, Jiali (2021) "Interaction Across Ideological Boundaries and College Outcomes." *Journal of Higher Education* 92(1), 56–83.

Lyall, Catherine (2019) *Being an Interdisciplinary Academic: How Institutions Shape University Careers*. London: Palgrave Macmillan.

Lyall, Catherine (2021) *Top Ten Tips for Working with Policymakers*. https://www.shapeidtoolkit.eu/wp-content/uploads/2021/05/Top-ten-tips-policy.pdf

Lyall, Catherine (2022) "Excellence With Impact: Why UK Research Policy Discourages 'transdisciplinarity.'" In Bianca Vienni Baptista and Julie Thompson Klein, eds., *Interdisciplinarity and Transdisciplinarity: Institutionalizing Collaboration Across Cultures and Communities*. London: Routledge, 13–26.

Lyall, Catherine, Ann Bruce, Joyce Tait, and Laura Meagher (2011) *Interdisciplinary Research Journeys: Practical Strategies for Capturing Creativity*. London: Bloomsbury.

Madjesberg, Christian (2017) *Sensemaking: The Power of the Humanities in the Age of the Algorithm*. New York: Hachette.

Mahoney, J., and K. Thelen (2015) "Comparative-Historical Analysis in Contemporary Political Science." In J. Mahoney, and K. Thelen, eds., *Advances in Comparative-Historical Analysis* (Strategies for Social Inquiry). Cambridge: Cambridge University Press.

Marks, Jonathan (2021) *Let's Be Reasonable: A Conservative Case for Liberal Education.* Princeton: Princeton University Press.

Marshall, Alfred. [1890/1920]. *Principles of Economics*, 8th Ed. London: Macmillan.

Martinelli, Dario (2017) *Arts and Humanities in Progress: A Manifesto of Numanities.* Berlin: Springer.

Martini, Carlo, and Marcel Boumans (2014) "Introduction." In *Experts and Consensus in Social Science.* Berlin: Springer.

Matthews, Mark (2016) *Transformational Public Policy: A New Strategy for Coping with Uncertainty and Risk.* New York: Routledge.

Mattick, Paul (2020) *Social Knowledge: An Essay on the Nature and Limits of Social Science.* 2nd Ed. Leiden: Brill.

Maxwell, Nicolas (2020) *Our Fundamental Problem: A Revolutionary Approach to Philosophy.* Montreal: McGill-Queen's University Press.

Mayer, Igor S., C. Els van Daalen, and Pieter W.G. Bots (2013) "Perspectives on Policy Analysis: A Framework for Understanding and Design." In Wil A.H. Thissen, and Warren E. Walker, eds., *Public Policy Analysis: New Developments.* Berlin: Springer.

Menken, Steph, and Machiel Keestra (2016) *An Introduction to Interdisciplinary Research: Theory and Practice.* Amsterdam: University of Amsterdam Press.

Merchant, Carolyn (2020) *The Anthropocene and the Humanities: From Climate Change to a New Age of Sustainability.* New Haven CT: Yale University Press.

Michael, O'Rourke, and Dena Fam, eds. (2021) *Interdisciplinary and Transdisciplinary Failures.* London: Routledge.

Mintz, Stephen (2021) "Policy Education and Public Advocacy." *Inside Higher Ed*, November 10. https://www.insidehighered.com/blogs/higher-ed-gamma/policy-education-and-public-advocacy

Mobley, Catherine (2021) "Building Connections and Broadening Horizons through Interdisciplinary Public Sociology." In Leslie Hossfeld, E. Brooke Kelly, and Cassius Hossfeld, eds., *The Routledge International Handbook of Public Sociology*, 104–117.

Moll, Ellen (2019) "Citizen Epistemology and Interdisciplinary, Inclusive Curriculum." *Journal of General Education* 16(1–2), 19–31.

Morgan, Stephen L. (2014) *Counterfactuals and Causal Inference: Methods and Principles for Social Research.* Cambridge UK: Cambridge University Press.

Morlino, Leonardo (2018) *Comparison: A Methodological Introduction for the Social Sciences.* Berlin: Barbara Budrich Publishers.

Muhonen, R., P. Benneworth, and J. Olmos-Peñuela (2020) "From Productive Interactions to Impact Pathways: Understanding the Key Dimensions in Developing SSH Research Societal Impact." *Research Evaluation* 29(1), 34–47.

Newman, Robert C. (2021) "How the Humanities can Flourish." *Inside Higher Ed*, September 3. https://www.insidehighered.com/views/2021/09/03/how-humanities-can-flourish-future-opinion

Nicolescu, Basarab (2002) *Manifesto of Transdisciplinarity.* Albany: SUNY Press.

Niemelä, Mikko A. (2020) "Crossing Curricular Boundaries for Powerful Knowledge." *The Curriculum Journal* 32(2), 359–375.

O'Leary, Zina (2007) *The Social Science Jargon Buster: The Key Terms You Need to Know.* Los Angeles: SAGE Publications.

Oliver, Paul (2010) *Understanding the Research Process.* Los Angeles: SAGE Publications.

Organization for Economic Cooperation and Development (2020) *Addressing Societal Challenges Using Transdisciplinary Research.* https://www.oecd.org/science/addressing-societal-challenges-using-transdisciplinary-research-0ca0ca45-en.htm

Pearl, Judea, and Dana Mackenzie (2017) *The Book of Why: The New Science of Cause and Effect*. New York: Basic Books.

Peterson, Erik L. (2020) "What Methods Do Life Scientists Use? A Brief History With Philosophical Implications." In Kostas Kampourakis, and Tobias Uller, eds., *Philosophy of Science for Biologists*. Cambridge: Cambridge University Press.

Pohl, Christian, and Isabel Fletcher (2021) *Top Ten Tips for Evaluating Inter- and Transdisciplinary Research*. https://www.shapeidtoolkit.eu/wp-content/uploads/2021/05/Top-ten-tips-evaluation.pdf

Ramadanovic, Petar (2021) *Interdiscipline: A Future for Literary Studies and the Humanities*. London: Routledge.

Rashid, Rafi (2021) "Updating the PhD: Making the Case for Interdisciplinarity in Twenty-First-Century Doctoral Education." *Teaching in Higher Education* 26(3), 508–517.

Reale, Emanuela et al. (2018) "A Review of Literature on Evaluating the Scientific, Social and Political Impact of Social Sciences and Humanities Research." *Research Evaluation* 27(4), 298–308.

Renn, J. (2020) *The Evolution of Knowledge: Rethinking Science in the Anthropocene*. Princeton NJ: Princeton University Press.

Repko, Allen, Rick Szostak, and Michelle Buchberger (2020) *Introduction to Interdisciplinary Studies*, 3rd ed. Thousand Oaks: SAGE.

Repko, Allen, and Rick Szostak (2020) *Interdisciplinary Research: Process and Theory*, 4th Ed., Thousand Oaks: SAGE.

Rodgers, Daniel T. (2011) *Age of Fracture*. Cambridge MA: Belknap Press.

Rosenau, Pauline Marie (1992) *Post-Modernism and the Social Sciences: Insights, Inroads, and Intrusions*. Princeton NJ: Princeton University Press.

Rosenberg, Brian (2021) "It's Time to Rethink Higher Education." *Chronicle of Higher Education Review*, April 2. https://www.chronicle.com/article/its-time-to-rethink-higher-education

Roseneil, Sasha, and Stephen Frosh (2012) "Social Research after the Cultural Turn: A (Self-) Critical Introduction." In Sasha Roseneil, and Stephen Frosh, eds., *Social Research after the Cultural Turn*. Berlin: Springer.

Ross, E. Wayne, Sandra Mathison, and Kevin D. Vinson (2013) "Social Studies Education and Standards-Based Education Reform in North America: Curriculum Standardization, High-Stakes Testing, and Resistance." *Revista Latinoamericana De Estudios Educativos* 1(10), 19–48.

Rust, C. (2007) "Unstated Contributions: How Artistic Inquiry can Inform Interdisciplinary Research." *International Journal of Design* 1(3), 69–76.

Sayer, Andrew. (2010) *Method in Social Science: A Realist Approach*. 2nd Ed. New York: Routledge.

Schaffer, Frederic Charles (2015) *Elucidating Social Science Concepts: An Interpretivist Guide*. New York: Routledge.

Schmidt, Jan Cornelius (2022) *Philosophy of Interdisciplinarity: Studies in Science, Society and Sustainability*. London: Routledge.

Sebastian, Isabel, Dena Fam, and Jason Prior (2022) "The Rise of Transdisciplinary 'boundary organisations' within the Australian Tertiary Education Sector: Beyond the Disciplined University." In Bianca Vienni Baptista and Julie Thompson Klein, eds., *Interdisciplinarity and Transdisciplinarity: Institutionalizing Collaboration Across Cultures and Communities*. London: Routledge, 89–106.

Schrödinger, Erwin (1944) *What Is Life? The Physical Aspect of the Living Cell*. Cambridge UK: Cambridge University Press.

Shape-ID (2021a) *What Can the Arts, Humanities and Social Sciences Bring to Inter- and Transdisciplinary Research?* Guide-AHSS-Contributions-to-IDR.pdf (shapeidtoolkit.eu).

Shape-ID (2021b) *Reflective Tool for Higher Education Institutions.* https://www.shapeid toolkit.eu/wp-content/uploads/2021/02/Reflective-Tool-Higher-Education-Institutions.pdf

Shapiro, Stuart (2016) *Analysis and Public Policy: Successes, Failures and Directions for Reform.* Cheltenham UK: Edward Elgar Publishing Limited.

Simonton, Dean Keith (1990) "Personality and Politics." In Lawrence A. Pervin, ed., *Handbook of Personality Theory and Research.* New York: Guilford.

Small, Helen (2013) *The Value of the Humanities.* Oxford UK: Oxford University Press.

Smelser, Neil J., and John S. Reed (2012) *Usable Social Science.* Berkeley CA: University of California Press.

Smiraglia, Richard, and Rick Szostak (2018) "Converting UDC to BCC: Comparative Approaches to Interdisciplinarity." *Proceedings of the International Society for Knowledge Organization conference*, Porto, Portugal, July.

Smith, Noah (2021) "When Disciplines Hit Dead Ends: The Academic Incentive Structure Leads Fields Astray." *Chronicle of Higher Education*, August 3.

Smith, Robert B. (2008) *Cumulative Social Inquiry: Transforming Novelty into Innovation.* New York: Guilford Press.

Smulyan, Susan (2020) *Doing Public Humanities.* New York: Routledge.

Sooryamoorthy, R. (2021) *Scientometrics for the Humanities and Social Sciences.* London: Routledge.

Steinberg, Theodore L. (2014) *Literature, the Humanities, and Humanity.* Albany: Open SUNY.

Stjernfelt, Frederik (2017) "Criticizing Erroneous Abstractions: The Case of Culturalism." In Claus Emmeche, David Budtz Pedersen and Frederik Stjernfelt, eds., *Mapping Frontier Research in the Humanities.* London: Bloomsbury Publishing.

Streek, Wolfgang (2015) "Epilogue: Comparative-Historical Analysis: Past, Present, Future." In J. Mahoney, and K. Thelen, eds., *Advances in Comparative-Historical Analysis* (Strategies for Social Inquiry). Cambridge: Cambridge University Press.

Swedberg, Richard (2020) "Exploratory Research." In Colin Elman, John Gerring, and James Mahoney, eds., *The Production of Knowledge: Enhancing Progress in Social Science.* Cambridge UK: Cambridge University Press.

Szostak, Rick (n.d.) *Basic Concepts Classification.* https://sites.google.com/a/ualberta.ca/rick-szostak/research/basic-concepts-classification-web-version-2013 [updated regularly since 2013]

Szostak, Rick (2022) *Making Sense of the Future.* London: Routledge.

Szostak, Rick (2021) *Making Sense of World History.* London: Routledge.

Szostak, Rick (2019) *Manifesto of Interdisciplinarity.* https://sites.google.com/a/ualberta.ca/manifesto-of-interdisciplinarity/manifesto-of-interdisciplinarity

Szostak, Rick (2018) "Interdisciplinarity and Adapted Physical Activity." *Adapted Physical Activity Quarterly* 35(3), 254–266.

Szostak, Rick (2017a) "Interdisciplinary Research as a Creative Design Process." In Frédéric Darbellay, Zoe Moody, and Todd Lubart, eds., *Creative Design Thinking from an Interdisciplinary Perspective.* Berlin: Springer.

Szostak, Rick (2017b) "Stability, Instability, and Interdisciplinarity." *Issues in Interdisciplinary Studies* 35, 65–87.

Szostak, Rick (2017c) "Facet Analysis Without Facet Indicators." In Richard Smiraglia, and Hur-li Lee, eds., *Dimensions of Knowledge: Facets for Knowledge Organization.* Wurzburg: Ergon.

Szostak, Rick (2016) "What Is Lost?" (Comment) *Issues in Interdisciplinary Studies* 34, 209–213.

Szostak, Rick (2015) "A Growth Agenda for Economic History." In Avner Greif, Lynne Keisling, and John Nye, eds, *Institutions, Innovation, and Industrialization*. Princeton NJ: Princeton University Press, 245–273.

Szostak, Rick (2011) "Complex Concepts into Basic Concepts." *Journal of the American Society for Information Science & Technology* 62(11), 2247–2265.

Szostak, Rick (2009) *The Causes of Economic Growth: Interdisciplinary Perspectives*. Berlin: Springer.

Szostak, Rick (2007) "Modernism, Postmodernism, and Interdisciplinarity." *Issues in Integrative Studies* 26, 32–83.

Szostak, Rick (2006) "Economic History as It Is and Should Be; Toward an Open, Honest, Methodologically Flexible, Theoretically Diverse, Interdisciplinary Exploration of the Causes and Consequences of Economic Growth." *Journal of Socio-Economics* 35(4), 727–750.

Szostak, Rick (2005a) "Evaluating the Historiography of the Great Depression: Explanation or Single-Theory Driven?" *Journal of Economic Methodology* 12(1), 35–61.

Szostak, Rick (2005b) "Interdisciplinarity and the Teaching of Public Policy." *Journal of Policy Analysis and Management* 24(4), 853–863.

Szostak, Rick (2004) *Classifying Science: Phenomena, Data, Theory, Method, Practice*. Dordrecht: Springer.

Szostak, Rick (2003) *A Schema for Unifying Human Science: Interdisciplinary Perspectives on Culture*. Selinsgrove: Susquehanna University Press.

Szostak, Rick (2001) "Putting Social Structure in Its Place, Schematically." *Issues in Integrative Studies* 19, 171–220.

Szostak, Rick (1999) *Econ-Art: Divorcing Art from Science in Modern Economics*. London: Pluto Press.

Szostak, Rick, Claudio Gnoli, and Maria López-Huertas (2016) *Interdisciplinary Knowledge Organization*. Berlin: Springer.

Thaler, Richard, and Cass Sunstein (2008) *Nudge: Improving Decisions About Health, Wealth, and Happiness*. New Haven CT: Yale University Press.

Tuckett, Jonathan (2018) *The Idea of Social Science and Proper Phenomenology*. Berlin: Springer.

Vertovec, Steven (2021) "The Social Organization of Difference." *Ethnic & Racial Studies* 44(8), 1273–1295.

Vicente, Paulo Nuno, and Margarida Lucas (2022) "Epistemic Cultures in European Intersections of Art–Science." In Bianca Vienni Baptista and Julie Thompson Klein, eds., *Interdisciplinarity and Transdisciplinarity: Institutionalizing Collaboration Across Cultures and Communities*. London: Routledge, 187–203.

Villa-Soto, Juan Carlos, Mónica Ribeiro Palacios, and Norma Blazquez Graf (2022) "Interdisciplinary Projects and Science Policies in Mexico: Divergences and Convergences." In Bianca Vienni Baptista and Julie Thompson Klein, eds., *Interdisciplinarity and Transdisciplinarity: Institutionalizing Collaboration Across Cultures and Communities*. London: Routledge, 43–56.

Wallerstein, Immanuel (1996) *Open the Social Sciences: Report of the Gulbenkian Commission on the Restructuring of the Social Sciences*. Palo Alto CA: Stanford University Press.

Watt, Gary (2011) "Hard Cases, Hard Times and the Humanity of Law." In Jonathan Bate, ed., *The Public Value of the Humanities*. London: Bloomsbury Academic.

Watts, Duncan J. (2007) "A Twenty-First Century Science." *Nature* 445(7127), 489.

Wernli, Didier, and Frederic Darbellay (2016) *Interdisciplinarity and the Twenty-First Century Research University.* Leuven: League of European Research Universities.

Wells, Cynthia A. (2016) *Realizing General Education: Reconsidering Conceptions and Renewing Practice.* New York: Wiley.

White, Alan (2014) *Toward a Philosophical Theory of Everything: Contributions to the Structural-Systematic Philosophy.* New York: Bloomsbury.

White, Hayden (1975) *Metahistory: The Historical Imagination in Nineteenth-Century Europe.* Baltimore: Johns Hopkins University Press.

White, P.J., and Colin Deevy (2020) "Designing an Interdisciplinary Research Culture in Higher Education: A Case Study." *Interchange* 51, 499–515.

Williams, Malcolm (2020) *Realism and Complexity in Social Science.* London: Routledge.

Zevin, Jack (2015). *Social Studies for the Twenty-First Century: Methods and Materials for Teaching in Middle and Secondary Schools.* 4th Ed. New York: Routledge.

Ziman, J. (2000) *Real Science: What It Is and What It Means.* New York: Cambridge University Press.

INDEX